Personal Finance
A Grouping of Financial Topics

By
Kirk G. Meyer

Personal Finance: A Grouping of Financial Topics
By Kirk G. Meyer

Final Expense Insurance

Disclaimer: Every effort was made to describe the information in this book in an accurate manner as of the publication date. The author makes no guarantees regarding the information of this book.

Personal Finance: A Grouping of Financial Topics
By Kirk G. Meyer

Table of Contents

Financial Plans

The next six topics will cover the basic steps involved in creating a comprehensive financial plan. Instead of creating a long single entry I have decided to break this subject up into six manageable ones that will not take that long to read and digest. Then after I explain the sixth and final topic, you will have an excellent basic understanding of what it takes to create a comprehensive financial plan. Of course, I do recommend that if you are serious about having a financial plan, it is best to seek out the services of someone who has been trained in financial planning. But regardless of if you have a financial plan or are in need of one this series of topics will help explain the overall basics.

Personal Finance: A Grouping of Financial Topics
By Kirk G. Meyer

Are you saving enough for retirement? Do you have your assets where they need to be to optimize taxes and potential returns? These are just some of the questions I am sure people ask themselves and if they are not they should be. While everyone's situation is different, and there is no one correct answer, these and many other things need to be addressed. It is important that you protect not only yourself but your family when it comes to financial matters. This topic is not about telling you or anyone what the best single answer is because that answer depends on you, and not everyone will or should receive the same answers. So let's begin looking at how a financial plan comes to life in some fundamental terms.

First in order to have an idea of your financial health you must first understand your income and expenses. The first step will be to determine what your total income is and what makes it up. For many, this is the wages that they earn from their jobs. But do not forget to overlook any bonuses you may receive from your job as well. If you have other outside sources of income, you will need to gather and list those as well, such as dividend income or interest income. This is also where you would record any gains or losses from investments that you have had sold over the past year. Also, if you have any business income or rental income, you would need to list it here as well. Add to these revenue sources up, and that is your total income that you will receive, and it is what we will loosely base the rest of the plan on. This exercise needs also to be done for your spouse if you are married.

Now the second step is a little more complicated as it involves all of your expenses that are either dedicated or discretionary in nature. The difference between these two has two parts. The first dedicated expenses are set, and they are expenses that are mandatory that they are paid such as a mortgage, all of the taxes one pays, and any insurance premiums. You would also include any debt reduction that you may have in the form of loans or credit card payments. It is also a good practice to list savings for your emergency fund and any retirement savings in the dedicated expenses as you should always pay yourself first in any system. As for discretionary expenses, those are expenses that may vary from payment to payment or they are expenses that are not considered essential. These expenditures can be adjusted as the need arises and provide a degree of flexibility in the amounts that are allocated for each. Expenses that are discretionary in nature can be such things as entertainment, clothing, food, and utilities. Again these are items that are not set and provide places where adjustments can be made. Where a mortgage is a set payment, the amount, someone spends on entertainment is something that can easily be adjusted. Some discretionary items could be considered dedicated such as food and some utilities but look at it this way. When it comes to food, you do not have to have a New York Strip steak for dinner when you could have a chicken breast. The same is true with utilities as in the winter instead of turning the heat up in the house put on extra clothes and save the money it would have taken to heat the entire house.

The first two steps in this process are primarily budgeting. Most people consider budgeting to be an evil thing but without a good budget it is impossible to start even on a financial plan or to get ahead financially in any manner. Budgets do not have to be elaborate or complicated in nature. If you have the desire, you can create your budget in any spreadsheet program such as Excel. If you do not want to create your own for free, you can get the one I have created that allows someone to track all of their income and expenses. If you are interested in such a spreadsheet that tracks and compares your actual expense to your budget go to www.kirkgmeyer.com and sign up for my free email newsletter. Then confirm your email address and send me an email with the subject "Free Spreadsheets" in the subject line. If you do not want to create or use a spreadsheet there are some web-based budget systems that will allow you to tailor your income and expenses and it will you access from any computer that has Internet access and Cash Control is one I recommend. To get it for a nominal annual fee go to Cash Control Budget. As an added tool, I have created a spreadsheet that can go hand in hand with either of these budget tools or any budget you have designed to use and that is a spreadsheet that will help anyone get out of debt by using the snowball method. You will need to list your debts, amounts owed, interest rates and minimum monthly payment owed. After you list all of your debts in the spreadsheet, it will tell you how long it will take to pay off all your debts and how much you will pay in interest. If you are interested this spreadsheet, please go to debt reduction.

Regardless of how you do it before we go on to the next stages in our financial plan, these first two must be completed. Take advantage of one of these two budget tools that have already been created, or you can take the time to develop one of your own. The key here is to do these steps so we can then move on to the next steps in our journey.

Personal Finance: A Grouping of Financial Topics
By Kirk G. Meyer

In our last topic, we examined how to start a financial plan by using budgets to establish the groundwork for everything else. Just remember that budgets are not the equivalent of a four-letter word. They allow all of us to be able to paint a picture of our financial wellbeing, and it will also enable us to move forward with our financial plans. Now that you have gathered all of your income and expenses it is time to turn our attention to the next step in our financial plan journey, and that is assets and liabilities.

This is known as your personal balance sheet as the budget would be your income statement. Just as you did with your expenses, it is now time to gather information on all of your assets and liabilities. For those of you who may not know, assets are things of value that you own outright or are buying through the use of a loan. Liabilities are debts that you owe someone else or a financial institution. As with anything, some liabilities are better than others, and some should be avoided. A mortgage is an example of a liability that is considered good as it is used to buy an asset that, in theory, is an appreciating asset meaning it should go up in value over time. While some may consider an auto loan a good liability that is not the case. As most autos are not appreciating assets but rather depreciating ones, meaning they will lose value over time and in many instances much faster than the loan that is being paid off. Credit card debt is always considered a bad liability as they have high-interest rates and have no asset associated with them. Try to avoid credit card debt if at all possible.

Now there are different types of assets and how they are categorized. First there are liquid assets such as cash in checking, savings and money market accounts. These assets are kept liquid because we may need to access them in a hurry for everyday expenses or emergencies. These assets are not considered to be tax advantaged as they are not intended to be used for retirement purposes. Next we have investment assets that can be equities, bonds, and real estate designed to be used for income production. These assets can be liquid to a degree such as equities and bonds or illiquid such as real estate. While these assets may be intended for retirement or just wealth accumulation, they are not going to be considered tax advantaged. Retirement assets are considered tax-advantaged because, in most instances, they are comprised of your 401(k) plans or individual retirement accounts of various types. These are also going to be considered illiquid at least until you reach age 59 ½ as there are stiff penalties and taxes associated with withdrawals prior to that age. If you have permanent life insurance policy, which has a cash value, that also needs to be considered an asset as would any college savings that may be in 529 plans or brokerage accounts. That pretty much sums up all of the assets of a financial nature.

Assets may also be in a more physical form, and many instances are considered illiquid as they may not be readily converted into useable cash. These include any real estate that is used as a residence and is not meant to be a source of income for you. An appraisal or tax assessment can value real estate. Vehicles such as autos and boats are also considered assets and would be considered at their current value as determined by comparison or through the use of a service such as Kelly's Blue Book. Collections such as art or coins go into this area as well as they are usually appraised for their value and need special riders for insurance purposes. The furnishings in your home have value and need to be included as assets as well. Determining the value of these assets may be more subjective and is open to debate. But it is better to estimate the value of such items on the more conservative side and always insure these items for actual replacement cost when you purchase your insurance policy for contents or in your renter's insurance policy.

Liabilities are a little straighter forward as compared to your assets. These are any debt you may have for any reason. Any unpaid balances on your credit cards appear here. The balance on your mortgage is also a liability as would any outstanding balance on an auto loan is you were to have one of those. Also, if you have student loans do not forget to list those as well.

Now the difference between what is in your asset balance and your liability balance is your net worth. If you are prudent and have been managing your finances, your net worth will be positive. If the number is negative, that means you owe more than you own, and we have some extra work that will need to be done for you to achieve financial prosperity. But do not get to down or beat yourself up too bad if you are young there is time to fix this issue and for older people you may want to seek a professional to see what steps can be taken to get you into a position that your net worth is positive.

The next step in our journey to a financial plan is the estimation of any goals that require saving for, any college expenses that need to be accounted for, and how to better manage your taxes by estimating what it is you will owe. These three areas may not be a primary concern for everyone, but it is a group of things that always need to be considered. Compared to the first two steps this topic will be shorter as these areas are relatively straight forward with the exception of taxes.

If there are any special goals that you or your family have, it is best to plan in advance for them and try to fund them over years and not at the end of your working years. Say you want to travel the country after you retire in a large fancy motorhome. Well, as you may have guessed, that is not an inexpensive purchase and will require either you save for the acquisition, or you will have to liquidate some of your existing assets to make the purchase. If you know that this is something you will want, the more logical course of action is to save for the large outlay of cash by estimating what the cost will be in however many years away the purchase will be. As an example, if you figure inflation will be 3.5% annually it will take more money to buy something in 20 years as it would be if you bought it today. That means the average cost of goods will increase at 3.5% a year every year over that 20 year period. This means that you need to have an after tax and after inflation adjusted returns that are at least greater than those two items combined. The reason taxes must be considered most goals are funded in brokerage accounts and not in tax-advantaged retirement accounts.

When saving for college there are some more options as compared to goals. One way to save for college is, in fact, the same way as a goal and that is in a taxable account that will have to produce returns that outpace not only taxes but the actual inflation factor of education, which over the past few decades has been greater than that of general inflation. Meaning your account will actually have to return significantly more than the next option. And the next option is a state-sponsored 529 college savings plan. These plans are tax advantaged and will grow tax deferred, and the proceeds will be tax-free if used for qualified education expenses. This is an enormous advantage over a taxable account as all the gains will continue to grow in these accounts and the return, in theory, will only have to keep pace with the inflation factor for education and taxes will not be an issue. In many states, they offer to reduce your state income taxes for any amount that you contribute to that state's 529 plan so check with your state to see what the tax advantages may be. But do shop around as different states offer different plans with different expenses associated with the investment options.

Taxes are more complicated, and we will not go into them too much here. Taxes are also a touchy subject for many, but this is one instance where everyone's situation is different. If you are someone who gets a large tax refund every year, you may be someone who needs to evaluate your tax withholdings. There is no need to give the government an interest-free loan every year. In these instances, adjust your deductions with your employer to withhold less in taxes from each paycheck.

But on the other hand if you are someone who uses your tax refund as a savings account it may be worth it to you to continue to loan the government this money especially of you are a person who has trouble saving. The goal with taxes is to pay very little at the end of the year or to get very little back in the way of a refund. Use your prior year's return as a guide to the current year and make your adjustments accordingly.

As we continue our path to a financial plan, the next stop is one that may get a little complicated, and that is in the area of insurance. Now there are many types of insurance and all are important and have their place in your financial plan. The central point of insurance is to mitigate the risks that you could not afford to cover on your own if something bad were to happen. Many insurance is now mandatory for either the government or financial institutions. But we will mainly be looking at life insurance, disability insurance, and long-term care.

Most people do have health insurance if they work for a large employer on a full-time basis through that employer's plan. But even if you do not get that benefit through employment, health insurance is now available through the Affordable Health Care Act. Now days there is no reason everyone in America should not have some form of health care. By having health insurance, it reduces the chances that you will be hit with a large medical bill that could wipe out your hard earned savings. No, I am not saying that by having health insurance you will not ever be hit with large medical bills because that does indeed happen, and it happens to a lot of people every year. But by having health insurance in place you will reduce the risk of large medical bills.

Insuring your assets is next on the list of insurance we will just briefly discuss. Most states require at least liability insurance on autos and if the vehicle is financed the lending institution will require full coverage of liability, comprehensive and collision insurance on the car. Houses are the same way with the lending institution requiring at least the amount of the loan is insured for their protection. It is a good practice to evaluate your residence insurance every few years to make sure that the cost to replace your home is not out of line with the amount of insurance you carry. Another type of insurance that goes with these two kinds is extra liability insurance or an umbrella policy that is done in conjunction with your homeowner's policy. Usually for a minimal annual premium you can get a million dollars in liability coverage for added protection. Remember the insurance is about managing risks you cannot afford to fund out of your savings in the event something bad occurs.

Life insurance is an insurance that is not required by any law, statute, government, or lending institution. This is a policy that is up to you as t if you do, in fact, need it. If you are young, single, and have little debt, there may not be a need for you to have life insurance or at least a significant policy. Also, when we are younger, we do not as a rule have much in the way of disposable income making a permanent policy cost prohibitive, but when you are younger you can purchase large amounts of term policies. These are policies that accumulate no cash value and expire when the term ends. The only way these policies will pay a death benefit is if you die during the period covered by the term. Permanent policies are in place until you die or stop paying the premiums. These policies will accumulate a cash value and will, in fact, stay in place for the rest of the insured's life. For a brief look at the different types of insurance, you can get my eBooklet from Amazon.com or by clicking the following link, The Basics of Life Insurance.

Now there are many ways to determine what kind of policy you need or the amount that you think you need to have in place. As a general rule, it is a good thing to remember that you are managing risk here, and there are many ways to get a correct answer. Personally I believe that many people may have a need to have a combination of policies to achieve their desired goals. As someone gets older they, in theory, require less coverage. This is because as you get older your expenses that need to be insured are decreasing. Think of it this way if you will. You bought your house when you were younger and therefore you needed to insure your family for the value of the mortgage in the event you were to die. The same goes for your children's college expenses. But after a certain age you will no longer need to fund your children's college or pay off the mortgage as you have already funded those expenses. Also, when you retire, you will not need insurance to replace your income as you are no longer earning any income. So it may make sense for the primary wage earner to have two term policies in place at the same time. Say one is for 20 years to help cover the cost of college for your children as well as any other bills you wish to be paid off when you die. The other policy should be a 30-year policy to match your mortgage. Now here is a third option, and that is to have a permanent policy in place to cover any final expenses or to cover any outstanding issues that you wish to be taken care of upon your death. As you can see, there is no one right or wrong approach to life insurance and in many instances a combination may be the correct answer. As for how much insurance you need that will depend on where you are in your life. Consider all aspects and take appropriate action to ensure you are covered and can mitigate the risks.

Now disability insurance is another that is not a required policy to have but one that is worth looking into also to help reduce the danger of lost income. These policies will replace a portion of your income either for short-term or long-term depending on what type of policy you buy. Short-term policies are for periods of less than two years and have a waiting period before benefits are paid. The longer the waiting period you have before benefits are paid, the cheaper the policy will be. For long-term policies, they will wait anywhere from 90 days to 6 months before benefits will be paid. These policies will also be particular in what occupations will be paid benefits. Some will pay you provided you cannot work your occupation while others will pay provided you cannot work in any occupation. As a general rule, these policies will not pay more than 60% of your salary and will end after a certain number of years or age 65 when social security will be available to the insured. This insurance can be expensive depending on how you set it up. For people who have shorter waiting periods, limit the policy to their occupation, and have long lengths for their payments will pay more than someone who chooses more lenient options. It is good risk management to have some protection on your income to cover you to a degree in the event you are unable to work.

Long-term care insurance is a more expensive insurance to have and again this is one that is not required by any law or statute. This insurance is somewhat similar to disability insurance as the premiums will depend on several factors. One is the age in which you take out the policy. The younger one is when they buy the policy, the lower the premium will be because in theory you will be paying the premium for a longer period. Another factor that has a large impact on the policy's premium will be the waiting period from the time you are first admitted into long-term care and when the policy will begin to pay. The longer the waiting period, the lower the premium will be but the more out of pocket expenses you will have to pay. These policies are also limited to a set amount that they will pay per day of care, and they are for a period not to exceed five years or a maximum dollar amount. The final main component is if the policy will have inflation protection that will adjust the amount the policy will pay in accordance with inflation. It is not uncommon for the premium of this insurance to run $400 to $500 a month for someone who is in their fifties. The premiums are much more reasonable for younger people but then again you have to remember you will be paying for a longer period.

Long-term care is one type of insurance where someone, in theory, can self-insure. This is done by someone who is diligent and has the will power to ensure that they do save the amount they would pay for the premium for the insurance. An example of this is if someone's premium $300 a month they can self-insure by investing that money in a low expense mutual fund or exchange-traded fund such as an indexed fund. By investing the money that would have been spent on the premiums in such a manner a person can expect to have a sizable amount saved that can be geared towards long-term care or in the event that they do not need that they have funds that can be used for other purposes or left to their heirs. While most people today will need some form of long-term care, the length and amount they will need will vary from person to person. But someone who is 25 and saves the $300 a month premium for 40 years and got an after-tax return of 5% would have approximately $450,000 to self-insure or leave to their heirs. This is an insurance that people need to think about and consider many factors prior to purchasing.

The next part of the journey in our financial plan is asset allocation. When we consider the asset allocation, we are talking about equities, bonds, real estate, commodities, and cash. Depending on what the asset class is, will determine the return one can expect. Historically equities have outperformed bonds. But it is always paramount to remember that past performance is no indication of what an asset will do in the future. But we use historical averages to help gauge what an asset may do in the future. I am sure you have heard the adage that "no risk, no reward". That saying will play a significant role in one's asset allocation depending on their risk tolerance. Obviously some assets classes are riskier than others and therefore they should expect higher returns for the added risk taken. Asset allocation, as a rule, will change as one gets older, and it becomes more conservative in nature.

When you are younger, you can afford to take more risk in your investing than someone who is approaching retirement. The reason behind that is due to the fact younger people have more time to make up for and correct any losses that they may encounter. As someone approaches retirement, they cannot afford to sustain losses of their principal in such a way as someone younger. That is because they will have a shorter period to recover from any such losses. When you are younger, or if you feel as if you can afford to take more risks, it would be wise to invest more in equities rather than bonds or commodities. Real estate is an asset class that takes a particular type of investor to own the actual property, but the use of real estate investment trusts is something that is more acceptable to the investing public, in general. Commodities such as gold and silver are viewed as hedges against inflation and can be owned either by having the actual metal in bullion form or through mutual funds or exchange traded funds. But again someone who is younger should focus their attention mainly on equities.

Now as far as equities go in America there are basically three types of classes for equities. The riskiest US equity class is small cap stocks that also have the highest returns of the three US equity classes. The next is mid cap stocks that are comprised of companies that are medium in size and they return the next best return. And finally the large cap stocks that most people know as the S&P 500 types stocks have the lowest return of the three equity classes, but it still is better than any other asset classes return. You can also invest in foreign markets to provide a broader base for diversification but it is advisable to do this by investing in mutual funds or exchange traded funds to reduce the risks associated with owning a single stock. While equities may have the highest risk, they also provide the highest returns. But by investing across the entire spectrum of equities with the use of mutual funds and exchange traded funds can reduce the portfolio's overall risk while maximizing your returns.

The next asset class to have reliable returns over the long haul are bonds. There are four categories of bonds that are sold and traded in the US, and there are government bonds that are issued by the federal government, municipal bonds, corporate bonds, and high-yield bonds or junk bonds. The lowest risk is in federally issued bonds as the federal government has never defaulted on any of its debts. As they are the lowest in risk, they also have the lowest returns of the four US-based bonds. Municipal bonds are next as far as risk as few issuers of these bonds have defaulted although in recent years it has become a little more familiar. These bonds will pay a little higher of a rate compared to federally issued bonds. Government bonds also pay lower yields because they are tax-advantaged as compared to the other types of bonds issued and the owner does not have to pay either federal or state income taxes depending on who issued the bond and where the owner lives. Corporate bonds will pay higher yields than government bonds, and they do carry more risk of default. A bond rating agency rates corporate bonds as with any bond and you will have an investment and non-investment grades. Most government bonds have investment grades unless you are dealing with a municipality that is in financial trouble. Investment grade corporate bonds have historically been decent investments, and as the bond goes down the grading scale the interest rate that they must pay will have to increase due to the additional risk associated with owning the bonds. Junk bonds are the riskiest and, therefore, pay the highest interest rates of the US-based bonds. Just as with equities, bonds are sold by foreign companies and governments and if you desire to diversify into foreign bond markets it is best to do so through mutual funds or exchange traded funds. Just as in US based bonds foreign bonds are rated by the bond agency rating companies.

As we reduced risk, we have also reduced the expected return. Again, someone who is younger should focus their attention on domestic and foreign equities with possibly a little devoted to other asset classes. As a person goes into their life and approach retirement, they tend to shift their focus from equities to safer income-producing assets such as bonds or blue chip stocks that pay dividends. The key for any investor is to assess their risk tolerance and invest accordingly. And then you must re-evaluate your risk tolerance on a regular basis and adjust your portfolio accordingly as well. This goes with assessing your assets allocation to ensure that your portfolio stays consistent with your risk tolerance and goals. That means if one asset class goes up or down by say 5% you sell assets that appreciated and buy assets that did not do as well. If you do not wish to sell assets if they are in a taxable account and you invest on a regular basis you can invest more in the asset that did not perform as well and less in the ones that did better. By investing this way you rebalance your assets, and you do not trigger any tax consequences.

Some financial advisors will say you need minimal equities as you enter your retirement years. I feel that equities still will play a major role in anyone's retirement portfolio mainly because someone may be in retirement for 30 plus years. If someone were to be in retirement for that long of a period relying solely on income producing, assets would make it difficult to ensure you do not run out of money before you die. That is why it is important to maintain some percentage of equities even in retirement. That is because equities tend to appreciate in value at a pace that one will outpace inflation and to provide your portfolio the chance to add to its principal base thereby increasing the overall value of your portfolio. Even in retirement it is not unreasonable for someone to hold about 30% of their portfolio in at least established large cap companies.

The final component of the outline to the basic financial plan is going to be estate planning. For the average married couple, federal estate taxes will not be an issue. As for state estate taxes, it is best to check your state's laws on estate taxes or seek the advice of a professional financial planner or estate lawyer. As far as federal estate taxes go they do not start until an individual has over $5.34 million dollars for 2014. That amount doubles for married couples to $10.68 million, but there are no estate taxes for a married couple when one spouse dies and leaves their estate to the surviving spouse.

If you exceed the federal limits for estates, there are certain ways to reduce your possible estate taxes. If you are lucky enough to be in this position of having more than $5.34 million if you are single or $10.68 million if you are married is by gifting assets while you are alive. But you must be careful in the manner in which you gift as to avoid gift taxes or generational skipping taxes. You can reduce your estate prior to your death by gifting up to $14,000 to any person regardless of age, relation, or reason. If you are married, you can do a split gift, and that will allow you to gift double the amount to $28,000 per person per year.

Other ways to reduce your taxable estate is to give to charity that is always a good thing no matter what your intentions are with regards to your estate. It is best to donate assets that have appreciated in value and the more they have appreciated, the better. This way you can reduce your taxable estate by the amount of the donation, and you are also able to reduce your income tax for the year in which you made the donation. And the final reason it is advisable to donate in this manner is to reduce your overall taxes as your cost basis in the assets is low and as it has appreciated in value you will not have to pay capital gains on the increased value of the assets. Remember you get to take the value when you donate the asset, not the value of what you paid for it.

And if you have grandchildren or nieces and nephews you can pay for their college education in addition to gifting them assets every year. This is done by paying the educational institution directly for college expenses and not by gifting the funds to the child. If you do it this way, you can gift more than the allowed $14,000 or $28,000 a year depending on your marital status. This exclusion also applies when you pay for someone's legitimate medical expenses when the funds are paid directly to the medical institutions such as a hospital. If you pay for either of these two items in this manner, it does not matter if the ultimate recipient is a relative or a complete stranger. They key to avoiding triggering a gift is that the funds are paid directly to the institution.

As you can now see creating a financial plan is a very detailed and most likely time-consuming endeavor. It also requires that you provide a comprehensive list of all sources of income, all expenses, all assets, all liabilities, all insurance policies, and you must determine your desired asset allocation based on your tolerance. Once you have accomplished all of these necessary steps, and many that I did not go over you will begin to see, the beginnings of a comprehensive financial plan take shape.

Budgeting

In the previous chapter, we have gone through the very basic steps of creating a fairly comprehensive financial plan. Regardless of if you will engage someone to help you with your finances and go the whole way and indeed create a financial plan there is one area that needs to be addressed for you and your family's financial health. No matter if you are financially oriented if you want to get ahead or move forward it is imperative to develop and maintain a budget. If you do not know exactly how much money you are bringing in on a regular basis and also do not know where your hard earned money goes how will you ever truly have a handle on your finances? In order to maintain a healthy relationship with your finances, it is imperative to be able to answer the previous question about your money. Think of it this way, once you know where your money goes you can begin to achieve financial freedom by budgeting, limiting, and managing your expenses. While it is true most people do not budget those who are getting out of debt and beginning to save for a house, a child's education, or their retirement have an excellent idea of where their money goes. In other words, they do in fact budget to some degree.

I owe a lot of thanks to my mother as she started with me and my sister at an early age to begin the budgeting process. When I was younger, of course, my budgets were very simple. I earned an allowance, made extra money doing odd additional money doing extra chores, and even did filing for my dad as he was a salesman who worked out of my childhood home. In the beginning it was very simple; I earned a little money, and I saved for things I wanted such as toys, then clothes, and finally my life beyond my parent's home and protection. This was before the age of personal computers and well before such helpful tools like spreadsheets and the age of the Internet. I started out with a single sheet of paper that was divided into what my income sources were and what my few expenses ended up being. Like most kids, and people, in general, I did not like doing the budget much less adhering to it but even at a young age I saw the benefits of developing a budget. Again thank you to my mom.

As times and methods have changed since my first budgets one thing remains consistent and the same, they help and they work. On the homepage of this very blog, I have a tab where you can buy a spreadsheet I developed that will help you budget in a fairly easy and painless manner. In it there is room for up to 90 expenses in addition to your income. You determine where your money goes and how much will be allocated to each line item. Daily or however often you want you simply input the amounts in one of the twelve month's tabs that are broken down by days. There is a tab in the spreadsheet that will show you how you did on your budget and it performs a comparison for you. It is a simple and direct approach to budgeting that I have used for many years. The main drawback is you need the file with you or access to it in order to input your expenses.

Enter web-based programs, and now you can achieve the same results from any computer with Internet access.

No longer are you tied to a single computer or forced to carry a thumb drive with your spreadsheet file with you. During the month of July I will use two methods to budget a mixture of my own expenses and income mixed with some fictitious figure to make things interesting to show how by budgeting and knowing where your money is going can help you get on top of things. I will purposely develop a budget that is negative on cash flow and as the month develops we will explain the adjustments that will be made. Now for the web-based programs I will be using Auto Budgeting, which has a nominal fee of $38 annually. For more information on this excellent program for budgeting visit Auto Budgeting.

I do recommend everyone budget, and yes, I will promote the two methods I am using on the topics, the spreadsheet I developed and Auto Budgeting, which is an affiliate of mine. Regardless of how you decide to budget the important thing is you do budget. Please try one of these methods or develop your own but do not give up on yourself and your finances. For more information on budgets, feel free to look at my Amazon books where I have an eBooklet available for $0.99 which helps to dispel the myths of budgets, Budgeting 101.

Part two in the budget monitoring blog that I am doing the month of July. While this is not going to be a very long series of blogs or comprehensive, it does lay the groundwork for anyone who is wanting to start the budgeting process. Last week I discussed my Excel-based budget that I think is excellent and efficient and a second that is web-based and also looked to be very efficient. Now the advantage of the web-based budget is it is accessible from any computer with Internet access.

Now I have used my spreadsheet since I developed it a few years ago with good results. It is easy to use and provides you with a snapshot of where you are financially at any point in time. The positives that I discovered this week in my spreadsheet are it tracks all expenses you make provided you enter them into the spreadsheet. Now you may do this daily or save your receipts and enter them every few days or once a week. Now the longer you wait to enter them the more likely you may forget one and your budget will be off by that missing amount. Also, it shows you exactly where you are with your spending and will detail if you are positive or negative in your spending at that point in time. There is a tab for each month and under that monthly tab there are the days of the month. The spreadsheet provides enough space for approximately 90 expenses and up to five sources of income. The negative of this spreadsheet is you must enter the data within the file, and there is no web-based component unless you subscribe to a service such as Dropbox to store the file for easy access. For a modest $5.00 charge, you may get my spreadsheet at the following link, BUDGET. All you need to do is sign up for my free email newsletter and send me an email with the subject "Free Spreadsheets".

The web-based program I utilized is a similar format but allows the user to determine if the expense is one-time or recurring. If the expense is recurring the program enables the user to determine how often it will recur. The program allows you to determine if the expense is one that is saved for in a "savings" bucket or is one that is paid for out of the "cash" bucket. Some of the positives for this system are that you can add as many expenses as you have and are not limited as in my spreadsheet. Also, you can access your budget from any computer that has Internet access for ease of entry of your expenses. Just as in my budget you are required to enter the expenses in a manner that you see fit and one that works for you best. Again it is better to update this and any budget on a regular basis to ensure that they are accurate. One of the things I noticed as a negative and was the only real drawback of the program was if an expense is in the cash bucket category it assumes you will spend that exact amount no more and no less in the designated period. While this is not necessarily a bad thing is may be an issue if you use cash on a regular basis and do not spend the full amount. That may cause you to have a budget that is just a little off. This week I will see if there is a way to take any savings from the cash bucket to the savings bucket as that is where they should go in theory anyway. For an annual membership of $38 this system will give you access to your budget, an eBook on how to get the most out of your budget, and emails with tips and encouragement to keep you focused. To get this budget click on the following link, Web-Based Budget. More on this method as I get further in the month and develop a better understanding of how it works and functions.

Now several years ago I came across a group of spreadsheets that I found useful to the point that when Excel updated several years ago I developed my spreadsheet. No mine is not 100% original but at the time the new Excel came out I had forgotten the name of the company that I bought my spreadsheets from. While this spreadsheet does cost a little more than mine, it is an excellent spreadsheet and worth the extra money in my opinion. One reason is it has a lot more than 90 fields for expenses where is mine is indeed limited. This company also offers two versions of their spreadsheet for budgets one being the basic and the second having daily tracking and a spending analyzer. The company also offers very well developed spreadsheets for retirement planning, net worth, mortgage planning, investment planning, and a 401(k) Planner. Another advantage is they do offer a budget planner in the following currencies: Euro, Pound, and Rand. The basic eight spreadsheets are sold for a reasonable $39.95 as a package at a savings of over $36 if bought individually. Another positive if for an additional $20 you can get the premium package that includes three licenses and on-line backup of your budget with free software upgrades. For this extremely well-developed suite of spreadsheets visit the following link, Simple Planning.

Of the three at this point I recommend the entire suite of spreadsheets from Simple Planning.

I started with two methods and last week added a third into the mix. While any of these three are more than adequate to accomplish one's needs in the budgeting process I have come to the conclusion that is really does come down to personal preference in what you are looking for in your budget and how you want to accomplish your goals. I prefer one of the spreadsheet methods as discussed last week and after buying the Simple Planning package again I do favor it even over my spreadsheet and the web-based program. As this whole process is up to you and your preference I will this week go over each of the three programs and detail what I did and did not like about each. Now one is not better than the other but what it boils down to is personal preference and for you to decide what works best for you.

The first method and least expensive is the spreadsheet I developed a few years ago based loosely on the Simple Planning spreadsheet. While my spreadsheet offers the main same essential features of Simple Planning it does not have many places to add and subtract more expenses and is technically limited to nine groups of ten expenses that are allowed to be customized. In this regard, it is somewhat limited over that of Simple Planning but it does come at a fraction of the cost at just $5.00. While Simple Planning is a better spreadsheet in my opinion it does come at eight times the cost of the suite of spreadsheets that is the best deal that they offer as there are some excellent tools that are not available in my limited spreadsheet. But I do offer a debt reduction tools that when used with the budget spreadsheet can help anyone get on top of their finances and reduce their debts. You can get both of the powerful tools for the price of one spreadsheet from Simple Planning at a cost of $10. If you are interested in the tools, I will develop I sell them as a single or double gig on Fiverr or at the following link, Budget/Debt Reduction. Sign up for my free email newsletter and send me an email with the subject "Free Spreadsheets" for a copy.

The next I will examine is Cash Control, which is the web-based system. While this system is very well designed and extremely comfortable to use, it has one main issue I had while trying to utilize it as an ongoing budget. The one area where I found it frustrating was that funds that were designated as a cash expense were limited to what was budgeted from what I could tell. If you input all your expenses as "big ticket" items you can manually input what you spent each week or month. But for cash items it was limited to what was budgeted, and there was little room to adjust the budget. A very nice feature of the system is that it does break down monthly expenses into what needs to be saved on a weekly basis that I did find very beneficial. The idea of separating items into one of the buckets was also very well planned and operated extremely well with the sole exception being the cash bucket that I have already discussed the shortfalls. And yes another of the main draws of this system over mine is that it is web-based and may be accessed from any computer with Internet access. This allows you to update your expenses at any time and not limit you to when you are on your computer or have your thumb drive with the spreadsheet saved on it. Some other benefits of Cash Control are that they offer 60 day money back guarantee, a very useful eBook that will aid you in setting up your budget and gives some excellent budget techniques and the company will even send you encouraging emails with helpful hints as well. You get all of this for a relatively small annual price of $38. Overall this is not a bad deal at all and can be powerful and valuable tool to be used in your budgeting processes.

Now on to what I believe is the best of the three options and is also the best value for the money. Simple Planning can be purchased as a single spreadsheet for say budgeting for $9.95. But the company offers a total of eight very useful and powerful spreadsheets. The spreadsheet by itself is an excellent value and as I stated earlier is a much better-improved version of the spreadsheet I offer. But that is just a small part of what Simple Planning has to offer. For $39.95 you can get all eight of the spreadsheets for your personal use. Let's look at them individually. As for the budget spreadsheet, mine is the same but this one has a spending analyzer that is very useful in giving you a snapshot of where you money is going. The quick budget and comparisons are done very professionally, and the spreadsheet is very easy to understand and use. There is a tax planning for 2013 that I am looking into adjusting for 2014, but I am not 100% certain it will be an active crossover, but it is worth noting that they make this available each year. There are three spreadsheets that can be used for your investments and retirement accounts, and they are a retirement planner, investment planner, and a 401(k) calculator. All three of these are very powerful and can help guide you to financial peace that may be many years down the road. What you need to be aware of while using these three spreadsheets is that you need to use reasonable and attainable goals for your assumptions. Two other useful spreadsheets are a net worth calculator and a mortgage calculator that can be used to get a good snapshot of where you are in an overall picture. A final spreadsheet that I have not used much is the calendar planner. From my limited playing in the spreadsheet, it appears to allow you to plan on a monthly and weekly basis and is good for many years to come. If you have many meetings, events or need to track items this is an excellent tool for you to have as well. You get all of this from Simple Planning for a very reasonable cost of just $39.95, or you can get the premium service for $59.95 that allows for cloud storage and access from any computer. This option combines the best of a spreadsheet with the web-based system.

When I started this series, I fully intended to have it last a full month and do a comparison but after three weeks Simple Planning is the apparent leader and advantage when developing and using a budget system. For more information on the budget process, feel free to click the link for Books on Amazon by Kirk and pick up a copy of my eBooklet Budgeting 101.

Personal Finance

Financial planning is not rocket science and the terms used are not entirely foreign. Why would someone who is educated need a financial planner then? The answer is simple, they remove the emotion that most investors experience. They act as your buffer to execute your plan nothing more. Well they can also advise you as to how to own individual assets or when to rebalance to maintain harmony with your plan so they do have a place and do serve to fulfill many aspects of your financial needs. Find one you trust, be honest with them, expect them to be frank with you, and always communicate with one another.

On that last point, communication. It is important that you and your planner are on the same page from the beginning. If your planner uses terms, you are not familiar with stop them right then and have them explain it further. The same goes for investments if you do not understand something they propose you include in your plan ask them for further explanation or clarification. Planning does not have to be confusing, and planners do not have to use big words to explain simple ideas when a simple term will work just as well.

While your planner may need to understand the big and confusing words because they have regulations to follow they should be able to condense these topics and ideas down into simpler terms for their clients. Also, it is important that a planner make it know to you as the customer that they are looking out for your best interests and are not just in this to make their money. Granted they are not performing these duties for free but be leery of planners who seem to avoid fees and commissions. Yes, that is how we make our money and like anyone who provides someone with a service we deserve to get paid but there has to be total transparency in this aspect of the relationship. They should show that they care about you and your needs above what they want you to do. You are their client, and they work for you. It is wise to remember that and use planners that remember that as well.

Remember all investors have access to the same information. Be leery of an advisor who claims to have a system or knows of a manager that is beating the averages. Chances are they do not have a legitimate system and yes that manager may have been doing good but chances are that is old news. As a planner never assume that your clients understand all the technical terms and try to use the simplest ones that will still convey your message. And as clients of planners never are afraid to ask a question, that is what your planner is there for. To answer that and address any other issue you may have.

Personal Finance: A Grouping of Financial Topics
By Kirk G. Meyer

There are some common financial terms that everyone needs to be aware of. In order to be on top of your financial game and to keep ahead, it is crucial that you know and understand these following terms. It is also important that you keep these in mind as you continue to grow and proceed on your financial journey. The key is to understand and maintain a good working knowledge of these terms and keep them in mind when going through your life.

The first is the concept of net worth. If you think about this one, it is clear this is important for you to know and understand. A person's net worth is the value of all their assets and then the deduction of their liabilities. The difference is your net worth. If it is positive, that is what everyone strives for in the end. A negative net worth is where you owe more than you own. This situation is not good and will require some serious work on your part.

Inflation is the rate at which our money can buy things at a future date. Let's face it, that 20 years ago we made less, and most things cost less in comparison to today. The average rate at which we need to make more and in turn we spend more has been about 3% a year in growth of the inflation rate. This means that the money we save today needs to grow at a rate higher than inflation so we will have purchasing power in the future. If we do not do, this our money will not be enough for us to have the buying power we will need.

Another term that is important to people is liquidity. As a former bank examiner liquidity is not only something, that is important to businesses but also individuals.

Liquidity for individuals is how easily you can get at your money. Cash is considered the most liquid of assets and keeps in a savings or checking account. Real estate would be an asset that is considered non-liquid as it may take a long time for you to sell and get your money out of the asset. Equities can be regarded as both liquid and non-liquid as they are easy to sell, but you may not sell at a profit every time. If you have an emergency fund, which everyone should, that needs to be held in a very liquid asset such as cash.

Some additional terms that many people interested in financial markets need to know and understand are bull and bear markets. These terms refer to how the United States stock markets are trending. If the markets are going up, economic trends are positive, and unemployment is low we are in a bull market. Today we are experiencing a bull market but how long it will last is anyone's guess. That is the nature of the markets they go up then at some point they reverse and go down. If the markets are not doing well, economic trends are negative, and unemployment is rising we are in a bear market.

Risk tolerance is very intertwined with the markets. How risky do you want to be in your investments? That is a crucial term for anyone who invests their hard earned money. Younger people tend to have a higher risk tolerance as they are younger, and if someone has time on their side they can afford to take more risks. The reason is simply that the longer you have to invest the longer you have to make back any losses. There are several websites that offer free risk analysis so to find one you like simply do a Google search for one that fits your needs.

A final term that is linked to the stock markets and can be used for any investing is diversification. This is not just limited to stocks, and you do need to be diversified in that area as it is never good to be heavily investing in one company or sector of the market. But you also need to diversify asset classes and own such things as equities, bonds, real estate, cash, and commodities. By doing this, you limit your exposure to any one asset class taking a downturn and by not exposing all your investments to one asset class. Also, by diversifying you will reduce your risk that is taken in your overall portfolio.

The final two terms we will look at are related, and they are interest and compound interest. Both of these concepts can work for and against you depending on how you use them or how they are used against you. Interest is what you are paid for loaning someone your money or what you will pay for someone to lend you money. It is the cost of money to you or the cost of using your money from the bank you use. Compound interest is what makes interest a powerful ally or enemy. If you are saving money, the compounding of interest means you will earn a set amount of money on a set basis. Then you will make money from not only your original money invested but the previous interest paid to you. It is the same with what you owe, and that is what makes loans, especially credit cards, dangerous. It is better to be on the receiving end of compound interest any time.

Those are some of the key financial terms everyone needs to know. While not terribly in depth this does give you an excellent overview.

Do you have credit card debt? Are you looking for an easy way to reduce your credit card debt? If so you can employ a technique that is used for mortgages on your credit cards as well. In order to keep your balances as low as possible try to pay off the card every month but in the event you cannot do that try making payments every two weeks on the card instead of a single monthly payment. If you do this you will pay smaller interest payments and more in principle as well as making an extra full month's payment that in theory will go directly to your principal balance as there are 26 two weeks periods in a regular year.

Most credit card companies will charge interest based on your daily balance and by making multiple payments you will reduce the interest on an average basis. The more you pay, the more you will reduce your principal balance.

If you are like me and most other people you want to see instant results for your efforts and multiple payments on a credit card balance will provide that for you when you review your monthly statement. Replace a luxury item or a simple want with a payment to your credit card instead and see that balance reduce even faster. Many banks will let you set up a payment schedule, and you can automatically make payments every two weeks or on any other schedule you can work with.

However, you should contact your credit card company and make sure they allow multiple payments in a billing cycle as not all do. Some allow payments on a daily basis while others limit you to what is on your monthly statement. If the credit card issuer does not allow, multiple payments do not make them as they may charge you a fee or change the terms of your card. Also, check and verify that multiple payments will be applied to your minimum monthly amount due before you make multiple payments.

Are you thinking about opening a custodial account for a child or grandchild? These unique accounts are set up for a variety of reason, some legitimate and some maybe not so legitimate. It all depends on the intentions of the person making the donation or gift to a minor who is need of a custodial account. Many of these accounts are established for schooling and college because the child has inherited a substantial sum of money, or in the days of the past because the parents or grandparents were looking for tax advantages. Before you establish one of these unique accounts for a minor, there are some things that you need to be made aware of and think about prior to creating the custodial account.

The first and maybe one of the most important things to know about the establishment of a custodial account is the money is no longer yours, and they irrevocably belong to the minor who the account was established. Now most parents or grandparents are the ones who create these accounts, and they typically name themselves the custodian or manager of the account. While these people are the custodians of the account and determine what the money will be spent on there is a rule that cannot be broken in this complicated process. The money has to be spent on and for the benefit of the child who the account was established. The money cannot be used to buy a car for the custodian as an example, and the funds also cannot be given to another child after the establishment of the account. The money is to be used for the minor in which the account was established and no one else although it can be a fine line when it comes to that child and other family members.

Be prepared to hand over control of the custodial account to your child or grandchild at a relatively young age, 18 or 21 depending on your state. All minor custodial accounts as established under one of the two methods, the Uniform Gift to Minors Acts (UGMA) or Uniform Transfer to Minors Act (UTMA). At whatever age your child ceases to be a minor they gain control of the account and whatever is in it. When children are young, we never have any idea what they will be like as a teenager or young adult. We all have heard the stories of children who are "trust" babies, and many of these stories stem from one of these two acts.

And the final area of concern deals with various tax issues. As in any case that involves taxes or complicated financial matters I urge you to contact a professional that can best help you in your situation. First depending on how much the custodial account makes in a tax year you may be required to file a tax return for the account and child. This provision begins when the account generates more than $1,000 in income. This tax provision also applies to state taxes so check with your state on how they deal with custodial accounts and their taxation. The exception to this is if all the income from the custodial account is from interest, dividends, and mutual fund capital gains you may be able to add that income to your tax return. For more information, please seek the advice of a professional in your areas and for further information, please look for IRS Form 8814, Parent's Election to Report Child's Interest and Dividends.

Be on the lookout for the possibilities of the Kiddie Tax. In previous years, money could be given to a child in a custodial account as the gains were taxed at the child's tax rate and not as it is not the parent's tax rate. That means what could have been only a tax of 0; 10; or 15 percent now may be as high as 39.6% depending on the parent's tax bracket. This tax rule will begin when the income from the custodial account is in excess of $2,000. For more information on this particular tax, please seek the advice of a professional and look at IRS Form 8615.

And the final tax we will see that could affect a custodial account is the gift tax. Now this is a tax that the person who makes the gift reports on their tax return and very rarely are any real taxes paid on gifts. People are allowed to gift up to $14,000 a year to an individual and if you are married that doubles to $28,000. In the event, you exceed that amount there is always your lifetime gifting amount of $5.25 million over a lifetime. If more than the annual amount is gifted IRS Form 709 must be filled. And be on the lookout for generational skipping taxes if the person is more than 34 years younger than you are at the time of the gift.

Do you want to retire early? Not looking forward to working until you are 62, 65 or even 67? Not sure what to do in order to retire early? With stocks on the fast track for all-time highs and housing on an improved recovery, you may not be alone in thinking you can now retire early. It seems that after the terrible financial years from 2007 to 2009 it seems things may be back on track. While the economy is not breaking records, unemployment is still too high, interest rates are at all-time lows but stocks and most likely your 401(k) are doing great. And prior to the implementation of the Affordable Health Care Act people who did not want to pay outrageous health insurance premiums before becoming eligible for Medicare now have options they did not have before. An early retirement not only seems likely, it is possible for many. But let's go through what you may need to consider before you pull the plug on the 40 hour week and shift to the golden years of retirement.

For many an early retirement was off the table before they even had a chance to take a serious look at it for one reason; healthcare had to wait until you were 65 and were covered by Medicare. And private companies are reducing pre-retirement benefits for those who have not reached age 65. And let's face it as we get older many of us are confronted with pre-existing conditions that made health insurance impossible or extremely expensive. And while people born after 1960 have a full retirement age of 67 most people retire at 65 when they become eligible for Medicare.

Welcome the Affordable Health Care Act which now makes health insurance available to older Americans at what they are calling much more affordable prices and you can now forget about pre-existing conditions as those will no longer keep you from obtaining health insurance. If you are 60, you will pay no more than three times that of a 20-year-old on the state exchanges. No one said getting old would be cheap but under the new law getting older does not mean sky-high health insurance premiums that prior to the new law were closer to five times that of a younger person. But the Affordable Health Care Act does not mean you should not shop around as many private insurance companies may actually beat the premiums on the state exchanges. Just as with any insurance there are many factors that will go into your premium but the new law will give those who were high risk or uninsurable a chance at an early retirement without losing your health insurance from say age 60 to age 65 when they become eligible for Medicare.

Start looking now and provided you are signed up by December 15th your coverage will begin January 1st. And as you will now be retired your income, in theory, will be lower, and you may qualify for a subsidy, and the quoted price may not be the final price you have to pay. To be eligible for a subsidy, a single person has to make less than $45,000 and a family of four it is $94,000. Again you have some homework to do prior to making such a decision.

Now the earlier you retire, in theory, the more money you will need as you will hopefully be living longer while you are in your retirement years. And most people who are going to retire want to invest in safe investments such as bonds. But with interest rates at near historic lows that are not a good combination for a fully funded retirement or at least one at the level you desire. So what do you need to do to retire early? It is estimated that in today's environment you need to start saving about 18% of your income from age 35 to age 65. Now that is an average so some years you may save more and in some years you may save less but the key is to start early. Money compounded over 30 years will grow at rates that would actually surprise you but if you were to start an extra five or ten years and say start at age 25 instead of 35 you would be shocked at how much larger your nest egg would be. The more you can put into your retirement accounts at an early age the more likely you will be able to retire early. In order to retire better you need to be willing to live maybe on less now.

Some keys when you are young or regardless of age do not live in debt and pay off the debt you have. And once the debts are paid off do not adjust your standard of living due to the fact you now have some disposable income save it. Get your house paid off and shop for deals on high-ticket items such as cars. Then save, save, and save some more.

Now that you are entering an early retirement it may also be time to consider selling your house that chances are is too big for you now that your children are on their own.

And with the housing market having rebounded fairly well in most major markets it may be time to lock in some gains and downsize if it does indeed make sense. Look for areas that have lower property taxes, as well as maybe cheaper housing, in general. The key to making this change work is to make your living expenses lower and do not only move and exchange costs with no benefit. But if your house is paid for and the costs are manageable there may be no legitimate reason for you to downsize. Consider staying put and retire right where you are.

Now at this part of your journey to early retirement it is time to plan the first ten years or so. Now you will be living on your retirement funds and if you are lucky you may have a pension. The key to a truly successful retirement is to delay taking your Social Security as long as you can. If you are like me and your full retirement age is 67 you can get an extra 8% a year if you delay until you are 70. So do not count on interest rates to outpace historical inflation as a ten-year bond is yielding less than 3% right now. And as you have retired early you will be living longer in your retirement so in the time between your retirement and when you will start collecting Social Security you cannot dip too much into your principal. If you do dip into your principal, you run a real risk of outliving your funds. As you will be in retirement longer you will need to be more active in your investments and fixed returns will not sustain you for 40 or so years in retirement. Equities are riskier, but they will allow for income appreciation and have historically outpaced inflation. Now retirees need to have a diverse portfolio but not one made entirely of fixed returns but one that may be reliant more on equities to produce enough funds to last you through your longer retirement.

Following this suggestion may not guarantee you an early retirement but they will not hurt. And it is never a bad idea to be insured for health issues, so point one is always a good idea no matter if you are in retirement or not. Living debt free and saving as much as possible for when you do decide to retire is never a bad idea either. And if anyone learned anything from 2007 to 2009 it is we should always live within our means as far as our housing is concerned. Start early and plan for things, and you will be able to retire a few or maybe even several years early.

Do you think about your retirement and how taxes will affect your situation? It is never too early to consider the role of taxes on your retirement, and if you are past age 59 ½ this blog is directed towards you. In fact, if you have someone close to you in this age range I recommend you read this thinking about yourself and them. Not only do people of retirement age need to consider their taxes in retirement, but younger people need to be aware of the implications as well. As I tell people all the time it is never too early to save, plan for retirement, and consider the fact that taxes are unlikely to go down in the future. Most people who are retiring today have IRA accounts as well as 401(k) accounts from their employers. The rules for both are very similar and regardless of what else you do or plan for you will be required to make Required Mandatory Distributions (RMD's) from both accounts at age 70 ½. So here are some tips and techniques to use along the way at different ages between 60 and 70 ½.

Now that you are 60 you can access your IRA with no penalties associated with the withdrawals. But there is more to consider before you should make any of these withdrawals. If you have been saving during your working years, these funds may have been growing tax-deferred for 30-40 years. Another ten years of growth in these funds will increase your account balance like you would not believe. If you need proof, go into Excel and use the Future Value (FV) function and run the numbers you. The longer the money is left in the account, the higher the value will be and as the program will show the contributions made at the beginning of the account will have the most dramatic effect on its value. Money that is allowed to compound over 40-50 years will increase the bottom line in an IRA's value.

Also, you will need to consider what assets are held where prior to your retirement and maybe even after you have retired if you did not do this sooner. The reason you have to consider the tax implications is because some assets are taxed at a lower rate than an IRA. Depending on the tax bracket, you will be in after you retire will determine where assets should be held. Taxable bonds and real estate investment trusts should be held in a tax deferred account as they are taxed as ordinary income in the year they earn dividends and interest. Dividend paying stocks and mutual funds along with equities that will appreciate in value should be held in taxable accounts as they are tax advantaged in the year payments are made, or a long-term capital gain is achieved. Regardless of what kind of gain is realized in an IRA it will be taxed as ordinary income in the year in which the withdrawal is made. While no one knows what taxes will be like in the future I think, it is a safe assumption that they will most likely be higher than they are today.

At age 60 and in many instances as soon as you change jobs it may be a wise decision to roll old 401(k) accounts into your new 401(k) account. Some people advise rolling old 401(k) accounts into IRA's and in many instances that do make sense. Regardless of what you do with older accounts a smart move is to consolidate them into one or two accounts to reduce fees and expenses. Also, it makes sense to continue to make contributions to your IRA between the ages of 60 and 70 ½ when RMD is required. And to better prepare for your RMD's project your future balance in your IRA and calculate what the RMD will be. This is a valuable tool in planning for your retirement and possible tax consequences.

Age 65 and 66 for current retirees or those born prior to 1954. For people in this age range now, it may make sense to withdrawal funds from IRA accounts now to live off of and lower your RMD's at age 70 ½. A strategy that this makes sense for where you will forego the additional 4-5 years of tax-deferred growth is to delay taking one's Social Security benefits until age 70. By doing this, you are getting a guaranteed 8% return on your money as that is what Social Security will increase your monthly benefit by each year for three years or until you reach age 70. That is automatic 24% raise in Social Security benefits, which you may not see in your IRA for the same period.

Also, there is a need to consider Medicare premiums as well. As most retiree's will be relying on Medicare in their retirement making withdrawals from an IRA having an adverse impact on the premiums paid by Medicare Part B. If you increase your Modified Adjusted Gross Income too much it could actually affect the premiums you will be forced to pay for Part B. Check with the IRS tables to see what the cutoffs are or consult a tax professional. But this is something that does need to be kept in the back of your mind if you are younger or examined now if you are nearing retirement age.

If you are age 70 ½ there are a few items to discuss as well. One is always trying to avoid making two RMD's in the same tax year. As you are allowed to make the first RMD by April 1st of the year following your turning 70 ½ it could cause you to actually make two RMD's in the same tax year with the second being required by December 31st. To avoid this make the first RMD in the year, you turn 70 regardless of when that is and make your second RMD in the year you turn 70 ½. That will make your tax base lower and could save you some pretty serious money depending on how big your RMD's are. And always make your RMD's avoid a very costly penalty as well. By doing that you will also create a stream of income that you can rely on and count on for your living expenses. And in the chance your living expenses are already covered by other means you can then turn your RMD into a charity gift avoiding the taxes on the RMD and reducing your Adjust Gross Income with the gift to your favorite charity.

Retirement can be a scary time in most people's lives, but it does not have to be. With a little planning and proper forethoughts, it can be the golden and happy years you have dreamed of.

Are you prepared to retire? Do you have everything in order so you can retire? You do not need to hire a bunch of professionals to manage your retirement nest egg. But at some point we all do need to consult a qualified financial professional to make sure you are doing everything that you can to ensure your retirement is the best it can be. What do you need to do in order to achieve this and retire in the best possible way? Here are some simple but effective ways to ensure your retirement is the best it can be.

The first thing you need to do is give an honest assessment of where you stand today with regards to your retirement. What are your total assets? What are your total debts? If your mortgage is paid for or nearly paid for now is not the time to refinance or purchase a new home. It is also not the time to be buying new automobiles so fix the one that is paid for up and use it a few more years. The average person who is about to retire has an average balance of $250,000 in their retirement accounts and if you have a pension that is a bonus that you can count on for a steady stream of income after you retire.

Now if you are a parent you have to not subsidize your children or their lifestyle. If you are retired or about to retire do not go into debt to fund your children's college expenses let them do that as they will have longer to pay for them, and they can do it during their peak earning years as compared to your retirement years. And after college do not let them move back home. Make them live on their own and support themselves to ensure you will keep on your retirement path. But if they do move back in with you at least charge them rent and share the expenses to teach them valuable life lessons on money and to help you out with your bills.

But if your children are out of college and out of the house it may be time to consider to downsize what you are currently in. If the house is paid for, and you can afford the taxes and maintenance I really do not see the need to sell and downsize, but the decision is really up to you and your family. But if your house is paid for and you can use the proceeds to pay cash for a smaller house that is more economical then it is something that does need to be considered. Regardless of the real estate market if you sell a paid for house at a lower price than what it was a few years before remember you are likely also to be buying a new smaller house at a reduced price as well.

Another attractive retirement plan is to go international and move to a foreign country. Latin America, individual European countries, Malaysia, and Thailand are all popular locations for Americans to retire. Most of these countries have a local population that is respectful of their elders and are relatively safe. But before you pull up your roots and move international make sure you do your homework and due diligence.

Another way to reduce costs and save on your retirement funds is to look for free entertainment and use senior citizen discounts. Check out what is available for free where you live at the local library or community centers. Then if you do feel the need to get out of town look for cheap or free attractions within a few hours of your house where you can visit for the day and return home at night saving on a hotel stay. But if you do feel the need to travel, look at AAA and AARP for discounts for its members. Also, look for government subsidies for seniors that may be available as well. Do not be embarrassed to look into these programs as many are underutilized because people do not know about them or are afraid to ask.

How can you ensure you get the most of your retirement income? Be realistic and save for retirement and even in your retirement years to get the most out of your retirement nest egg.

The best way to preserve your retirement income is to eliminate as much of your debt before you retire as you can and avoid getting new debt after you retire. And in the event you cannot pay the debt off try to lock in the rate at a fixed interest rate rather than a variable rate in the event that rates rise which with them at all-time lows is very likely.

Evaluate your insurance needs. The amount of insurance you need in your pre-retirement years may very well be different than that of your retirement needs. As you approach retirement, you need to assess what you need in the way of life insurance. Also as you get older, the need for long-term care insurance will increase, but these are policies that it is better to buy when you may be a little younger than retirement age. And shop around and make sure all the insurance you get meets your needs and is affordable in your retirement years.

As I touched on above when you assess your situation you need to consider any pensions you may receive, social security, other streams of income you may receive and figure out what will need to come from retirement accounts and investments. Another thing that needs to be considered, at the same time you assess your financial income streams, are the tax consequences that you will face. I know we all think that we will be in lower tax brackets when we retire but at this point I am not sure if taxes will indeed be lower for people in their retirement years. In order to preserve your capital consider less traditional and liquid investments in exchange for security and higher yields, but do not chase yields stay with high grade safer investments.

Retirement does not have to be a scary situation if you properly plan for it now and do not wait until you are within five years of retiring. It is never too early to start planning for your retirement years if you want to have the best of your golden years.

If done properly saving for your retirement can be a process that spans many decades. I hope that everyone is saving for their retirement now and is not putting off this crucial aspect of one's life. As I have said before the key to a happy and successful retirement is to save as much as you can and to start as early as you can. Money that compounds over 30 years will grow to a figure that may alarm some of you.

Let us look at a hypothetical person who is 25 and will retire at age 67 when they reach their full retirement age. In the first scenario, this person will begin saving in an IRA with $5,500 a year for the full 42 years until they retire. In these calculations, we will not take inflation into account just as long as you are fully aware it is a reality and will have an effect on your purchasing power when you retire. In both these scenarios, we will assume a moderate 6.5% return over the life of the IRA. Now if you were to start investing at age 25, you would have approximately $1,256,000. Now consider you wait ten years before you begin saving, you would have almost $627,000. Simply by waiting ten years you cost yourself nearly half of your retirement account. So you can see that by saving early and often you will set yourself up for a better retirement.

Now that you can see the importance of how and when to save there are some things that many people do to themselves that can ruin one's retirement. One of the primary concerns is that will I take out more than I can afford to by eating my principal balance. Now one knows how long they will live in their retirement years although

I hope everyone has a very long and healthy retirement. Some of the issues that you need to consider when calculating what amount you can afford to withdrawal are the length of your retirement, how well your investment will grow, and what the inflation rate will be over your lifetime. While no one knows the answers to these questions you and your planner need to make the best assumptions that you can make. Look at historical averages for returns and inflations as a guide and your family tree to answer the question to how long you may expect to live. It is better to be conservative in your estimates such as inflation may be higher than historical levels, returns will be slightly below that of historical averages and you will live longer in your retirement that maybe your family history suggests. You will make these more conservative assumptions help ensure you do not run out of money in retirement.

Do not simply look at the figures when calculating what it is you will need in retirement. In addition to having enough funds to live a fulfilling life monetarily you need to consider a healthy and full life. I order to do this you must have good family and friends to surround you in addition to your retirement funds. And it is also important to make sure you are healthy both emotionally as well as physically. Take the time now to lay the groundwork for having a full set of family and friends that you can surround yourself with in your retirement years because let's face it who want to sit all the time alone.

And lastly do not fall into the trap of comparing yourself to others or chasing after unrealistic gains. No matter how much you save, there will always be someone who has more money that you. So save yourself the trouble and be content with what you have and make sure it is enough to cover the expenses you have. Unless you are Warren Buffett chances are you will worry about your retirement, just do not get worried if someone has more than you. Their situation will be different from yours and with that in mind, please understand the only people who you have to answer to are your family and no one else. And when many people are busy doing this when they should not be they are also on the lookout for the next easy way to increase their gains. Please, remember that by the time an actual tip that is based on reliable information reaches you the majority of the profits have already happened. Never chase potential gains with your retirement savings. Develop an investment plan with a financial planner and stick to it unless there is a credible reason for any deviations.

Make time work for you with the compounding of money. Use conservative estimates when you are calculating things and, above all, be realistic. And finally do not compare your situation to others and never chase golden opportunities. When you think you need help do not be afraid to seek out the help of qualified financial professionals.

Personal Finance: A Grouping of Financial Topics
By Kirk G. Meyer

Are you already preparing for your retirement? Do you understand some of the pitfalls associated with your retirement? Most people figure that if they save that they will be covered in their retirement. That may or may not be the case depending on what it is you are doing with your savings. The following are some areas that you may want to think or research some more prior to your retirement.

Be alert and fully understand saving on autopilot. Today many businesses will automatically enroll new employees into the company's 401(k) plans. This may be anywhere between 3% and 6% of one's salary. Is that enough for a comfortable retirement? To me personally I doubt that those percentages are sufficient for someone to save and ensure a comfortable retirement. I along with most financial planners suggest saving between 10% and 15% of your salary prior to any company matches that we will look at a little later in this blog. But they key here is when you receive any raises try to live on what you made prior to the raise and increase your percentage that you contribute to your 401(k).

As I mentioned previously, you need to contribute 10% to 15% of your salary prior to any company matching. But under no circumstance should you leave free money on the table by not contributing at least the amount that your company will match at a minimum. They key here is to understand how your company matches funds and understand the program that the company operates under. If you have any questions about your company's plan, it is best to talk to your benefits specialist or the company's plan administrators.

Also it is very important to understand the fees associated with any investment you may have, be that a 401(k) plan, an IRA, or an investment such as a mutual fund or exchange-traded fund. All of these investment vehicles do, in fact, charge some fee and depending on how they are managed the costs may be substantial. Actively managed funds and investment vehicles will have higher costs than those that are passively managed. Read the prospectus of any fund you invest in and understand the fee structure prior to investing. 401(k) plans and IRA's have fees as well so read and understand the "fine" print on these plans. Fees over the life of your investments can eat away substantial portions of your retirement when you consider these fees over 30 to 40 years.

Be leery of retiring too early or not saving enough prior to retirement. As people are living longer, it is imperative that we save sufficient amounts of capital to last us for our entire retirement. As most people will rely heavily on Social Security, it is important to understand how that funding source works for and against you. Most baby boomers will reach full retirement age at 66 and for those born after 1960 your full retirement age will be 67. Wait you say! I want to retire at age 62 when I am eligible for Social Security. Excellent provided you understand that one you will not qualify for Medicare so you will need some form of health insurance, and two your benefits will be reduced about 25%. For those who do reach retirement at age 67 if you wait until you are 70 to retire you will increase your benefits 8% a year for a 24% increase in your retirement benefits. If you have any questions about Social Security, it is best to contact the Social Security Administration by visiting an office, calling them, or visiting their website.

Those are five areas that you need to consider when you are thinking of retirement. For some of these things, you will contact specific individuals such as your company's plan administrators or Social Security for more information on your particular needs.

Are you planning your retirement? Will you be retiring in the next 20 to 30 years? If you are indeed planning your retirement and it will be in the 20 to 30 year time frame there are some things you need to consider as you invest and plan for your future retirement. We will touch on a few areas that a young worker would need to study and then a few tips on how to maximize your tax-advantaged retirement accounts.

As painful as it is to say this but younger workers may need to consider the fact that Social Security may not be an option for your retirement. Also, in the event it is still operational it replaces on about 25% of your income in a best case scenario. Consider the fact that for many years the fund operated with a surplus of money; however, the government did not leave the excess money in the Social Security fund but rather spent it to help balance the US budget. And now because of this poor stewardship in utilizing the excess funding Congress will be placed in the position that it may have to reduce benefits or even phase out the program. Currently, Social Security funding is not in that bad of shape or at least not as bad as people tend to make you believe. The main drawback to keeping the benefit around is the Medicare portion of Social Security that provides health care to retired seniors. These are the costs that are hurting the entire Social Security program. Overall, between Social Security and Medicare benefits they are the single biggest source of expenditures the federal government incurs.

A second area that young and middle-aged investors needs to consider is investing outside of the US. While most large corporations in the US have significant overseas positions to consider, they are not in fact foreign investments. They are, in fact, domestic companies that may or may not have a significant portion of their profits generated outside the US. A genuine foreign investment is one that is not necessarily regulated by the Securities and Exchange Commission. Where domestic companies may pay a dividend on a set quarterly basis and that dividend is usually based on the prior quarter's dividend. Foreign enterprises will pay a dividend once or twice a year, and they are based on profits and not prior payments. Then like their domestic equals who earn money in foreign currencies, actual foreign companies will need to be converted to the US dollar making them seem more volatile than a domestic company. However, both will experience a currency risk to some degree. Now foreign markets are a better value than the US markets due to a host of reasons. One as the Federal Reserve continues to cut back on its bond buying smaller foreign markets and some foreign markets, in general, are finding it harder to find funding for their continued operations and growth. Also, local and regional politics in foreign countries tend to make investing in them more volatile and to a large degree it does. But with a little research and planning there are some excellent investing opportunities abroad.

And finally while it currently does not pay to have a substantial cash position it does make sense in the fact you need readily available cash at your disposal if you are to take advantage market opportunities. If an investment you like takes a hit and declines in price without a cash reserve, you will not be able to take advantage of the opportunity without the liquidation of another position. And that liquidation could have tax consequences, or you may be placed in a position where you are having to choose between the new opportunity or keeping another existing position. There is a reason Berkshire Hathaway under the direction of Warren Buffett keeps large amounts of cash and cash equivalents on hand, and that is to take advantage of market conditions that are favorable when investing.

Now if you are planning for your retirement as you should be there are some things to consider with your retirement accounts and are like some additional guidelines. If you want to own a limited partnership or a REIT, it is best to own these in a retirement account. First they are corporations that do not pay taxes provided they pay at least 90% of their profits out as dividends to shareholders. While these are considered dividends, they are not taxed like dividends but rather as ordinary income. But before you but one of these investments it is best to understand the company and what it does. You also need to make sure you understand the balance sheet and income statement so you can be sure they will be able to continue the payments without issuing extra equities or taking on debt.

Also, it is never a good idea to put a mutual bond in a tax-advantaged account as they are stated, and income tax-free provided the bond was issued in the state you live.

If another state issues the bond there are state taxes but not federal. These tax breaks are built into the interest rate a bond will pay and thereby municipal bonds, as a rule, pay a lower interest rate than a corporate bond. And speaking of corporate bonds, with interest rates so low they are paying similar returns as municipal bonds. But owning a corporate bond in a tax-advantaged account makes sense as the interest earned on these bonds is like that of the dividends mentioned in the earlier part of this paragraph, and they are taxed as ordinary income. But there are still some incredible investing opportunities for high quality smaller companies that are issuing bonds which pay higher interest rates due to their size and not by their ability to repay the bonds. With some research and digging you can find these hidden gems and use them in your portfolio.

And finally it is a good idea to have some exposure to precious metals. Now this can be through ETFs or funds that invest in the metals by owning then in physical form such as SPDR Gold or iShares Silver. Right now, the cost of gold and silver is at or below the production costs making it an excellent opportunity for investments. Also if you wanted to own the actual gold or silver bullion it makes sense to be buying these assets now while the price is advantageous as selling them outside of a tax-advantaged account results in a 28% tax on precious metals and collectables. If you want to own the actual metal yourself, you can put it in a qualified IRA provided it is done through a company acting as the trustee of your IRA. But shop around when looking for such companies and always make sure that they are endorsed or approved by the Better Business Bureau.

As you know, I am a firm believer that saving for retirement is essential. The more you can save earlier in your career the better off you will be later in life. That and the money you saved earlier in life will earn much more for you than money you save later. The power of compounding is incredible and not something that should be ignored by any means. But here are some more saving tips for those who are focusing on their retirement.

If you work in certain fields such as a public school teacher, healthcare worker, nonprofit employee, or other public sector jobs you have an opportunity to double your workplace savings. In 2014, you were eligible to save up to $17,500 in your 403(b), and you can save an additional $17,500 in a 457 plan.

Now if you are over the age of 50, there are some special provisions for saving for retirement that are designed just for you. If you are 50 or older and have a Traditional or ROTH IRA, you are allowed to save an extra $1,000 for a total of $6,500 for 2014. In regards to work plans, those over 50 are allowed an additional $5,500 for 401(k), 403(b), and 457 plans for a total of $23,000 in 2014.

If you are self-employed, there are some additional saving opportunities for you. This strategy will apply even if you have a regular 401(k) or similar plan at a full-time job. If you are self-employed, you have two basic choices, and that is a solo 401(k) and Simplified Employee Pension (SEP). You are allowed to make tax-deductible contributions to both, and they then grow tax deferred until your retirement. In a SEP account, you are allowed to save up to 20% of your net self-employment income with a limit of $52,000 in 2014. If you are over 50, there is also a special provision for these savings tools that allow you to save up to $57,500.

If you earn more than what is allowed to make contributions to a ROTH IRA, there are some ways to navigate around these restrictions. For single people, the maximum you are allowed to make in your adjusted gross income is $129,000 and for joint filers the maximum is $191,000. However, there is no restrictions on making non-deductible contributions to a Traditional IRA and converting it into a ROTH IRA. There is also no timeframe in which the funds have to be in a Traditional IRA prior to it being converted into a ROTH IRA. So if it is done immediately, there will be no further tax implications to deal with.

Just because your employer has enrolled you in the company's 401(k) plan, chances are it is at 3% of your salary, and that is not sufficient for your retirement. In most instances, the 3% that you are setting aside does not even begin to meet the maximums that your company will match meaning you are leaving free money on the table, and that is never good. Also, I would recommend setting aside at least 10% of your salary in your 401(k) before the company match is considered in the equation.

There is a tax credit for low-income wage earners who save for their retirement. For those who qualify the credit can be 10%, 20% or 50% of the contributions depending on your adjusted gross income with credit of up to $1,000 for individuals and $2,000 for joint filers. In 2014, the income limitations are $60,000 for those who file as joint, $45,000 for head of household and $30,000 for those who file single. Not a bad deal or incentive for those who are not high-income wage earners to save for their retirement.

A unique way to save for retirement, lower your current taxes and pay for healthcare costs later is a health savings account (HSA). This is available to people who have high deductible health care plans and provides a triple tax advantage as mentioned earlier. The contributions are tax deductible, grow tax deferred and if used for medical expenses are tax-free. Now it does not get much better than that when saving for retirement as we all know medical expenses will play some role when we reach an advanced age. And best of all you can use it while you are working on qualified medical bills provided you keep good records.

And finally where you retire can also be an active retirement tool. Seven states have no income tax at all; many do not tax Social Security or pension benefits. While it does not help you while you are working and may be an added expense in retirement to move for many it is worth it when they do retire to ensure they pay as little as they have to in taxes.

Are you thinking of your retirement? If you are like me, or even younger, you may be pondering how you will retire and under what circumstances. If you read my blogs on a regular basis, you are well aware I am a firm believer of saving early and often to ensure you will have enough when it is time to retire. To be honest, it never is too early to consider your retirement. When I first started working for the government one of the best things I did was attend a retirement seminar where I was working. Granted it was aimed at people that were going to retire within five years but even the instructor said that was too late for someone to get the proper information. First if your employer offers a retirement seminar I highly recommend everyone attends it to get some valuable information that is aimed at younger workers who are not near retirement. As someone who will be assisting people gauge how much of their income they will need to replace here are some of the key expenses retiree's encounter.

The single largest cost is someone's housing and housing related costs. Hopefully, by the time you retire you no longer have a mortgage but in the event you do I recommend trying to pay it off before you actually retire. A mortgage is an enormous expense for everyone, but it could become a burden when you no longer have an active income. It is estimated that as much as 40% of your income may go to pay for housing and related expenses. And considering that even if you do not have a monthly mortgage you will still have insurance, property taxes, and utilities to pay. So if you can eliminate the cost of a monthly mortgage, you will be better off when you retire.

Healthcare is an expense that when you are early on in your retirement years you will pay less than later in life. Typically someone in their 50's can expect to pay about ten percent of their income to medical expenses. This will increase to 20% or more when you reach your 80's and depending on your situation could go much higher. If you are in your 40's or earlier, I do not recommend long-term care insurance as it is very costly over the life of the policy. Find out what the premium would be and invest that amount on a monthly basis to an indexed fund of some kind for the rest of your life. By doing this, you will self-insure yourself for long-term care needs. If you are older, it may be more economical to purchase a long-term care policy from a reputable insurance company rather than try to self-insure. I know there are very few insurance companies that still sell this type of insurance that were selling it 15 years ago. When you purchase a long-term care policy, it is critical to do your homework on the company issuing the policy.

Taxes never seem to go away but in your retirement one tax that will disappear if you no longer work is the FICA or Social Security Payroll Tax. Depending on other factors such as how much Social Security you receive, if you have interest income, investment income, a pension or are making withdrawals from an IRA or 401(k) you may have some tax liabilities. Not all states tax retirement accounts the same so check with a tax professional in your state for more information.

Now you are retired, and no longer will be commuting to and from work. If you are married, your spouse may no longer be working either, if that is the case, consider selling one of your cars as you no longer have a need to be a two car household. It will save you on maintenance, insurance, possible taxes, and gas. Why pay for two vehicles when you only have a need for one. In some larger cities where public transportation is good, safe, and reliable you may not even need the one car.

Now the last area is one that is very dependent on the people and what their desires are as far as travel goes. Some Baby Boomers estimate they will spend upwards of $8,000 a year on as many as four trips. While there is nothing wrong with that and after all you have worked hard your whole life, so it is time to enjoy the fruits of your labor. But consider scaling back from five-star hotels to nicer chains. And take advantage of going to see your children and grandchildren where you can stay with them and avoid the cost of a hotel altogether. This expense is the only one that is 100% discretionary so if you spend a lot or a little it is up to you.

Are all states equal when it comes to taxes and retirement? The answer may surprise you and may have you double thinking where it is you want to spend your retirement years. Regardless of where you live everyone will always owe and pay federal income taxes. Depending on what types of retirement accounts, you will have will determine how much in federal taxes you will pay. Social Security while not 100% taxed may be taxed to some degree at the federal level. The accumulated portion of an annuity, withdrawals from traditional IRAs, 401(k) plans and pensions will be taxed as ordinary income. Taxable brokerage accounts will indeed be taxed but at rates that are better than those of straight income with a maximum of 20% for dividends and long-term capital gains. Of course, any withdrawals from ROTH accounts are tax-free. As you can see just because you retired does not mean the federal government will not get its fair share of taxes. With proper planning, federal taxes can be reduced but rarely do they go away entirely. Personally I do not see taxes going down in the future; so proper planning in this regard is essential so consider using a financial planner to assist in your asset allocations and locations.

As for state taxes in retirement you will need to do some homework in your state and any state you are considering living in during your retirement years. Not all states tax people in retirement in the same manner. Currently, there are nine states that have no income tax at all with two of them only taxing dividends and interest. But that does not mean that the other 41 states are not tax friendly for retirees. Again do some research on a state by state basis and compare things such as income taxes, sales taxes, and property taxes. Those combined with each state and city's standard of living need to be considered. Mississippi and Pennsylvania are the most retiree friendly as they do not tax any retirement income including public and private pensions. Many of the remaining states offer some degree of tax breaks for retirees while six offer no tax breaks at all.

Most states are much more generous when it comes to taxing Social Security than the federal government. On a federal level, Social Security benefits may be taxed at rates up to 85% and in many states these benefits are 100% tax-free. As states become more and more dependent on internal revenue to make up deficits this may change over time and states may begin taxing these benefits. Besides the nine states that already have no income tax an additional 27 and the District of Columbia do not tax Social Security benefits. The remaining states do tax these benefits to some degree. Here it is imperative to check the tax codes of the state you are living in or thinking of moving to.

While most of us do not have to worry about estate taxes as the personal exemption is $5.34 million, and that doubles for a married couple states can be vastly different. Many states do not have an estate or inheritance tax 19 states and the District of Columbia have one or the other. Maryland and New Jersey impose both of these taxes. The difference between these two taxes is an estate tax is paid by the estate before assets are distributed, and inheritance tax is paid by the heir of the assets. Like income taxes and taxes on Social Security benefits check your state's tax code to see what the tax implications of these two taxes are for you.

With a little planning, most of these taxes can be limited but maybe not eliminated. If you are concerned about the tax implications, seek a tax professional or a financial planner for assistance.

Personal Finance: A Grouping of Financial Topics
By Kirk G. Meyer

With a new year, it is time to think once again of retirement and take some proactive steps in that regard. Are you one to plan early? If so these are ten areas that you may want to focus on in 2015 to ensure, your retirement is as good as it can be. If you have followed my topics, you are aware I honestly believe it is never too early to think about your retirement planning and to save for your golden years. So what are the ten areas that I feel are important for your retirement? Well, none are rocket science, and we will now touch on the ten areas I think everyone can focus on to make sure they have prosperous golden years.

The basis for most of us in retirement is Social Security. While this is especially true for people such as my grandparents and parents, I do believe it will play a significant role for me as well, I am 43 now. If you are in your 20's or early 30's Social Security may not be the same when it comes time for you to retire so while you can count on it do not rely on it being the same that we see today. After all you and everyone else has spent their entire working lives paying into this system, and we all expect to see the benefits at some point. To maximize your benefits make sure you have worked the required years and consider the age at which you will start taking your benefits. With people have later full retirement ages taking early Social Security may not be the best move as we are also living longer so consider your options and if you are like me, and your full retirement age is 67 and you wait until age 70 to begin your benefits, you will receive a 24% raise in your benefits as well.

In retirement, health care costs can be extremely high, so there is Medicare. Unless you are one of the lucky ones who will continue private health insurance in retirement such as a government worker, Medicare will be your primary source of health care insurance. You can sign up for Medicare up to three months prior to your 65th birthday and by doing so you may get lower premiums as compared to waiting. However, if you retire prior to age 65, you will have to make arrangements to buy private coverage until such time that Medicare will take effect and cover you for your health care needs.

A Traditional 401(k) is also a primary component of any retirement plan these days. And with companies contributing a portion of the funds through matching contributions it is important that everyone take advantage of these while they can. Also, there are significant tax advantages to making contributions to a 401(k) as well. Consider someone who is the 25% federal tax bracket, and they can contribute the full $18,000 in 2015 to their plan. That equates to a tax savings of almost $4,500 alone. Workers over the age of 50 are allowed an additional $6,000 in contributions to their plans.

A Roth 401(k) works the same, but the money is contributed on a pre-tax basis meaning there are no current tax advantages to the account. But provided the account is at least five years old when you retire the proceeds are tax-free upon their withdrawal. These work best for workers who are younger and in lower tax brackets making the benefits better.

An IRA is another tool for your retirement needs. These act similar to a 401(k) but are done on an individual basis and have much lower contribution limits. In 2015, an individual may contribute up to $5,500, and those over the age of 50 can contribute and additional $1,000. These accounts also can reduce your tax basis provided you meet the income guidelines. Many people have enormous IRA balances because they roll over old 401(k) accounts into these when they change jobs. IRA accounts can be invested in just about any type of investment provided the IRA is set up correctly.

A Roth IRA accounts have the same characteristics as a Roth 401(k) and an IRA meaning they are not tax-advantaged now but are when the funds are withdrawn. The same applies to these when it comes to younger workers and savers as the benefits will most likely be more advantageous upon retirement, and they could be in a higher tax bracket. It is possible to convert a traditional IRA to a Roth IRA provided you pay the proper taxes on the contributions and any gains in the year you make the conversion. Also, like a Traditional IRA, Roth IRA's have income limitations that must be adhered to in order to be legal.

Everyone needs to have a savings account that they keep their cash that they plan to spend over the short run as well as to keep their emergency funds. No matter what age you are, everyone needs to have an emergency fund that is equal to about six months worth of expense. This not only provides you the ability to meet any unexpected needs but also provides you piece of mind when it comes to knowing you are in a liquid position.

If at all possible have a house that is paid in full by the time, you retire. This means no mortgage payments that are the main expense for those of use who are paying on our houses now. In retirement, you do not want this large monthly payment hanging over your head thereby freeing up what could amount to a substantial sum for other needs and wants. Also, if you needed to you would be able to tap into your home's equity in an emergency or even consider a reverse mortgage if that is something that appeals to you.

Something that many people are now doing that may not have planned for it prior to the 2009 collapse of the economic situation is getting a part-time job. Not only do they get us out of the house and keep us active they provide us the opportunity to interact with others outside of the home. As we get older, this becomes imperative and best of all it also provides additional money that allows us to enjoy life more. And it may delay the spending of precious retirement funds until a later date when a part-time job is not an option.

If you are one of the few Americans who will receive a pension, this is just as important as Social Security in some aspects. A pension is like Social Security in the fact we cannot outlive it, and it is additional money that we can utilize for everyday expenses. Younger workers will most likely not have this aspect in their retirement, but some older workers still have these powerful and precious benefits. I know those who work for governments or some older larger companies you may be lucky enough to count this as part of your retirement plans. Otherwise, concentrate on the other nine aspects of this topic.

Are you at the age where retirement is a real possibility? Are you looking at the size of your retirement accounts and figuring you are all set? If you are going to retire in the next few years, there are some areas that you need to consider in addition to your retirement assets. Retirees need to consider not only the amount that they have accumulated in their accounts but must also take into account the market cycles, expenses that will be incurred in retirement and your possible tax bracket in your retirement years.

First one does indeed need to have enough saved in 401(k) plans, IRA's and brokerage accounts to support them in their golden years. That is a given regardless of what else is occurring at the time. Let's face it without having substantial savings retirement will be difficult to achieve. But timing is also important when you are going to retire. If, as we have been experiencing the last few years, we are in a bull market at some point there is going to be a correction or a full blown bear market that will affect your retirement accounts. If you are heavily invested in equities, a change in market conditions could have severe impacts on the overall value of your assets. If you are worried about bear markets or severe market corrections and are considering retirement it is not a bad idea to have several years' worth of expenses on hand to avoid having to sell assets when the price is depressed.

Which lead to the tax consequences of selling or making withdrawals from accounts, if you are dealing with ROTH IRA's or 401(k) accounts these funds will not be taxed. However, if you are dealing with Traditional retirement accounts, these withdrawals will be treated as ordinary income. If you do have any assets in brokerage accounts the gains on these assets will be capital gains that are considered either short or long term in nature. It is best to try to go into retirement with a little in each of these asset classifications as you can take from one when the tax advantages are in your favor and others when it is in their favor. It is best to consult a tax specialist or a financial planner to maximize your accounts and the tax advantages of each.

Expenses are another component that you need to consider when you are planning to retire. Most people project what they will be required to replace income wise in their retirement years. While it is true your assets are designed to replace the income you are losing by retiring another way to calculate this is by figuring out expenses you will no longer have to pay. Hopefully, if you are retiring, you will not be paying a mortgage payment so that should be an expense that is not required to be paid. Also if you are not working you will not be paying taxes in the form of income or social security, again expenses you do not need to replace in retirement. If you remove the expenses that you are not required to replace in retirement and consider your social security payments when you decide to start taking payments you may see you only have to replace between 60% and 80% of your income.

Retirement is more than your savings. It is a combination of savings and wise planning. As I hope, you can see one without the other is only poor planning and will lead to a retirement where you may run out of funds before you die. It is best to save and consider many aspects of your retirement before you retire. It may be wisest to seek the help of a financial planner to ensure you are in the best possible position you can be in prior to retiring.

Are you thinking of your retirement? At some point, everyone will be retiring and enjoying their golden years. But there are some common mistakes that many people make when thinking of or planning what their retirement will be like. How is this possible you ask? Well, it is all in how we look at our retirement, our planning, and how will it be funded. In previous generation's retirement was supported by pensions from companies that people worked at for their entire careers and social security as the full retirement age was lower. Think of my grandparent's generation. They could retire at age 65 so taking Social Security at age 62 did not reduce the benefits as much as it does for someone my age who has a retirement age of 67. Now we will look at three areas where many people make some very common and in some instances costly mistakes.

One of the biggest mistakes people who are planning for their retirement make that they do have some control over, is how much they save and what they use for an expected rate of return on that money. One way to ensure you will have the money you need for retirement is to save as much as you can as early as you can. Someone who starts saving in the mid-20's will have to save considerably less than someone who starts in their mid-30. The reason for this is the power of compounding interest over 40 years instead of 30 years. For this part of the example, we will assume a savings of $400 a month for the entire period, and we will assume a conservative 7.5% return on your investment. Now the 30 something will have at age 65 or 30 years a total investment with a valued of about $542,000. Now that same investment made over 40 years with the same assumptions from a 20 something would be worth about $1,200,000. As you can see the power of compounding just over the additional ten years over doubles your investment.

The second part of people's saving is the amount they save and the return they expect. We will use the same assumptions as before but now the 30 something wants to have the same $1.2 million. In order to do that one of two things, or possibly both, need to occur. One they will need to save more every month or two they will have to have a higher rate of return on their investment by taking on additional risk. In many instances, the 30 something will have to do both of these in order to reach the same $1.2 million. If you take on no additional risk, you will have to pay $885 a month to achieve this goal, an increase of $445. Now let's say you take on more risk as you cannot afford to save an additional $445 a month, and you project a return of 9%. Now you would have to save $650 a month or an additional $250. But is 9% realistic with your investment choices and your risk tolerance? As you can see, one or the other will need to occur, most likely both, in order to reach the savings goal of $1.2 million.

A second area that many people make mistakes with as it concerns to their retirement is the possible income of employment after they retire. In some recent surveys, a majority of individuals who are in the initial stages of planning their retirement they plan on working at least part-time in retirement. While there is nothing wrong with the concept what is not a right retirement tool reduce your savings amount due to the fact you anticipate income in retirement. It is never a good idea to try to make up for savings and the power of compounding of interest with a post-retirement income. First as with the returns you will make on your investments, making enough money to retirement is not guaranteed. While I plan on working past my retirement age in some capacity I will not use any projected income in my planning as that is not a given and who knows, I may even change my mind in the next 25 years.

Lastly, there is the favorite subject of Social Security. While in recent years the number of people who are taking early retirement at age 62 is declining it is still the most common age at which people take their benefits. For someone like me that means a decrease of around 30% from what I would get at my full retirement age of 67 as they reduce your benefits by about 6% a year that you take the benefits early. On the other side if you are set to retire at 67 and wait until age 70 to take your benefits you will get an additional 24% for delaying your benefits for three years as they will reward you with an 8% a year increase. With proper planning in regards to Social Security, you can maximize your benefits of yourself and your spouse. Consult a financial planner and visit with a Social Security specialist for more information.

While retirement is going to be in everyone's future as you can see it does take some realistic planning to ensure you get the most out of yours.

Personal Finance: A Grouping of Financial Topics
By Kirk G. Meyer

Are you preparing for retirement? Are you afraid that you may not have saved enough to retire comfortably? Then there are some techniques that older readers can try to increase their overall savings. One is the obvious method of saving more, and the second is to be more aggressive in your investing plan. Most financial advisors will recommend that you have eight to ten times your annual salary saved prior to your retirement in order to retire comfortably. Of course, many factors can go into what each of you will need to save in order to retire in the manner that is suitable for you.

Now the longer you wait to start saving the more you will need to set aside to achieve your goals. If you are in your 20's and are saving at least 10% of your salary for the first several years of your career, you will be much better off, in the long run. That is because your money will earn a return over 40 plus years allowing the power of compounding to work in your favor. Someone who starts in their 30's and has two times their annual salary saved would need to save about 10% of their annual salary to retire comfortable as well. Fast forward to someone in their 40's with the same two times their annual salary saved will need to save 16% or more of their salary to achieve the same results. The power of time and compounding is the most powerful tool in your retirement savings arsenal. And worst off if you are in your 50's and only have two times your annual salary saved you will need to save almost 30% of your salary to achieve your retirement goals.

But how much you need to save is an answer I am not able to give you at this time for many reasons. As a general rule, you need to save at least 10% of your salary before you add in any company matches on your 401(k). Once you factor in the company matching, you need to be saving between 12% and 15% starting out in your career. If you do this, chances are you will be comfortable in your retirement. The later you wait to start the higher the percentage will be that you need to save in order to retire comfortably. Now there are other factors that will need to be considered when deciding how much is enough to save. Some of them are your personal health and any health related issues you may have or think you may experience in the future. Knowing your family's health history comes in handy here and can assist you in your planning. Also, if you come from a family that has a history of longevity, you will need to consider that when saving as chances are you will need to save more to make up for your longer life. And with a longer life comes the increased chances that some form of long-term care may be necessary so that must be considered as well either through additional savings or an insurance policy.

As for how much you are allowed to save that is dependent on your age, for 401(k) accounts in 2014 workers under the age of 50 may save $17,500 and those over age 50 are allowed a catch-up contribution of $5,500 for a total of $23,000 that can be saved. If you are also saving in an IRA as well, savers under the age of 50 can save $5,500 in 2014. For those savers over the age of 50, they may contribute an additional $1,000 in catch-up contributions for a total of $6,500.

Now if you are an older worker and you need to save extra in addition to keeping more you may also want to consider investing more aggressively. While many people tend to shift from equities to bonds as they near retirement I, along with many other advisors, find a fatal error in this strategy. As people are living longer in their retirement years, they still have a need to not only preserve their capital but in many instances they still need capital appreciation. Only you can decide what you are comfortable with as far as your investing plan but consider that more exposure to equities does increase your portfolio's return and in many cases does not increase the portfolio's risk as much as you think. History, while not a prediction of the future, does give us a good idea of how the markets may perform in the coming years. Yes, equities are much more volatile than bonds, but the rewards far outweigh the rewards of bonds at this time. If you want to know how volatile your portfolio is or how volatile it could be if you were to change the asset allocation consult a financial advisor for more information.

So for savers who are over the age of 50 and either think that they have not saved enough or know that they have not there is hope for you still. One is you must invest or save more of your annual income in order to catch up with your overall portfolio value. And secondly you may have to re-evaluate your investing plan and consider becoming more aggressive in your investment choices.

While more volatile equities will return more than bonds and if done the risks properly can be mitigated to a great extent.

Are you about to retire? If so there are some things that you need to make sure you address while you are still employed and working. By addressing these issues, you can have an easier and possibly better retirement.

Before you retire, it is important that you get dental insurance in some form. Medicare does not provide any dental coverage so without some dental insurance you may be out some serious money in the event you have dental issues. It is best to get dental insurance while you are working and have as much of the dental work you need done prior to retirement. If you know you will have some dental expenses when you are retired make sure you save up properly for them as you will most likely not continue the dental insurance into your retirement years due to the costs associated with it. The same will apply to vision insurance as it did with dental insurance. These are two areas where people can adequately plan for and in many instances have work done while they are working and insured.

If you plan on buying a house or second home in retirement, you should consider doing that while you are employed. Mortgages are difficult to qualify for regardless, but it is easier to be eligible if you have a reliable income source. Also, many lenders do not want to enter into long-term loans with people that are older as the likelihood of them passing before the loan is repaid is higher.

Life insurance while important, when you are younger and have people depending on you for financial needs, may not be required when you retire. The key here is to remember that life insurance is meant to replace lost wages or income to the family after the insured dies. If you have little debt, no mortgage and are retired there is little need for continued life insurance. Of if you do need life insurance you may not need as much and can lower your death benefit.

These are just some of the things that you need to consider before you retire. There may very well be others depending on your situation. As always it is best to consult with a financial planner to get a clear picture of your retirement, what your needs will be in retirement, and where you stand now prior to your retirement.

Are saving your money in a regular savings account? Do you have your emergency fund saved in a safe, accessible place? Well, most people would answer that they keep their checking, savings, and emergency fund money in their regular bank. The only problem with this scenario is that banks in the traditional sense have high costs that are passed on to you, the customer. Never fear there is a safe and reliable option for regular banks, and that is true on-line banks that do not have any a physical presence.

Yes, credit unions are an alternative to large and smaller banks which are technically for profit whereas a credit union operates as a non-profit with any such profits being passed along to it members or customers. As a general rule, credit unions have lower fees, charge lower interest rates on loans and pay higher interest rates on savings deposited in their institution. But credit unions still have overhead an on-line bank does and has lower fees than a bank but they for the most past still do not compete with on-line banks.

Now to just clarify something that some of you may be thinking. If you log into your on-line account at say Bank of America that is not the type of on-line banking, I am referring to here. There are many on-line banks that have a presence only on the Internet. Some that come to mind are Capital One 360 which I had used for years going back to before they bought out ING Orange. In this case as well as other on-line banks, they do not have an actual brick and mortar building in which customers can go. By not having a brick and mortar building, this is cost savings number one for the on-line bank. Now many people fear that because they cannot go to the bank their services may be reduced, and that is not the case in most instances. And just as a regular bank your deposits are insured by the FDIC.

A second reason banks and some credit unions, to a degree, have higher fees than on-line banks, is they are fighting for customers in the first place in order to gain market share. In order to get more clients, banks, run specials where they may offer a higher interest rate for a specified period or provide a credit card with a bonus of some sort after they spend a certain amount of money. These incentives do come at a cost, and that cost is passed along to the existing customers in the form of higher fees, higher interest rates on loans, and lower interest rates paid on deposits. With banks, it all boils down to what makes the bottom line look the best it can for the bank's owners or shareholders.

While on-line banks are not for everyone, they do offer some very enticing features. Most on-line banks offer ATM users with no fees which can save you upwards of $4 a transaction, lower or in many instances no overdraft fees, no charges for low balances on accounts, no monthly maintenance charges, higher interest rates on deposits, and with smartphone apps you can even deposit checks from your phone. I cannot speak for all on-line banks but as I have used Capital One 360 for over a decade, I have never had to pay any fees of any sort. And recently I started to use their mobile app for the iPhone to deposit checks. It is real easy to use, and the hold is only two business days on checks deposited in that manner. And for those who like to use bill pay that is also a free feature at most on-line banks as well. Are you a check writer? Capital One 360 has a solution for that as well as for a small fee you can order actual checks that you can use in any manner you need. Here is where Capital One 360 will separate itself from other on-line banks, over the next year 360 account holders will be able to make cash deposits at Capital One ATM's and they will have same day access to the cash they deposit.

While it is true that many on-line banks do lack the local conveniences of a local bank or credit union, you may not leave them altogether. But consider at least moving your savings and emergency funds to an on-line counterpart if for nothing else the higher interest you will earn on your money. With interest rates being at historic lows and some as low as 0.01% there, really is no reason to leave your money in such a situation. Consider you have $10,000 in your savings account earning 0.01% or a dollar after a year. Comparable on-line banks are paying as much as 0.95% on savings accounts and in many instances there is no minimum deposit requirement meaning that same $10,000 deposit will earn you $95 in a year. Now you will not be getting rich on a savings account but $94 is a difference worth pursuing if you ask me.

On-line banks are making banks and credit unions take a hard look at their fees and the way they treat customers. It will take a lot before they can compete with an on-line bank's interest on deposits due to the significant difference in expenses they both incur. To find on-line banks all you need to do is perform a Google search and research your results.

While I mention Capital One 360 quite a bit in this blog, it is because I have used them for over a decade and have never once had an issue with them during that time. I am not endorsing Capital One 360 or being compensated for what I have said, but I have extensive experience with them and can discuss their service with confidence.

Personal Finance: A Grouping of Financial Topics
By Kirk G. Meyer

Do you know what questions to ask when it comes to your personal finances? Chances are you are like most people and keep your personal finances, well personal. It is not a natural feeling for us to discuss our personal finances with people who are not in our innermost circle. It is important to have a person with whom you can discuss your financial situation with, and if that is a financial planner then you need to have one that you trust completely. If you do not have a planner find a family member or good friend who is financial savvy who can be your sounding board. Here are several questions that everyone needs to be aware of and answer when looking at their personal finance situation.

What is the cost of this investment at the end of the day? Fees can come in all shapes and sizes and if they go unchecked can erode your financial position in ways you never considered. If you are investing on your own, you have fees associated with the buying and selling of the securities or commissions on each transaction. Also mutual funds and exchange traded funds have fees associated with their daily management. Here passively, managed funds such as an indexed fund will have much lower fees than an actively managed fund. Also, some companies are known for lower fees over other such as Vanguard, who is the leader in low-cost indexed funds of both varieties. What you pay in fees can add up over the long haul in some serious money loss or gains for you so pay particular attention to what you are paying in various fees.

How much do I need to retire and is there a chance I can save that much? Just about any financial website has a calculator that will assist you in figuring out how much you will need to save in order to reach a particular goal, but that is about the end of their usefulness. These calculators only tell you what you will have at retirement assuming an initial sum saved, an inflation rate, and savings rates to give you what you would technically have at the end of a pre-defined period. That will answer the second part of the question, and that is if you can save enough of what you think you will need for retirement. As for how much you will need that will take some additional work on your part or better yet the consultation of a qualified planner. Here you need to figure out your post-retirement budget and spending levels. You will also need to estimate how many years you will be in retirement to spend your money. A good planner can help you budget your post-retirement years and help make adjustments in the event there is a significant event that could affect your retirement such as a stock market decline. If you are detailed oriented and can do decent projections you may be able to accomplish this on your own but it is better to consult a financial planner.

Am I taking too much or too little risk with my investments? Here the answer is one that is best accomplished when you can work with a financial planner. Many people will buy a security when it is hot and normally at a higher price and when the market turns they panic and sell at the worst possible time. This is not a unique situation but rather one of human nature.

By hiring a financial planner to advise you on these matters it takes the emotional side out of the equation because they are helping you make these decisions and they can look at the situation as a whole and not as individuals do in the heat of the moment. Also, financial planners can assist you in selecting appropriate securities that will match your risk tolerance levels and build a portfolio that will handle the changes in the markets with minimal effects on your returns.

Is my insurance coverage adequate on my residence? This is a paramount question that needs to be addressed on a regular basis. The best thing to do in this situation is to review your policy on an annual basis to ensure that it is adequate for your needs. If you have a life event or a significant change in circumstances, it is always good to revisit your policy coverage after these events. At a minimum, you need enough coverage to replace your residence in full. Additionally you need to make sure you have adequate insurance to cover your contents as well. Be aware that some high dollar items and collections need special riders to provide sufficient coverage in the event of a loss in these items.

What surprises might come back and bite me in my coverage? Here is it good to sit down with your insurance agent and go over the possibilities that could affect your property. An example of this is a home owner's policy will protect your house against rain and wind damage but you need a particular flood policy to protect you against flooding. A second area that is often overlooked is liability coverage. Normally for a nominal cost anyone with a home owner's can get an umbrella policy that will provide a million dollars in coverage, and you may even get more depending on what your needs are. I know my policy costs about $135 a year for the basic million in coverage, a wise insurance for minimal costs that provides a world of comfort in today's world of lawsuits.

Are my investments tax efficient? Not all investments gains are treated the same way or in the same manner. Any security that you sell that was not owned for at least 12 months will be processed as a short-term capital gain and be taxed at your ordinary income tax rate. For those investments held longer than 12 months the gains will be treated as long-term capital gains and for most people will be taxed at 15%. If your tax rate is less than 15% long-term, capital gains are not taxed at all allowing many retirees the ability to sell these long held assets with no tax consequences.

How can I minimize my taxes when I have to take a withdrawal from my IRA? Before you elect to take Social Security, calculate what your RMD will be for your IRA at age 70 ½. Then you can calculate what your social security would be at age 70. Here is where the tax savings comes into play. For someone who is in the situation such as myself their full retirement age is 67. By delaying social security until age 70, you will increase your benefit 8% a year for an additional 24% in benefits. For the period, you are not taking Social Security make withdrawals from your IRA to replace the missing social security. Then at age 70 ½ your RMD will be lower, and you will now also be collecting social security at an increased amount. And the tax brackets are much broader than most realize with the 15% rate being anything between $18,150 and $73,800. Then it bumps up to 25% up to $148,850. But taxes are bracketed, and if your income was $100,000 the first $18,149 is tax-free, then from $18,150 to $73,800 will be taxed at 15%, and the final amount will be taxed at the highest 25%.

While these are not the only questions that you need to be aware of they are some of the most important ones that should be addressed.

Personal Finance: A Grouping of Financial Topics
By Kirk G. Meyer

Do you have a financial planner? Are you satisfied with your working relationship with them? Do you wish you had a better working relationship with your planner? As a newer planner myself, I can only speak as to what I believe will enable you and your planner to have a healthy working relationship. What is important for people to understand that there is no cookie cutter process to developing a financial plan for someone. As everyone is different with different goals and expectations, it is thereby reasonable to assume that what may be a complete plan for someone may not be in fact what you need in order to achieve your goals. Both parties need to express to the other what the objectives and expectations will be in this partnership. And it is important to remember that the more you are willing to tell and share with the individual you chose as a planner the better they will be able to serve your needs. But here are some questions that you may want to consider when looking for a planner.

What will be the expectations of this working relationship for each party? It is imperative that both you and your planner are on the same page with what is expected of them and what your expectations are for their services. A planner can only help you and keep you on a path that fits your needs if you are effective in your communication with them. It will never end well if you have the desire only to invest in government bonds and want returns of the S&P 500. No matter how good your planner or well developed a plan may be this is a receipt for disaster. You need to communicate your risk tolerance and return expectations with your planner so they in turn can create a plan that will achieve your goals.

Building on some of the expectations question it leads directly to how do you manage to get our desired returns? This answer will depend a great deal on how honest you are with your planner on your risk tolerance. Beware of a planner that tells you he can outperform the markets as no one knows what they will do in any given period. Historical performance may be used a guide, but that should be about as far as you would want to rely on historical returns as they are no guarantee of future performance. A good planner should be able to explain things such as market risks, diversification and asset allocation to prospective clients. While returns are necessary, it is sometimes more important to have a diversified portfolio that covers several asset classes.

Is your planner willing to be a teacher and help educate you in your finances? Not everyone will begin at finance 101, and not everyone will have an advanced degree knowledge. As you are reading this blog, you may be at one or the other end of the spectrum or more likely you are somewhere in the middle of most people. But your planner needs to be able to explain what it is they are proposing in your plan, and it is up to you to understand it as well. That way the first question is always satisfied which is expectations. Planners may not know everything but they need to have a comprehensive knowledge base and be able to explain the plan that they have developed to you in a manner in which you fully understand.

Taking from the last question it leads to the next one. Can you please speak English? While you do want to hire a competent planner that has the needed education remember that as a general rule the more educated someone is, the more likely they will speak in technical terms. While there is nothing wrong with this as long as you understand what the terms mean. In the event, you are not familiar with something never be afraid to stop your planner and ask for a simplified explanation. Also, not everyone needs a comprehensive plan so only ask for what it is you need and have that delivered to you in a manner in which you will understand.

Who is all on your team? While some planning services are offered through a group of professionals, many planners are small independent operations. Never be afraid to ask them who they work with on such issues as taxes, charity gifts, trusts, estates or research analysis. Also, it is worth noting if they have a backup in the event they are not available when you are in need. While a planner may be a one-man shop, it is good to know who they work with and respect in other related fields who may be called on in certain situations. Also, it is a good idea to have specialist available for those unique situations when one is warranted.

How can my taxes be minimized? This is a question that may be an important one depending on the size of your portfolio and the income it produces. A good planner will look at ways to minimize your tax liability, and they may work in conjunction with a CPA or tax advisor to ensure compliance. A trained planner is aware or some basic methods that can minimize or reduce their client's tax liability. In order for them to help devise an investment plan that will aid in your taxes it is imperative that you give them access to prior year's returns to get a feel for your unique situation.

How often will we hear from you? This is a question that may have several different correct answers. Some clients prefer to meet face to face a few times a year to discuss things with their planner. Others may want a call to give them an update on things in general terms with an annual meeting. This is a question you need to discuss with your planner, so he knows what is expected of them, and they will also know what it is you expect in the way of communication. Do not be afraid to tell your planner what it is you want in the way of communication and hold them to that standard.

And look for a planner that is willing and in many instances insists on to both the husband and wife be present so that everyone is on the same page. Also, it is important that both parties are engaged in the process because you never know when something might happen to one party leaving the other to make all the decisions.

While there are other questions, I am sure you may have for prospective planners these are just some that I feel critical and some that need to be asked regardless of others you may have.

Personal Finance: A Grouping of Financial Topics
By Kirk G. Meyer

Do you want to become rich? Do you have dreams of being able to afford the nicer things in life? If you answer yes to these questions, there is one word that can help you achieve these goals, SAVE. Now in order to be able to save you must first not be living paycheck to paycheck and thereby giving you something to save. What is the key to becoming wealthy? That is saving early and often and let the money compound over time that will enable you to see the wonders of compound interest. If you are 21 years old and right out of college let's say, you put $5,000 in a ROTH IRA for the next 38 years until you can withdrawal the funds penalty free. That initial $5,000 if invested in something that returns an average of 6% a year which a good equity fund ETF should be able to do will grow to over $45,000 and if you left it there until you reached your full retirement age of 67 it would be over $72,000. Now if you opened a ROTH IRA with $5,000 at age 21 and ignored any adjustments by the IRS on contribution amounts and stayed with $5,000 a year at age 59 you would have over $725,000 and if you did the same until your retirement age you would have over $1,205,000. And that all relies on a very conservative 6% return. Now you can see the power of compound interest and how it works for you from a young age. Now if you waited until you were 30 to begin saving in a ROTH IRA with $5,000 a year for your retirement age, you would only have about $679,000 in the same account. Those extra nine years made you almost double on the same investment.

Now that you are saving for retirement it also helps to control spending and make wise investment choices. Do you need a $500,000 house when one that costs $300,000 will work? That is an extra $200,000 you can invest and make work for you instead of having an extra room or two. As we learned in the Great Recession real estate can and will go down and in some instances in a high percentage as compared to its current value. While real estate has come back in most parts of the country, it is not back to the levels that occurred prior to the Great Recession. Now if you had invested money in equities you not only would have gotten your losses back but you would have had some impressive gains. Now I am not saying to try and time markets or real estate but rather make wise and intelligent investments that are geared towards a long-term nature. A stable steady return will outweigh a fast profit over the long haul.

The more you save, and the better a return you can achieve on your savings will have a direct effect on you becoming wealthy. And as I showed you save early and save consistent and you will have a nice nest egg when it is time for you to retire later in life. Remember always to pay yourself first.

Personal Finance: A Grouping of Financial Topics
By Kirk G. Meyer

I am guessing that if you have been following my blog chances are you may have read that it is imperative that someone save for their retirement. And the key to someone who is younger is to save early and often save. In an earlier topic, we looked at Generation Y workers as they compared to some other generations, and it was revealed that on a whole they are doing a pretty good job. But someone in their 20's may be asking themselves why it is so important to start saving now. Also as discussed in another blog someone who is 25 and saves for 42 years until their retirement age will have about $1.2 million as compared to the same person who waits until they are 35 to start savings, they will only have about $600,000 in savings. Remember always to pay yourself first.

Depending on what kind of plan you are saving in, a 401(k) or an IRA can have some effect on your current taxes. Some employers offer traditional 401(k) plans that will reduce one's taxable income in the year in which the contribution is made. The same holds true for a contribution to a traditional IRA. In both of these scenarios, you are given a tax advantage today, and your money will grow tax-deferred and will be taxed as ordinary income when you retire.

I would seriously consider contributing to a ROTH 401(k) if your employer offers one and a ROTH IRA. While you will not get the tax advantages in the year, you make the contributions all of the earnings that have accumulated tax-deferred are withdrawn tax-free upon retirement. Consider this when reaching this decision. As you are younger and are not in your prime wage earning years your tax bracket is relatively low now negating the advantages of getting the tax deduction now. I think that paying the taxes now and letting the money grow tax-free for 40 plus years is far more advantageous to the minimal tax advantages a younger worker can experience today. That and I do not see a realistic future where tax rates will be reduced although they, in theory, should be lower in our retirement years. But even if you go back to your tax bracket that you were in when you first started working using the example from above a ROTH account would save you taxes on the entire accumulated amount.

How do you start to save in the first place you are asking? Well, the answer to that has been discussed many times in various blogs, and that is to budget yourself. How can you save when you do not know where your money is going in the first place. Under the Financial Tools Tab on this blog's homepage, you can find links to two well-prepared spreadsheets that can assist you in ways you cannot imagine.

When you are in doubt, you need to know that It is okay to ask for help. When you are first starting your careers, it is wise to ask for advice on 401(k) plans or how to invest what you are saving. Many private employers will offer financial services for employees to assist them in these matters. And in the event yours does not take full advantage of what the Internet has to offer or find a financial planner who will assist you for a flat fee. The latter will be difficult to find, but there is no harm in asking or looking. Also, it is always important that you understand what it is you are investing in. If you do not understand the investment, do not invest in it no matter how good it looks. It is difficult enough to manage a portfolio of securities you understand but how in the world can you expect yourself to manage something you do not understand? There are numerous websites that for a small fee will actively manage your funds mainly through the use of exchange traded funds. I will be examining these services in an eBooklet that I hope to release in the next few months.

No matter how much you save, it is imperative that you always save in your company's 401(k) plan up to the amount that they will match. Never leave free money on the table as that is an instant gain on your investment. Another thing that is a good idea is when you receive a raise or increase in your salary it is also a good idea to raise the amount you are contributing to the 401(k) plan. Also, it is wise to look at your retirement accounts on a regular basis to ensure that they are performing as you want them to. Unless you have invested in target date funds, you may have to evaluate your asset allocation. From the time to time, you will have to change things and reallocate assets. But do not confuse this activity with trying to time the markets that you should never do.

Starting early and saving as much as you can is the key to anyone's retirement but for someone who is still in their 20's this can provide tremendous opportunities. Like to the tune of an extra $600,000 in a single account. Don't believe me try the math yourself.

Are you between the ages of 21 and 35? If you are here are some tips that can help you in your quest to retire rich. Typically at this point in your life you are not thinking of retirement but I think you may want to retire at least rich. By making at least modest contributions to your IRA and 401(k), plans the power of compounding will amaze you in ways you never imagined. If you do not believe me go into Excel and use the future value function and plug in some returns and contributions and see for you.

As an example of this I started your first job at age 22 with you saving $200 a month. Not an unrealistic goal with some proper planning. Now we will assume a return of 8% that is not entirely unreasonable over a long term investment in equities. After ten years you will have about $37,000, after 20, it will be $122,000 and at age 67 you will have an amazing $1.2 million in your retirement account. Not too bad for just saving $200 a month and never increasing the rate of savings. If you get to the point where you can contribute the full amount allowed in an IRA which currently is $5,500 you would have about $2.8 million at age 67. Talk about having your money work for you and yes this is the power of compounding.

Many financial planners suggest you save at least 10% of your salary and no I do not include any company match here when calculating the savings rate. You need to put 10% of your salary into your 401(k) plan but under no circumstance should you not contribute at least the maximum that will have a company match. Therefore, if you company matched the first 5%, you contribute at least contribute that amount. Then get it to where you are contributing 10% of your salary and with the match it would be 15%. Not a bad way to save and retire rich. By contributing to your 401(k) in the same manner as your IRA, you will be amazed again by the power of compounding. The main key to a company 401(k) is never to leave any free money on the table and get the most out of your work retirement accounts.

If you do not have a work 401(k) and your adjusted gross income allows, it funds a ROTH IRA. As you know from my previous posts I am a huge fan of the ROTH accounts. And as a side not if your work offers a ROTH 401(k) contribute to that as well as there are no income limitations on a ROTH 401(k).

If you are self-employed look into a SEP-IRA as the contributions are higher than that of a Traditional or ROTH IRA. Check with your CPA on the limits for any particular year and the tax advantages that you may get with your company. This is also an option for employees you may have as you are allowed to fund their SEP IRA's as well. But make sure you follow IRS rules and regulations as they may nullify your IRA if they are not followed correctly.

And when possible pay off student loans as fast as you can to start saving for a house, a child's education or your retirement. And look into ways that will reduce your interest rates on the loans such as automatic drafts and never missing a payment. Also, make sure you take advantage of any tax breaks that you may be eligible for as they are dependent on your adjusted gross income.

Check with a tax professional for additional information or contact a financial planner.

It is never too early to start saving, planning, and thinking of your retirement. Start early and develop good habits that you will not break over time. With proper planning and good solid work, you will be more than able to retire rich. If you have any questions or need any help feel free to contact me and I will do my best to help you.

Personal Finance: A Grouping of Financial Topics
By Kirk G. Meyer

Are you fresh out of college? Are you already thinking 30 or 40 years into the future? While most people who are not even 25 yet rarely think about savings here are some helpful tips for those who do and are thinking about their future. As you know if you read my blog on a regular basis, I am a true believer that it is never too early to plan for and start saving for your retirement.

First we will look at the concept of saving to begin with from the start. First it is important to create an emergency fund of about six months' worth of expenses that one keeps in a safe and accessible accounts such as a money market account or savings account. This money is not what I consider savings or money that you do keep in a savings account that could and you invest. By keeping these funds in a savings account, you are earning almost no return on these funds and not a return that will outpace inflation. Saving for retirement should be done in a tax-advantaged way such as a workplace 401(k), an IRA or if you are self-employed a SEP IRA. These are considered investments and, in theory, should outpace inflation that has averaged about 3.9% a year. Your investment needs to make a return that is larger than 3.9% a year just to keep even with inflation. Now it is true that by keeping your money in a savings account or a CD, it is safe, but I can almost guarantee that inflation will eat at everything you have saved not leaving you with as much money as you need. By investing and taking on extra risk, you should be able to save enough money that will allow you to retire and have a nest egg that has outpaced inflation.

Now some basic terms that you will need to know and understand at least to some degree. A security is simply a financial instrument. Now there are different types of securities but when you hear the term most people think of stocks. There are two fundamental types of securities, debt security where money is owed to you such a US government bond and equity security such a share of stock in a company that is a small piece of ownership. Stocks are traded on exchanges, and many are tracked by indexes such as the DOW or the S&P 500 which are merely a collection of companies that are traded on that particular exchange. An example of an exchange is the NYSE or spelled out the New York Stock Exchange. Bonds can are bought and sold as well, and the prices for them can be found in certain publications and through people who are authorized brokers of bonds. Another key to investing in securities is diversification that simply means spreading your investments over several assets or security classes. It is best to own some stocks in different sectors or business lines, bonds in different companies or governments and commodities such as silver and gold. What is the best percentage to put in each security? That answer depends on how old you are and what you risk tolerance is. No matter what never put all of your investments in one asset or security.

Now on to some other items that you will need to be aware of when investing. When investing fees, and commissions are paid to brokers. If you invest in a stock, you will be paying commissions to buy and sell the stocks. If you own an exchange traded fund or a mutual fund, you will be paying commissions to buy and sell as well as management fees to the company that actually manages the funds. And if you do not want to pick individual stocks the funds are the way to go as they will get you the returns of stocks with instant diversification as well. Investing in tax-advantaged accounts such as an IRA, 401(k) or annuity will provide you in your retirement years, and a 529 will give you a tax-advantaged saving for college expenses. Know and look for ways to invest that are advantageous to you tax wise.

How to invest may be a good thing to look at now that we have covered some of the more basic things you need to know. Starting in your 20's will give you a major advantage over someone who even starts at say 30 or 35. The power of compounding interest is something that you want to work in your favor and time will allow just that. Just a word of advice and no this is not something that is to be ignored do not buy the hot stock or make a purchase of a stock tip. Before you buy any security, you need to do your homework on it to understand how the company makes it money and how sound the company is. There is nothing worse than investing in a company that has poor financials, and you lose your money. But if you are to lose money the time to do it is when you are young, and you have time on your side to make it back through the power of compounding interest. Also, you need to think long term and avoid short term investing which is risky and can be costly to your account. It is also wise to put money that will be needed a liquid account and invest money that can be kept invested for at least five years.

Now this is the final bit a basic information that everyone needs to understand and not just someone who is 25 years old. And that is no one can predict the future of where the stock market or any investment will go in the future. It is also important to understand that past performance is by no way an indication of what future performance will be. History does not guarantee future performances by any asset or security. And no one knows everything about the market or asset class. The best we can do is always do our homework on a security and keep current on how it may do. When in doubt seek the advice of a professional who can help you and help keep emotion out of your investments that are vital to the success.

Personal Finance: A Grouping of Financial Topics
By Kirk G. Meyer

Are you like me and in your 40's? Are you preparing for your retirement to happen in the next 20-25 years? If so you are like many people who find themselves in this pivotal decade for workers and families. If you follow me on Twitter or Facebook in the past few weeks I have posted money mistakes that people make in their 20's and 30's but I felt compelled to write something for those who are in their 40's mainly because I am 42, and I know many people who are in the same shape as I am. In your 20's and 30's you can save in different manners and spend in different ways. In your 20's chances are you are just starting your career and not making much in the way of an annual salary. In your 30's you may be making more at work, settling down and starting a family, and maybe buying a first house. Your 40's are a transition decade that sees you are going after more possessions, and you are entering the earnings apex of your career. The following are some common mistakes that people make in their 40's that you can avoid with some proper planning and a common sense approach.

Many people and couples who are in their 40's may feel that they have outgrown their smaller starter house and have the urge to supersize to a new larger house. Here I am not telling you not to buy the larger house but rather if you do opt to buy a bigger home do not buy one that is too big or out of your comfort zone as far as price and mortgage payments. The reason I advise you to not buy too big is because in many instances when you do retire and the children are out of the house people have the urge to then have the urge to then downsize their homes. Also, many times, when people upgrade their homes in their 40's they, do so at the expense of college savings if they have children and in many instances at the expense of their retirement accounts. It is never wise to sacrifice your retirement accounts for any reason at this point in your life. But if you are dead set on getting a larger house buy one that is a minimum of what you think you need and do not go to the biggest house in the neighborhood or on the street. Modest homes that accomplish your needs is all that is needed, and excess is a waste at this point.

Just as with the house it is not wise to put your children's college education expenses ahead of your retirement. The best thing to do is put some money in a 529 plan when you are young and first married in your 20's or 30's along with funding your retirement accounts. Then let time and compounding of interest and earnings work in your favor for both accounts. But if you are like many people and have not started saving for your children's college until your 40's it is never wise to save for their expenses at the risk of your retirement savings. Always pay yourself first in the way of retirement accounts and if there are funds left then use them to fund a 529 plan for your children. And 529 plans can have anyone contribute to them not just you as the parents. And it makes more sense to have your children take a greater responsibility for their education as they will have a much longer period to repay loans while they are younger and working. But it is important that they also save for their retirement at the same time just as it was for you when you started out in your career. And never overlook scholarships, grants, and having your children work while in college to help cover the expenses.

When you reach your 40's it is important that you no longer are saving like you did in your 20's and 30's. You are now technically within 20-25 years of retirement, and you need to step up your savings in such a manner that will allow you to retire in a manner in which you are comfortable. When you are younger, you can save a little less because you have time on your side and the longer the money is saved in a retirement account, the more it will grow. Compounding is a real wonder of the world. In your 40's the money you save will have a shorter period to grow, so you have to save more to accomplish the same result. The goal when you are younger is to save 10% of your salary for retirement, and that percentage needs to increase as you get older. Try living on the same as you did before as your salary grows and save the difference.

Another problem that goes along with the savings is how you invest your funds. Most people in their 40's are investing in a manner that is more conservative than is practical. Now I am not saving to invest outside your risk tolerance level or in a manner that is not prudent or safe. But as we are living longer in retirement we need to invest in a manner that will allow for our funds to continue to appreciate and allow for capital appreciation of our assets. In past generations, people retired and could expect to spend 15-20 years in retirement prior to their deaths. Now people are living much longer, and your retirement funds may need to last 30-35 years or longer. Find a happy medium for your risks and rewards when it comes to your retirement accounts to ensure that your funds to run out prior to your death. In today's world of financial instruments, there are several options for people to choose from that will allow them to achieve their financial goals and ensure you do not run out of money in your retirement years.

Now that you are in your 40's chances are you are married, have children, and have bought a house. There is no reason now to avoid the inevitable which is your death. In order to ensure your wishes are carried out and to protect your family it is imperative that you draft a will. Better yet if you are married, you and your spouse both need to have this vital document done to protect each other and your children if you have any. Also, this is a good time to make sure your insurance is at an adequate level to protect your family in the event you die prematurely. And for those who are on top of their game go all in and see a professional and develop an estate plan to protect your family and all of your assets. And never overlook the use of a power of attorney for medical and financial purposes in the event you become incapacitated.

If at all possible avoid tapping into 401(k) loans and home equity lines of credit in your 40's. Many people are changing careers in their 40's and if you have an outstanding 401(k) loan you must repay it in a short amount of time or face penalties and taxes on the outstanding balance of the loan. And if you are laid off the same applies. As for home equity loans, you are placing your home at risk if you cannot repay the loan for any reason. 401(k) loans also affect your earning power as you are taking funds out of your account, and this potentially will have a negative impact on your long term value. Again if possible avoid both of these loans and do not use them as a piggy bank.

Your 40's are a pivotal decade as far as family and retirement. Avoid these traps, and you can make the most out of your hard work up to this point. But do not stop here consult a professional and see what changes you may need to make to ensure you have a dream retirement.

Are you over 50 and thinking of retiring? Do you know what your options are in the area of retirement? Well, I hope that you at least are saving in some form for your eventual retirement. Most of us do work somewhere that offers a 401(k), and I do hope you are taking advantage of the opportunity to save some for your golden years. And if you are lucky enough to work for an organization that offers a match for your contributions I hope that you are at least contributing the full amount that will receive the match. It is never a wise move to leave free money on the table when it comes to your retirement. Think of it another way, it is an instant positive return on your investment. Either way make sure you contribute at least the amount that your organization will match if not more.

If you have reached the age of 50, you need to make some changes that will protect you and your family in your retirement years. The first is you have to make saving a non-negotiable item in your household budgets. You have to save and pay yourself first because in retirement I would not count on Social Security to be enough to cover your expenses. One way to do this is to contribute to your work's 401(k) as that is an automatic deduction from your pay and in essence you will not even notice the money is gone because you technically never saw it in your bank account. If you are already contributing to your 401(k), then consider making automatic contributions to an IRA that will be deducted directly from your bank account on the same day you are paid. Again this is almost like you never had the money to spend because the funds are directly taken from the account before you even notice that they were there. In a simplistic term make saving for your future as automatic as you can and it will be relatively painless. Remember that individuals over the age of 50 are allowed extra contributions to 401(k)'s and IRA's. Pay off high-interest credit cards instead of paying them the high interest that they charge on almost all credit cards. This is another way to pay yourself instead of paying financial entities.

So how much will someone need when they retire? That is the question all of us would like to know along with what is the return on my invested money going to be. If we had the answer to those questions, retirement would not be a stressful event and require years of diligent work to save enough to live comfortably. As far as how much you will need to save that will depend on a few factors. The most common are what will be the return on your investments, how much will you need each year to cover your expenses and how long will live as a retired person. Now that last one is right up there with the other two questions we would like to have the answers to when it comes to planning our retirement. But let's face it no one can predict the future so make the most educated guesses you can with the best possible information you can find. As for how long you may live in your retirement years you can look at your family to maybe get some insights into your longevity. If your grandparents and parents lived into their 80's, there is a good chance you might as well. Now as for how much you will need to save some say about 25 times the amount you will withdrawal each year. While this may sound good, you will have to know what your expenses will be and how many years you will be taking the money out of your accounts. Another way to calculate what you will need is to take the amount you have saved and project what you may expect to earn on the investments. Here it is better to be conservative rather than aggressive when it comes to returns. If you have a million dollars saved and it earns a conservative 6.5% a year, you will be able to take out $65,000 a year without depleting your principal. Also, when you are figuring out what you will need in retirement it is not only important to be realistic in your returns but you must also consider inflation. A safe assumption for inflation is about 3%, so your real return on a 6.5% return is 3.5% adjusted for inflation. Remember a million dollars today will not purchase the same amount in 20 years due to inflation. Keep that in mind when you are trying to calculate your needs.

With all of these things being taken into account for it can be a safe assumption that the following age groups should consider saving these amounts. If you are smart and start saving in your 20's, you can expect to have a relatively safe retirement putting away 10%. Each decade you decide to wait you can increase that amount by 10% so as you can see it is best to save early and often save. Now consider it is estimated that two-thirds of Americans use Social Security as their primary source of income. Then you must consider that the other third of Americans it is their only source of income in retirement. And on average Social Security payments are about $15,000 a year.

Also, you need to consider that you may have expenses now that you will not have in retirement. One could be the Social Security tax itself. Another may be life insurance as retired people have much less of a need for life insurance than working people. Also, it is a good idea to save with your future health care needs in mind. Do not make the mistake of thinking Medicare is free or will cover all your health care needs. Medicare premiums are deducted directly from your Social Security payments and then even after considering this you can really only count on Medicare to cover about 60% of your health care costs.

With all of these things to consider, it is always the best idea to start thinking of your retirement early. Save as much as you can and try to make it as automatic as you can. With proper planning, anyone can have a truly blessed retirement.

Turning 50? Are you about to consider retirement? There are some particular rule and laws that allow that closer to retirement to use catch-up contributions to preparing better for a better retirement. Many people who are working today have not prepared for their retirement and are going to rely on Social Security as their primary source of funds after they stop working. This is not an ideal situation and one that can be avoided if you plan correctly starting now. No matter how old you are it is never too late to start saving, step up your savings to a higher level, or continue saving the way you are if that is at an adequate level to begin with. I personally do not expect much help from Social Security when I retire in about 25 years as I hope to wait until my full retirement age of 67 or if I can delay my checks even until I am 70 years old. That way I will increase my benefits 24% from the age 67 levels for an instant return on my money. That and I do not plan on retiring at 62, 65, or maybe even 67 as I love what I do but plan on doing more financial planning after I retire from my government job.

If you are over the age of 50 the first place, you need to begin increasing your savings in your Individual Retirement Account or IRA. For everyone who saves in an IRA in 2014, they are allowed to save $5,500 on an annual basis. Here is where being over the age of 50 is essential to saving the most as you are allowed an extra $1,000 in annual savings for a total of $6,500. The amount that is allowed to be saved in an IRA is set on an annual basis by the IRS and largely depends on the rate of inflation. As inflation was low the last few years, the IRS has not raised the annual limit from 2013 to 2014.

401(k) accounts are also an area where people over the age of 50 are allowed a catch-up contribution. For 2014, those under the age of 50 are allowed to contribute up to $17,500 in their work sponsored 401(k) or equivalent account. But just as with the IRA the IRS allows those over the age of 50 to contribute an additional $5,500 a year for a total of $23,000 on an annual basis. Also, just as with the IRA the IRS examines these funding levels on an annual basis.

For public sector workers, there is a special savings tool and an example of this is a 457 plans. These allow a pre-retirement catch-up where they are allowed double the maximum allocation for a period of three years prior to their normal retirement or up to $35,000 in 2014. This works well when people are paid large lump sums for un-used sick leave or annual leave that is paid upon retirement. However, you are not allowed to use this in addition to the standard catch-up contributions. People who use some 303(b) plans are allowed to make extra catch-up contributions after 15 years of service, but these rules are tricky and it is best to consult a professional prior to trying to do these contributions.

I plan on examining the does and do not's for those who are in their 50's in the next few weeks. Until then if you have any questions or concerns feel free to contact me, and I will be more than happy to help you in any way I can.

Insurance

I shared an experience that some friends of mine had with a life insurance agent. The interesting part is that the day before that topic was discussed I came across an article on Yahoo Finance about; you guessed it life insurance agents. While I will provide the general information from that well written and very informative article, I will also explain how it relates to my friends yet again and my experience as a life insurance agent. While I am a registered life insurance agent in my home state of Tennessee, I am also completing my MS in Financial Planning and have a goal of becoming a Chartered Financial Planner one day. So let's not waste any more time and get down to what a life insurance agent won't tell you.

The first thing they will say is that you are most likely under-insured. While it may be a fact that about 30% of American households have no life insurance, there may, in fact, be a real reason for the lack of insurance. Let's take my parents as an example. Both are retired. They own their house outright with no mortgage. And have very little debt that they have to service. They would be part of the 30% that does not have a life insurance policy and for good reason, they do not need it. Single adults who are just starting their careers are also prime candidates for not having life insurance as they have no dependents and no one relies on them for their income. The only reason a single person would need a life insurance policy is to handle any debts that they do not wish to burden their family with. What is bad is that it is estimated that as much as 60% of the policies sold are whole life policies that are some of the most expensive while being the most lucrative for the agent. As for what is the correct amount of insurance that is needed that is a question you need to address with your situation being the only factor that helps you decide. At a minimum, if you have a family you need enough of a death benefit to pay off your mortgage and possibly fund your children's college expenses. Other than that it may be necessary to use the policy to help replace your income. In these instances use the much cheaper term policies and not the more expensive whole life policies.

What out for insurance agents who are selling life insurance as a security as they are limited at best. Many universal life policies are marketed as indexed policies. The issue here is they will pay a minimum interest rate to lure a customer in and sell the fact it is an index say to the S&P 500. What they do not divulge in great detail is that the indexed interest rate that is paid is capped and could result in a lost opportunity cost to you, the policy owner. In these instances, it is vital you understand what it is you are buying and that you have a trusted agent.

Children do not need a life insurance policy as there is no income to be replaced. Also, these are whole life policies that agents sell to people as investments for their children's college fund. Do not fall into this trap as you would be much better off savings the premiums in a state authorized 529 plan that offers tax benefits, as well as much better returns than a whole life policy. And do not let an agent sell you on the fact that your child may be uninsurable when they need to take a policy out. Many employers offer term policies for their employees and to be honest unless there are some serious health issues getting a life insurance policy for younger people is not all that difficult.

While I do not sell variable annuities, they are an expensive group of mutual funds. While I do believe that these instruments do have a place in someone's retirement planning as it have no limitations on what can be contributed. Also, they allow for you to buy and sell within the annuity with no tax consequences at the time of the buying and selling allowing for a good way to rebalance one's assets without having considerable tax implications. If you are an average investor, it is better to look at an indexed annuity or a fixed rate annuity as they are much less complicated. Chances are your agent does not fully understand all the complexities of a variable annuity or the fees associated with it so how in the world will they be able to explain this all to you? Chances are they will not be able to.

One of the selling points of a whole life policy is that the accumulated cash value will earn interest that it does and that in time you will earn enough interest to pay the premiums. Many people are finding out that this is not the case as interest rates are at historic lows and have been for some time. And in many instances it may take years for the policy to accumulate any cash value even at all. What insurance companies generally like to keep as quiet as possible is that the first few years premiums go pay the high commissions that they policies have, marketing and management fees just to name a few of the items.

And finally beware of agents who tout the long-term care aspect of a policy. Chances are it is not a good policy for you or them. As insurance products go these are relatively new to the insurance world and most companies are still trying to figure out the numbers. If they do not know what the total costs will be how do they expect you as the consumer to make an informed decision? The answer is they don't. While most people can expect to need some form of long-term care, there are some viable alternatives to an insurance policy. Take the premiums that you would have spent on the policy and invest them in a low-cost indexed exchange traded fund. These are tax efficient investments that can experience real returns over extended periods of time. And the best part of this approach is that if you do not need long-term care you have not paid years' worth of premiums and have a nice nest egg you can spend on anything or leave to your heirs.

Keep these things in mind when someone tried to sell you a life insurance policy. Better yet keep these things in mind and think along these lines when you buy any insurance product.

Despite recent legislation are you needing to reduce health care expenses? If you are like the majority of people, the answer to that is yes. No matter how someone has gotten their health insurance chances are the costs are higher than they should be or how we want them to be. Due to this, chances are good that every consumer of health care is paying a higher percentage of their health care expenses. Premiums and out of pocket expenses seem to be going up every year with no end in sight. But there are some steps that can be taken to reduce out of pocket expenses associated with health care and health insurance. Some may seem obvious and others not so much but taken together they can save you some of your hard-earned money.

One step that can be taken to keep out of pocket expenses lower is to stay in the plan's network of doctors and hospitals despite the fact these networks are shrinking. According to healthcare experts, going outside of your plan's network may be the single costliest mistake that an insured person can make. In some plans, there is no out of network option or the co-pay is raised substantially. But in today's world of insurance many plans are saying no out network options except emergencies. And an outside provider is not bound to charge plan prices and can set them how they determine, and your policy will only pay the predetermined amount leaving the insured to cover the difference. In the case of a planned surgery, it is best to make sure all parties are within the policy's plan as not everyone involved may be in the network. Always check to make sure. Check to see if your insurance plan even has super-preferred providers that are care providers who display excellence in service and a commitment to reducing costs.

Shop around for the best prices as not all facilities charge the same prices. When it comes to radiology depending on where you have, your test can have vast differences in prices that you will be required to pay. On average an MRI or CAT scan can be between $1,300 and $1,650 at an outpatient clinic or hospital. The same tests can be as little as $450 to $725 at a radiology center that is independent. When it comes to radiology, it does pay to shop around and in many instances your insurance provider may offer assistance in locating the best prices. The same can be done for clinics and hospitals as not all charge the same price. If your doctor is a member or associated with one or more hospitals, it may pay to ask them what one has the best prices for their part of the procedures. While the doctor's fee will be the same regardless of where you are seen or have the procedure done the center, or hospital can charge vastly different fees.

If at all possible avoid the emergency room. In some instances, it may be advisable to visit an urgent care facility or a walk-in clinic instead of making a visit to the emergency room. For minor illnesses or injuries, it is much cheaper to visit one of these types of places as compared to an emergency room. On average an emergency room visit will run about $1,500 during an urgent care clinic is about $125, and a walk-in clinic can be as little as $55 in many instances. So depending on what is the health issue let that help guide you in where you will go for your health care. In some cases, the emergency room is the best bet but for some things a clinic will work just fine.

Similar to where you get your health care is what types of prescriptions you get. When it comes to prescription drugs if the option is available go with a generic formula over the name brand drug. In many instances, the use of generic prescriptions can save you 80% or more in costs. And when you can purchase generic over name brand the co-pay is less as well. Keep an eye out for when name brand drugs have the patent expire, and generic ones can start production as this is always happening. Most of the time, your insurance company will make the switch for you or even ban the use of name brand prescriptions, but that is not always the case. And shop around as not all drugstores will charge the same price for the same medicine. And sometimes the insurance company will offer mail order prescriptions that are much cheaper than your local store so check with the insurance company to see if they do indeed have more reasonable service.

Another way that will enable you to save some money is through the use of a flexible spending account. If your employer offers a FSA, it is wise to take advantage of them as they can save money in two ways. The first it will reduce your income taxes by the amount you contribute to the FSA. This means if you were to contribute $2,500 to a FSA it would reduce your income taxes by that same quantity. The drawback in this is if you do not use all the funds you put into the FSA on an annual basis the funds will be lost. And in the past any FSA money could be used for non-prescription drugs so get your physician to write a prescription for over the counter drugs to be able to get the advantages of the FSA.

Look at these steps and try to reduce your health care expense. There are many other ways to achieve lower costs, but these were some of the more common and some of the ones that are available to more people. As health care is always changing so keep up with the changes and that will enable you to stay on top of your health care expenses.

Are you looking to buy life insurance to protect your loved ones? Chances are if you are you are looking at the differences between a few policies. The main two types are term and permanent, such as a universal policy for the purposes of this blog. Now I am a licensed life insurance agent in the state of Tennessee; however, I am also finishing a Master's of Science in Financial Planning, so I have a conflicted approach to this particular subject. As a life insurance agent, I prefer you would buy the universal life policy from me as the annual premium is higher than that of a term policy thereby allowing me to make more off that sale. As a financial planner I would advise you to buy the term policy and invest the difference between what you are paying for the term policy and what you would have paid for the universal life policy thereby making a smaller commission on the sale due to the fact a term policy can be purchased for lower annual premium. As I told you earlier, we will compare a universal life policy and a term policy and assume the following conditions. First we are insuring a 42-year old male who is a non-smoker and has no health issues. The policy is for a death benefit of $250,000 as that is about the maximum that an insurance company will issue a policy for without a medical portion of the application process. The term policy will be of two lengths, a 20 year and a 30 year fixed premium. Those two policies will be compared to a universal life policy from the same primary insurance company.

Many financial advisors who also appear on national television shows will advise you of the same thing I would and that buy the term policy and invest the difference of that, and a universal life policy would cost. So who is telling you this besides me? Most of you have probably heard of Dave Ramsey or Suze Orman. They advise this approach all the time on television and in their books. Now I have read many books by both of these well-known and respected individuals but I do not recall them showing me the math behind their advice. Well, I will show you what the numbers look like when you purchase a term policy and invest the difference. Once you see the numbers, I think you will agree with the well-known professionals and myself. Now you are most likely asking yourself what is the catch? Well, that is simple, you have to be disciplined and invest the difference to make this work.

Now had you purchased the universal life policy you would be guaranteed a death benefit of $250,000 for life provided you continued to pay the premiums on the policy. And most insurance agents will try to sell this policy as not only an insurance policy but an investment as it does generate a cash value that you can use to borrow against or pay the premiums in your later years. While it is true that most policies that are considered permanent policies will have a minimum guaranteed return and you will not lose any of your principal. About now you are telling yourself this sounds pretty good; I get life insurance and it generates a cash value that I can borrow against. What most agents neglect to tell you is that the guaranteed return is most likely not going to keep even up with inflation and if you do borrow against the cash value you have to repay the loan with interest or it will be deducted from your death benefit. Now it does not sound quite as good is it? And this final piece of information will seal the deal for you most likely. And that is this policy will cost you $252 a month for the rest of your life and the cash value that is accumulated cannot exceed the death benefit. In most cases where that does occur you get to keep the insurance and not pay the $252 a month while still being insured.

Now let's say you go with a term policy over the universal life policy. In the example I will put before you we have two choices, a 20 year and a 30-year policy. The good thing about term policies is that if you need additional coverage for 20 years but still want the coverage for 30 you can purchase both at a relatively inexpensive price. While in this example either a 20 or 30-year term policy is purchased it is still affordable to purchase both if you have a need for both. What would cause such a need you ask? Say you just bought a house with a 30-year mortgage and wanted to ensure the house would be paid for in the event of your death. Simple you buy the 30-year term policy. Now say you have a child and want to ensure they have money for college. Now you would buy the additional 20-year term policy when they were about five years old to cover their college years. Now unlike the universal policy these two policies will end at the end of the term, and they accumulate no cash value. If you die, they will pay your beneficiary the $250,000 but if you outlive the policy it just ends, and the insurance company keeps your premiums. Now I am sure you are asking what the policy costs if the universal policy was $252 a month. The same death benefit for a 20-year term policy is $46 a month, and an extended 30-year policy is $76 a month. Both of those premiums are vastly different from the $252 a month cost of a universal life policy.

First we will look at the difference between the 30-year term and the universal life. Now you were a careful and mindful person who always pays their premiums for the universal life policy. At the end of the 30 years, you would have a cash value in the policy of $121,552 at a cost of $90,720. Now had you purchased the term policy you would, of course, have no cash value, but the cost of the term policy would have only been $27,360. If the difference of $176 was invested every month in an indexed fund that gave you a 7.5% return, which is lower than the S&P 500 return for the last 30 years, you would have an account with $237,150 in it. In this case, you can afford to have no insurance on your life at all and self-insure as by saving the same $176 a month for an additional ten years would give you an account of $532,193. And depending on how you invested these funds they could be tax-free if they were invested in a ROTH IRA. Regardless, buying the term policy and investing the difference is the better option in the end provided you stay right and always pay the premiums and invest the difference. The comparison between the 20-year term and universal is the same with a lower cash value and paid a premium for the universal life policy and a smaller account balance for the invested term difference.

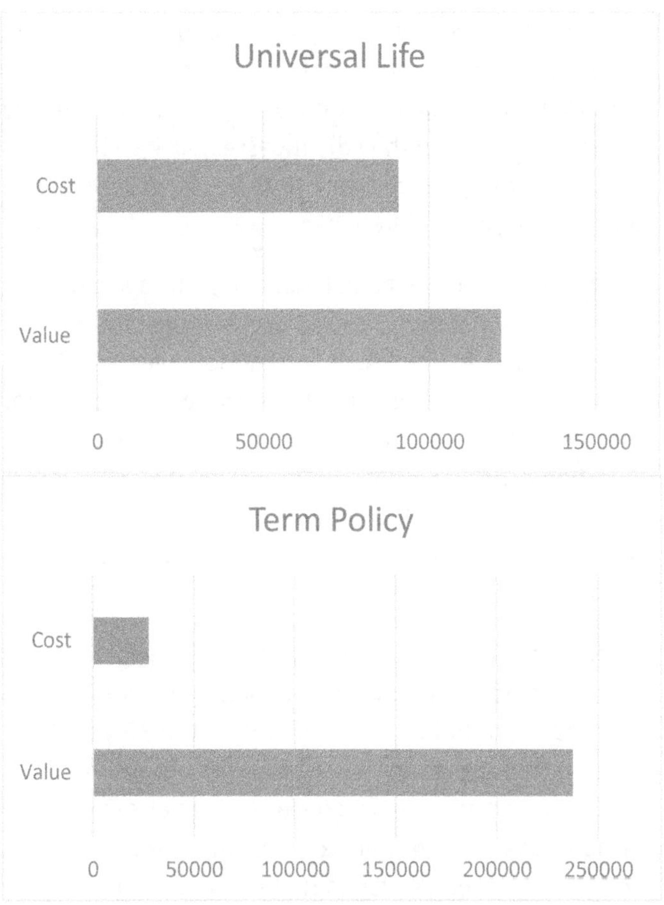

Now I know you are thinking to yourself that life insurance proceeds are tax-free. That is true but if you are worried about your spouse they pay no federal estate taxes on anything you leave them anyway. And in the event it is left to your children provided you, your spouse and the children did some estate planning the proceeds can be tax-free if the funds were invest through a ROTH IRA and can continue to grow tax-deferred if the proceeds are placed in an inherited IRA by your children. They will then be required to make minimum annual withdrawals over their lifetime and if there is any money left in the IRA when they die it passes tax free in a lump sum to your grandchildren if there is proper estate planning by your children.

As you can see by the actual numbers, I have laid out it is better to buy the term policy and invest the difference in premiums in a ROTH IRA. If you cannot invest in a ROTH IRA due to the income restrictions, there is a solution for that as well. Make non-deductible contributions to a Traditional IRA and immediately convert it to a ROTH IRA. By doing that you will have minimal taxes and get the tax-free advantages of a ROTH IRA for your spouse, children and possibly grandchildren.

Think about the bottom line after say 40 years. If you purchased the universal life policy, you would leave $250,000 your heirs. Had you bought the 30-year term policy and not died for 40 years while always investing the $176 a month you would leave your heirs over half a million dollars. And if done with some estate planning and the use of beneficiaries that half a million would be tax-free the same as the life insurance policy.

Do you need life insurance and are not certain what kind you need? If you have read my blogs in the past you know I, am a firm believer that the term is a much better value for a permanent policy. While I still believe, a term policy is better for most people provided they invest the difference of the two premiums in a low-cost mutual fund or exchange traded fund. But there is a point for some high net worth people where a permanent policy does have its place in someone's financial plan.

First, let me explain my preferred method of buying life insurance and explain some of the numbers. If you are a non-smoking male age 40 and in good health you can get a $500,000 30-year term policy from a major insurance company for about $152 a month. The same person could get a universal life policy for a monthly premium of $502. That is a difference of $350 a month that could be invested in a low-cost fund that is almost guaranteed to outpace the accumulated cash value of a permanent policy. In the policy, I quoted in the example above the guaranteed interest return on the policy was 2% that does not even outpace inflation that is currently at about 2.2%. That means the value of your cash value is not going to outpace the inflation rate, and you will, in essence, lose money. But if you were to invest the $350 difference in premiums in an indexed fund in something similar to the S&P 500 it would have a pre-inflation return of about 8.5%. That means the adjusted return would be 6.3%, and that invested $350 a month would grow to be $367,000. And if you invested that $4,200 a year in a ROTH IRA that is money that would be tax-free for you or your heirs. And to be honest with you, most people in their 70's do not need large life insurance policies as their homes are paid for, and there is no income to replace.

As you can see for younger people who are healthy there, is little incentive to purchase a permanent life insurance policy when by using a term policy and a smart investment plan the same objective can be achieved with much more flexibility for the insured. Regardless if you buy a term policy and invest the difference or purchase a permanent policy, it is all pointless if you do not or cannot pay the premiums for the policy for the life of the policy or the insured. Now we will take a brief look at some instances where a permanent policy may make sense depending on the time in which it is maintained.

If the permanent policy is kept, less than five years it is basically a waste of your valuable resources. As many insurance agents will sell a permanent policy as a hybrid of insurance and an investment that is simply not the case. For the first year or two about all of the premiums, go to pay the commission to the agent that sold the policy and will build very little in the way of a cash value. In reality the cash value of a policy less than five years old will be minute in nature as during that period most of the premiums go to pay commissions, fees, and the insurance portion of the policy. So if you cannot pay for the policy for at least five years, it is a much better proposition to purchase a term policy from the beginning.

In the sixteenth year of the policy is to the breakeven point. This means that the cash value and the value of the life insurance provided to that point are about equal to what was paid into the policy. This is the earliest you can cancel the policy and not lose the vast majority of what you have paid into the policy. Again, if you do not think you can afford the higher premiums for at least this period, it is better to go with the cheaper term policy.

If you can maintain the policy for twenty years and are wise with the use of any dividends paid by the issuing company, a permanent policy can be advantageous. Dividends will be the subject of a the future blog as they can be somewhat complicated but if you reinvest them they can actually make the death benefit and cash value an attractive vehicle for financial planning. If a permanent policy is held long enough and dividends are reinvested, the cash value portion of the policy can compete with similar risked investments.

Now the term policy would have expired at age 70 and taking out a permanent or another term policy at that age may be prohibitive for most. However, if you had the term policy and invested the difference in premiums, you would have a sizable amount of money at your disposal. And yes It is also true that you would no longer have any life insurance death benefits that will be paid upon the insured's death. But as I stated earlier a large death benefit might not be needed if you invested wisely, have paid off your house and are not replacing lost income. And in many instances the value of the investments can return a large portion of the death benefit. A positive of a permanent policy is that they will continue to insure the person anywhere from 100 to 121 years of age provided the premiums are paid on the policy. Depending on at what age a permanent policy is taken out it is apparent that this type of insurance can be extremely expensive depending on the longevity of the insured.

Term policies and permanent policies both have their advantages and disadvantages, so it is wise to consult an expert when deciding what is best for you and your family.

Are you a retiring baby boomer? Are you one of the thousands of baby boomers who will turn 65 every day for the next 20 years or so? If you are in retirement or nearing retirement, it is likely you may be concerned with long-term care (LTC). It is a known fact that nursing homes are very expensive in the present and like everything else in today's market the price will not likely be going down. And do not count on Medicaid to provide much comfort as their benefits do not start until you have expended all of your assets in many cases leaving a spouse with very little. Ten years ago the principal players in the LTC market seemed stable but one look at the same market today shows very few of the companies that provided LTC are still producing policies. And those who are in the LTC market are scaling back benefits, making their eligibility stricter, and charging higher premiums. And women see the largest increases in premiums in today's marketplace.

People who are in their mid-40's and even into their 60's do have some options when it comes to LTC. It is true that the premiums paid for LTC will be lower the younger you are but that also means you will be paying the premiums for a longer period. If you are a prudent saver and are consistent with your ability to save you can figure out what the premiums would be for a LTC policy when you are younger and just invest those funds in something relatively safe that will give you decent returns such as an index exchange traded fund. Remember the insurance company is taking your premiums and investing them for the same period but unlike you, they have restrictions placed on them as to how they invest your premiums. This combination of your premiums and their expected return is what will fund your LTC in the event you need it. So if you are younger why not self-insure and take the amount you would pay in premiums and invest the money yourself. Provided you can get a return as good if not better than the insurance company you will have enough money by the time you retire to pay for any LTC you may need. And in the event you do not need to go into a LTC facility you will leave your loved ones a beautiful legacy as the money you would have paid to the insurance company is your to leave behind and not lost to pay the insurance company. However, this strategy will only work if you are diligent in ensuring you save the money and get a decent overall return. This is a good strategy for someone who is in the 20's or 30's as it will give them in most cases 30 plus years to accumulate funds.

For those who are in the 40's or later, LTC insurance may be a better choice as the amount of time you will have to self-insure is considerably less. But depending on the insurance company and type of policy you decide to buy will determine what your premiums will be. The longer wait period you have between being admitted to a LTC facility and when the insurance company starts to cover the costs will significantly influence the amount of your premium. The longer you delay the insurance company in what they will pay means lower premiums for you but greater out of pocket expenses. Also, if you decide to buy the inflation protection rider that will increase your premiums as well, so you need to consider that in your factoring of a LTC policy. And most policies will limit the amount they will pay on a per day basis and for how long. When LTC coverage started, it was more common to have longer periods that benefits would be paid now it is mainly up to two years or so that an insurance company will pay the benefits. Also, many policies will pay $100, $200 or $300 a day in benefits. Obviously the more per day that is paid in benefits and the longer the benefits will last and result in higher premiums as the chance is greater that the insurance company could be paying out more in total benefits. It is wise to consider that a private nursing home room rate averages a little over $200 a day or about $73,000 a year and the average stay in an LTC facility is just over two years. Of course depending on where you are living in the country could significantly affect the cost of a LTC facility as some parts of the country are considerably cheaper to live in and result in lower LTC costs as well. An average LTC facility on the west coast could run well into six figures a year. So if you lived in a high cost of living area, a LTC facility could run you $150,000 a year or if you were to be there for the average two years at least $300,000 that either you or the LTC insurance company would pay.

If someone were about 30 years old and invested $100 a month at an 8% return, they would have about $230,000 at age 65. If a person were 40, they would have to invest $250 a month to get the same $230,000. As you can see, it is possible to self-insure for LTC if you plan properly and get a return that is sufficient to grow your investment to a desired amount. And again the best part of self-insuring is if you do not need to spend the money on LTC you can leave it to your loved ones. Of course, you would have to earn more than 8% on your investment as it will be taxed and must outpace inflation as well. But there are strategies that can be used to minimize the taxes that have to be paid on the investment. If you have concerns about a strategy, seek the guidance of a financial planner.

No, neither LTC or saving $100 a month for 35 years will be sufficient if you are diagnosed with a disease like Alzheimer's which can lead to a LTC stay of well over the two-year average. In this case, you will be forced to find an insurance company that offers a longer period of benefits. In these instances, it is best to consider savings, pensions, social security, and a LTC policy to cover the costs associated with a prolonged LTC stay. Of course, no one knows if they will develop an illness such as Alzheimer's but such illnesses and things such as debilitating strokes do occur and will require possibly extended stays in a LTC facility. The best advice is to consider all of the assets that will be available to you for LTC and buy a policy that will cover the difference taking into account an extended stay in a LTC facility.

As women frequently outlive men they now pay higher premiums. But if a married couple buys a LTC policy together they may get a discount up to 30%. Also, it is a wise idea to check with your employer to see if they offer a LTC policy as many group policies will provide a unisex rate. Also not all insurance companies offer the same products or the same benefits so regardless if you are a man or a woman make sure you shop around and get several quotes.

Investing

As an individual investor, you face the prospect of protecting your investments with little or no support from a professional advisor. If you are like me, you have to ask yourself what should I do about rebalancing my assets? Should I sell my winning stocks now to rebalance into lower yielding bonds? Should I let me gains ride and rebalance when bonds have made some of a rebound? Only you can truly answer these questions, and only you know if you feel comfortable in rebalancing your assets in your portfolio.

Chances are if you do own a mixture of stocks and bonds your stocks are outperforming your bonds by a significant amount. Over the past year, the S&P 500 index was up 16% prior to the government shutdown and will most likely go back to the pre-crisis levels provided Congress does not have another showdown on the debt ceiling limit. If that happens your guess as to what will happen is as good as mine but chances are the stock market will go down and the yield on US Treasuries will go up due to the inability of Congress to act and thereby creating an environment where it will cost the US more to borrow.

But as of today I can honestly say I am not certain I would own bonds in my portfolio or at least I would not add to that position. Why do you ask? The current yield on a ten-year Treasury is about 2.6%. While, that is up from the start of the year that the return will not even keep pace with inflation over the long run. If you were to look at bonds for your portfolio, I would highly recommend a high percentage in high-quality corporate bonds and a small proportion of riskier high yield bonds. This will help diversify your portfolio not only between stocks and bonds, but a mixture of these kinds of bonds will further diversify your overall portfolio as well as the portion of your portfolio invested in bonds. Unless you are actively buying and selling bonds looks for high-quality bonds that have attractive interest rates and hold them until they mature eliminating your need to adjust the bond's principal for rate sensitivity. Do the same for high yield bonds but pay particular attention to the company's financials because in these bonds your interest payment and principal payment may both be at risk at a higher degree than high quality corporate bonds.

I recently read an article in Money magazine where a portfolio of 70% stocks and 30% bonds were purchased and examined over a 187 year period between 1826 and 2012. The result of not rebalancing surprised me to a great deal as the adjusted for inflation return on the rebalanced portfolio was just 0.23% better than the portfolio where nothing was done. Depending on the size of your portfolio that small of an amount would have been eaten up by the costs and fees associated with your rebalancing. After all, it is not free to buy and sell these assets in order to get to your desired rebalance ratio. Clearly rebalancing on an annual basis may not be the best strategy and in most cases for us as individual investors may not be practical on a cost basis as well.

While buy and hold may be out of favor with many I am starting to take a hybrid approach to investing. Warren

Buffett is the best investor in the world and is known as a value investor. His track record speaks for itself, and I will not even attempt to explain his in-depth strategies. But a fundamental and simple approach is to find a company you understand their core business. Do your homework on the business and see what the numbers tell you. And this is a Buffett aspect of the research but does the business enjoy a wide moat meaning it has distinctive advantages that is has created over time that will give it advantages over its competitors. And finally is the stock selling at an attractive price or a discount. Or once again to take an example from Buffett what is the stocks intrinsic value? Once you know the stock's intrinsic value, you will be able to determine if it is selling at a discount, premium or if it is fairly priced. Now do not place all of your emphasis on the price of a stock at the time you are doing your research. It is entirely acceptable to buy a stock at a premium if you believe in the core fundamentals, management and business in general and from doing your research you believe the stock will go even higher. If you have done your research and are comfortable with a company's stock there is no reason why you cannot buy the stock as a long-term investment or as I like to say a buy and monitor approach. It is imperative to keep informed on the businesses you invest in and at any point you see something that causes you to be concerned it may be time to sell. But rebalancing for the sake of rebalancing may not make sense when things are all going according to your original investing plan.

Now if you have a portion of your portfolio in quality bonds and you are comfortable in your stock positions, there is no need to rebalance what appears to be working. But if you want to get back to your desired ratios try this. Instead of selling one asset to buy another, when you invest new capital in your portfolio use the new funds to buy the asset class that is no longer at the desired ratio of your desired portfolio balance. For example, say you are needed to buy bonds because the stock market has outperformed bonds during the year. Do not buy and sell current assets but use the new capital to buy new bonds and by doing this you will help to bring your portfolio back to the desired ratios. And if that still does not get you back to where you are comfortable try rebalancing every three or five years to avoid unnecessary costs and fees. But chances are you will be able to adjust the portfolio balances by investing in the lagging asset class for a few years with new capital while you continue to let the winners continue to win and adding quality assets in the lagging asset class.

Are your investments not in the proportion you have as targets? Is one asset outperforming another? If you answered yes to these two questions, it might be time to take a look at your investments and rebalance. Now many people rebalance either at the beginning or the end of the year but there is no reason someone cannot rebalance when the advantage it to their benefit.

While investing is meant to be a long-term undertaking, there may from time to time be advantages to taking certain moves that are tax advantageous. As equities have been moving in an upward direction since mid-2009 it may be time to harvest some of the gains that have been experienced and in contrast to that it is a good tax practice also to harvest losses to offset the gains. There is no reason always to wait until the end of the year to perform these tasks as the gains may not be there as well as the losses. Take advantages of these situations when they occur and do not be a slave to a calendar. While almost all equities have seen tremendous increases in the last five years, there are some areas that have been lacking in gains over the last few years where someone can harvest losses. Emerging markets have been hit hard as the Federal Reserve eases its bond buying causing it to be more expensive for these markets to obtain cheap capital resulting in a decrease in their market prices. Also, fund or ETF that is associated with gold or the production of gold has been hit hard over the last three years. And finally what used to be fast growth smaller companies have seen a decrease in their market value in the last year. If someone were in need of losses in equities, these three areas would provide excellent opportunities for loss harvesting. If someone does harvest losses, they need to remember the wash sales rules by the IRS. And that is if someone were to sell an equity at a loss they must wait at least 30 days before buying the equity back. If someone does repurchase the equity prior to the wash-sale rule completing the 30-day wait period, the loss is negated for tax purposes. A way around this it to sell an equity that operates in a particular industry a fund that invests in equities in that industry is an acceptable replacement for the original equity.

Another reason it is important to rebalance is it does increase the returns on your portfolio by as much as one percent a year. Over time that can make a difference in the value of the portfolio. Over the last five years, equities have seen double digit returns on average while bond funds have been relatively flat. That means that if someone has a desired asset mix of 80% equities and 20% bonds their portfolio is now very much out of balance depending on when it was last rebalanced. If it has been more than two years since the portfolio was last rebalanced, the significant increase in the value of equities alone will trigger the need to rebalance. Some people rebalance annually other more often. The key factors to rebalancing are how much is the desired asset allocation off and what are the costs associated with rebalancing. As a general rule when an asset has gains or decreases of 5% or more it may be time to rebalance. As for how often one should rebalance the commissions and tax implications need to be taken into account before any trades are made.

And finally there are needs to rebalance as one's risk tolerance changes. When an investor is younger, they may feel comfortable have a higher concentration of their assets in equities. As they get older, they may want to reduce the risk by shifting assets to an asset such as bonds. As one approaches, retirement their risk tolerance changes and they become more interested in the preservation of capital and not as much of growth. But as people retire they do need to remember that many will spend 30 plus years in retirement so equities will still play a vital role in one's retirement plans.

As costs are a factor in rebalancing as well as taxes, it is best to start rebalancing in tax sheltered accounts. Many 401(k) plans and IRA's are the best places to begin with rebalancing as the taxes are deferred or not even an issue. Also in many of these plans the commissions on trades are less than one may expect in a brokerage account.

Personal Finance: A Grouping of Financial Topics
By Kirk G. Meyer

Are you invested in the equities markets? Are you worried that equity prices may be inflated? Are you concerned that the bull market will make a correction? If you answered yes to these questions, you are not alone by any means. Since the financial crisis, the markets have been on a path that has lead almost straight up. Yes, there have been a few dips but on a whole we have seen some significant gains from the lows of 2008 and 2009. According to Money, the January indicator has been wrong 4 of the last ten years and over the last five years the S&P 500 has about tripled. Now February of this year was good compared to January overall lending that the market may not be done with its run. So what is it you need to focus on to try and keep up with the market?

First we need to keep an eye on revenues and understand them and what they mean. While the average S&P earnings for a company was up 15% revenues for those same companies were only up about 2.5%. With such a disparity between the two it must be asked how these companies achieved such earnings growth on such modest revenue. To understand that, one must look at the underlying numbers and examine the income statements of the companies involved. In most instances companies increased their earnings through cost-cutting and savings on expenses, in general. Also, many companies reduced the outstanding shares through stock buybacks that many companies have been doing in recent years.

By looking at the price to sales ratio you can use that as a historic guide to where the markets might go next.

Currently, the S&P is at 1.6 and since 1993 in the three years following a 1.6 ratio the average return on stocks has been about 1%. Now if the ratio were to hit 2.0 that is a huge sign of trouble ahead for the markets. In 2000, the ratio hit 2.3 and over the next three years equities lost 44% of their value.

If a few stocks result in new highs that is a sign things may be changing. In 2000, it was estimated that about 50 companies are what drove the S&P to record highs then. To track this yourself, all you need to do is to examine the advances and declines on a daily or weekly basis. If the market sees significant moves and there are few companies that advanced, this is the sign that should make you worry.

And finally there is the advice of the greatest investor of the modern age, Warren Buffett. And that is, "Be fearful when others are greedy." If people think the outlook is bearish the markets will lose value the following year. And when the long-term outlook is somewhat high the markets are modest in their returns.

There is no way to predict the markets with any success, but historic data is useful for spotting possible trends. Use common sense and never try to time the markets but rather be watching what they tell you. When you see an anomaly, it may be time to take action.

Personal Finance: A Grouping of Financial Topics
By Kirk G. Meyer

Are you an investor that is worried about the latest bull market? Are you concerned about the valuations of equities? There is no denying the fact equities in recent years have been advancing at an alarming pace. But that does not mean that they will be slowing anytime soon. As any investor knows there is no way to predict the market's next move or how far it will go either up or down. What investors should know is that it is not wise to try to time the markets as many studies have shown. In the last ten years, if someone missed the top days the markets moved and timed those days only, their portfolios returns a fraction of the ones who stayed invested and did not try to time the markets.

As the US markets continue to set record highs, there appears to be no end in sight. But again that does not mean the markets have to continue to set records nor does it mean that there will be a correction. But it may indeed be wise to take some profits now provided there are some losses that can be taken as well to offset the gains. But as more and more firms report marginal earnings or IPO's are held for companies that have little or no earnings these are areas of concern. For older investors placing some of a portfolio in safer assets or cash may be a wise move for those who are nervous. For younger investors, the risk may not seem that serious as they, in theory, will have much more time to regain any losses they may experience.

In recent years, investors have seen returns that are not to be considered the typical returns one can expect. In a conservative 60% equity and 40% bond portfolio, an inflation-adjusted return of 3%-5% can be expected while the long-term average is closer to 5.5%. The reason for this is bond funds are producing returns that barely are keeping up with inflation while equities are giving investors double-digit returns.

As I have discussed in other posts rebalancing is key to one's long term success. In the recent bull market, anyone who has equities in their portfolio is going to be out of balance if they have not rebalanced in the last few years. There is no way a portfolio that includes a large portion of assets in bonds is still in balance in today's markets. Provided it is affordable, and there are no significant tax implications rebalancing is merely selling assets that have appreciated and sell those that have depreciated. If you do not want to rebalance in that manner, it is possible to add new funds to the assets that depreciated until you are back at your desired asset allocation thus avoiding any taxes.

Are you an active investor? Do you only invest in equities and bonds? Then chances are placing a small percentage of your overall portfolio into a commodities exchange traded fund, or mutual fund may have a place in your investment plan. If you consider the modern portfolio theory as many financial advisors do, they have a place in someone's portfolio. By owning assets that are uncorrelated in this manner their prices are independent of each other and move in an independent manner. By having such assets in your portfolio, it will reduce the portfolio's overall risk. As equities rise and fall, the price of commodities does not necessarily follow as they move on their accord.

The most common commodity that people wish to own is gold. Gold serves as a haven for investors who fear inflation as they view it as a hedge. And historically commodities during periods of inflation have performed better than equities and bonds. And depending on the period you are examining the performance of commodities have performed significantly better than most other asset classes.

However, in recent years the most common commodities that people wish to own such as gold and silver have lagged most other markets and asset classes. In fact over the last five years commodities have not performed anywhere near equities peaking in 2010 and falling consistently ever since. In fact, if you consider the two most popular commodities in gold and silver they are nearly half of what they were selling for per ounce just four years ago. In other words, with the equities markets considered expensive in the United States and bonds not producing yields that were found attractive it may be time to consider such commodities as gold and silver.

As an advisor who preaches saving for retirement, I think this is a good time to consider investing in physical gold and silver in IRA's. There are many ways to invest in IRA's and placing actual gold and silver in them is one such method. Now you could buy bullion coins that are not minted by official mints, but if you are going to invest long-term in gold and silver bullion I recommend coins minted by the United States Mint in the form of gold or silver American Eagles. Not only is the content of the coin guaranteed by the United States Government it is the most collected coin currently in the world. Check with particular IRA trust companies that will hold your physical bullion coins as you are not allowed to possess them personally. And right now with these two commodities being as inexpensive as they are it to me is a splendid buying opportunity.

If you do not want to invest in actual bullion, there are some options for you as well. With exchange traded funds and mutual funds, there are opportunities for investors to participate in these commodities as well as others. Now actively, managed funds tend to have higher management fees, and other fees associated with futures contracts as these funds tend to not own the metal. Other funds own the metal and avoid the higher fees. Depending on what you want to own you need to do some research on what the fund does as far as holding the metals or any commodity.

As a disclaimer on commodities, while they can reduce the overall risk of a well-balanced portfolio, they are extremely volatile on their own. In some years, they may double in value and others they may lose all the previous gains. Investing in commodities is not for the faint of heart and in many instances is a long-term strategy.

Do you track your investments? Are you diversified? Are you too diversified? These are some of the questions we must ask ourselves when we are investing in 401(k) accounts, brokerage accounts, or IRA's. While all financial planners will advise their clients to become diversified, they also warn against becoming too diversified. There are risks with both aspects of this, and they are the same, by being under or over diversified you may increase your risks and decrease your returns. How do you keep an eye on things and not get to a position where you are over diversified then? Keep a watchful eye on these areas and keep these issues in mind while you invest your hard earned money.

If you worked at three different jobs, you very well might have three different 401(k) plans in your name. While it is very possible to have a diversified portfolio within a 401(k) account and even within three 401(k) accounts you have to know what is in each account. Say you invested all three in the same fashion you should be diversified to a degree as no one plan is exactly the same as another. However, if you say invested each 401(k) plan in blue chip stocks or larger firms that would make up the S&P 500 you are not really diversified as you own the same stock just in three separate accounts. Also, if you were to chase returns, you would find that one year you may have invested in international equities and the next in small and mid-cap equities in the US. Many people tend to invest this way in their 401(k) plans as they offer ease of investment changes, and the fees are fairly low. But as you can see just because you have three different 401(k) plans depending on where you invested the money in them will determine if you are diversified, not the actual number of accounts.

If you do find yourself in a position where you have said several 401(k) accounts, a few IRA's and say some brokerage accounts you must look at all of them as a whole picture and not as individual accounts. With today's investment choices, it is very easy to buy ten different ETFs or mutual funds. But by doing so are you diversified? In order to determine the answer to that question, you will have to examine what the different funds you own invest in. A fund in the S&P 500 may share similar equities with a fund that is invested in growth, and that fund may have same equities as a fund that invests in technology. As you can see there are three very different investment strategies but when you look at what the fund owns it may paint a picture that looks very similar to the others. When you invest in funds, it is important that you as the investor understand what the fund invests in and what its investment strategy is. In many instances, funds that sound vastly different are, in fact, very similar to others. That is why it is imperative for individuals to do the research into their investment choices and know what each is made of.

If your portfolio is large enough you can diversify by owning individual stocks. In these instances, I would say the average position in each equity should be at least $5,000, and there should be 20 to 30 different ones. That will allow you as an individual investor to invest in enough different companies that can be spread over several asset classes and industries. While people tend to invest in sectors that they understand, it defeats the purpose to invest in 30 different companies if they are all tied to say technology. If you did this you are not diversified at all, and rather you would be concentrated in a single sector or industry. Never a good thing. And also the reason I stated a position of at least $5,000 in each investment within your portfolio is that way it is large enough that any changes will indeed make a difference. Also, if you invest in individual equities, ETFs or mutual funds you need to be able to reposition and do asset re-allocation when things get too far out of balance. This is important as it has been shown that by rebalancing your assets you will actually increase your overall returns.

Do you need to diversify your holdings? If you are not diversified to at least some degree, you are taking on risks that are unnecessary in nature. About 10 to 15 years ago the only real ways to diversify for the smaller investors was to own a variety of individual stocks and bonds. A second more accepted practice of smaller investors was to own an actively managed mutual fund or an indexed fund. Over the last ten years, exchange traded funds (ETF) have become extremely popular with investors of all sizes for several reasons.

In recent years actively managed funds have not necessarily outperformed their benchmark index while charging much higher management fees as compared to an indexed fund or ETF. In a recent report on performance of actively managed funds, three out of five large-cap funds did not outperform their benchmark. And small-cap funds had an even worse performance with three out of four failing to beat their benchmark. And with the popularity of ETF's it is creating a shift in investing with ETF's now having over $2 trillion invested at the end of 2014 as compared to $4 trillion in mutual funds. And every year the gap between the two narrows as more investors are opting for ETF's.

When deciding if you should invest in a mutual fund or an ETF one of the primary considerations is the cost of the fund itself. Actively managed funds that are designed to beat the market on average charge 1.14% in management fees a year. This means that for a $100,000 investment for any profits or losses in the fund $1,140 will go to the fund itself. In a passive fund that tracks an index, the management fees average about .35% or $350 a year, about 70% cheaper than the actively managed fund. Now compare those to an indexed ETF in say the S&P 500 the management fee is .05% or $50 a year. Compound those savings over a 20 or 30 year period, and you are looking at tens of thousands of dollars in lost income. So when diversifying it is always a good idea to consider the investment first to see if it meets you needs and then take a close look at the management fees the investment charges. A cheap investment is not everything if the overall investment itself does not contribute to your diversification and investment plan. Both are critical to examine when deciding what to invest.

Another consideration that must be taken into account is the cost of transaction fees to buy and sell the investment. Many mutual funds can be purchased and sold commission free through the issuing company or a number of brokerage firms. If you buy in a larger block, this is not as big an issue as someone who invests in smaller denominations. When you invest in smaller denominations commissions can take a big portion of your investment as compared to buying larger blocks of a fund. In recent years, however, many issuing companies and some brokerage firms have started offering free transactions on certain ETF's as well. Investigate what the investment fees or commissions will be on a fund prior to purchasing the fund. IN many instances, you can find a brokerage firm that will offer discounts or even free trades on a family of funds. The key here is to keep as much as you can invest instead of paying transaction fees.

Finally, ETF's are more tax advantageous than mutual funds that are actively managed. In most actively managed funds, the turnover rate of assets can be as high as 40%. This means that the fund is actively buying and selling securities throughout the year and by doing this the fund creates a capital gain situation that is passed along to the shareholders in the form of taxes. ETF's and indexed funds have a much lower turnover rate and by that create a lower or in many instances no capital gains situation within the fund itself. Taxes are always present when a fund or ETF makes a distribution of dividends to the fund's owners.

It is now possible for even the smallest investor to diversify in an adequate manner through the use of ETF's. As with any investment perform your due diligence on any investment prior to investing.

Do you need to diversify beyond the S&P 500? Are you looking for dividend paying equities that are outside the S&P 500? Dividend are taxed at a maximum rate of 20% and for high-income earners they can have a tax rate on ordinary income of 39.6%. So regardless of where you fall on the tax tables dividends can give anyone a good return on a tax basis. The lower your earnings are the lower the taxes will be on dividends earned. Also, equities that pay dividends will lower the overall risk and volatility in a portfolio as compared to one that does not pay dividends. And the reason for that is mainly due to the fact companies that pay dividends tend to be more stable and older established firms as compared to younger companies that are re-investing in themselves for growth. In general the average yield on the S&P 500 is 1.8% that is not all that great but it is still better than short term Treasuries.

But the low return of the S&P 500 is due to several factors. Some are simple such as companies are doing stock buybacks instead of returning money to the shareholders through dividends. By buying back shares, a company can increase the average price by reducing the number of shares outstanding. Acquisitions of other companies to enable some growth in more mature firms is another use of capital that can replace the payment of dividends. Or in the case of some firms the taxes they would have to pay to bring the money back into the United States is more expensive than leaving the money overseas. But something that the financial crisis of 2008 and 2009 many firms just wants to save in the case of another downturn.

Large cap equities are still the best way to find dividend paying stocks, but the S&P 500 is not the only place in which to find them. There are many Exchange Traded Funds that specialize in dividend stocks and most instances they focus on large cap companies. While most small and medium sized companies will reinvest in the company's growth, some do, in fact, pay dividends. In smaller specialized companies growth may not be an advantage or even a desired activity so instead of keeping or re-investing they have decided to pay their shareholders a dividend. And, believe it or not, there are more small caps that pay dividends than you might think as seen in WisdomTree's small cap dividend ETF as they own almost 700 individual equities in the ETF. And that one ETF has a yield of about 2.4% that is excellent considering the number of equities it owns. But the Price to Earnings in a small cap company is much higher than on an established large cap equity resulting in an inflated price at the moment.

And if you own both large and small cap dividend ETFs also consider an ETF that owns equities from established and developed foreign countries. For the past decade, these markets have returned a yield that on average have been over a percentage point higher than those companies based in the United States. And currently foreign equities seem to be priced lower than United States equities also resulting in a higher yield. But there could be tax issues in owning an ETF of foreign equities so read any prospectus prior to investing and if you are not sure of the consequences consult a tax professional or financial planner.

Are you one of the many that think that the stock market is set to fall? Are you hesitant to invest in the market? Well, many people believe that the stock market is too high at the present values and is set for a significant correction or even a switch to a bear market. As I have written previously I, do think that many of the individual stocks in the overall market are priced fairly while some are on the expensive side. There are sectors that have not seen as much appreciation as others developing investing opportunities still to be had. But reliable companies, which are paying good dividend yields do deserve a look as well. And if the prices of stocks do decline then this high-quality dividend yields will look even better.

If the markets do go into correction mode, then intelligent investors will not be selling their top dividend stocks but will rather see this as a buying opportunity to acquire more. By taking this strategy, it is a move that can pay off over the long term. Since 1929 half of the S&P 500's return, has come from dividend paying stocks. These dividend paying stocks have historically been a valuable source of income for people in retirement as until recently it has outpaced inflation.

By investing in high-quality dividend paying stocks, this can help offset the possible correction that many predict in the overall markets. While many do not see the markets making a complete collapse as it did in 2008 and 2009 but rather a slowing of growth from around 10% closer to 7.5% for large-cap stocks. If that interests you then consider that the S&P 500 since 1929 has had a return of about 9.5% annually with dividends being reinvested. Now consider that dividends are not reinvested that return slips to around 5.2%. The power of dividends becomes apparent here as compounding is an investor's greatest ally. Here is an example of the power of dividends in the S&P 500 since 1929. If you invested $100 back then it would be worth a little over $7,000 today but if you take dividends into account and had reinvested them you would have over $178,000 from that same $100 investment.

If the power of compounding dividends is not enough on its face value, then consider that most dividend paying companies are sitting on piles of excess cash. Yes, many are reinvesting the money into capital improvements or share repurchase programs but at some point, there is more cash than these projects can handle. Excluding financial institutions companies held over $1.6 trillion is cash reserves just half way through 2014. With that much money sitting, idle shareholders will begin to demand dividend increases. Considering that historically the S&P 500 had a payout of around 50% it currently is less than 40%. At some point, the system will revert to the norm and approach the 50% payout again.

With low-cost exchange traded funds and indexed mutual funds, it is easier now than ever in the history of investing to become truly diversified. And please remember that dividends are also tax-advantaged in the US with most being treated as long-term capital gains and not ordinary income as is the case with interest on bonds.

Regardless of where stocks go, a high-quality dividend paying stock is worth the investment. Do not only chase a high dividend yield but seek out quality dividend paying stocks instead. I guarantee that if you do this you will not be sorry.

What do you do if you are a younger investor looking for the opportunity for some serious growth and can handle more than average risk? In my opinion, I would look to emerging markets now as they have been hit hard be recent economic conditions and the overall environment in emerging countries. I am a firm believer in ETF, and I recommend investing in equities in emerging markets through the use of ETF's to achieve this goal. When you think of emerging markets you tend to think of China, India and Brazil as the leaders in foreign investments. Over the past three years, the iShares S&P India has lost almost 9% annualized. In comparison, if you had invested in an S&P 500 Indexed ETF you would be over 60% for the same three years. As Warren Buffett says the time to buy is when people are in a panic and over the last several years investors have been in a panic in emerging markets. So if you have some extra money you can take some added risk with now may be the opportunity to look at the emerging markets for some possible serious gains.

As I said the main three emerging markets that have been considered in the past are China, India and Brazil but other countries that deserve a look are Mexico, Indonesia, Malaysia, Chile, Peru and too many others to list. The key is to know the strengths and weaknesses of each country you are thinking of investing in, the political climate in each and how stable are its trading partnerships. You need to be aware of the social environment, as well as the political one for each. That is the key to success in investing in emerging markets. So after you find a country or maybe a few that you will want to invest in, and then you will need to find an appropriate tool in which to invest. I recommend ETF's for a few reasons with the top few being they are inexpensive mechanisms that will give you real diversification without having to own a lot of individual stocks. I am not saying do not look at mutual funds because there are several good ones that exist and in many of those you may get an added diversification benefit of the fund owning bonds in the local country.

Regardless of what country you decide you want to invest in remember always to stay informed on the news and conditions in the country you choose to invest in. While things in the US may not be ideal currently you have to admit for the most part things are stable, not desirable, but stable in comparison to emerging countries. If you look at most emerging markets, the majority of them have younger workforces that will be able to help support more growth. Most also have lower debt to GDP as compared to the US as well and in the case of China its debt is 23% of GDP compared to the US at 102%. And a third reason is China, India, Indonesia, and Brazil are four of the top five countries in terms of population accounting for almost half of the world's population.

As you can see from this basic evaluation of emerging markets, many countries outside the US have plenty of room to grow and expand. If you are younger or able to handle some extreme risk in your portfolio, do look at emerging markets and make them part of your investment strategy. But always remember when you invest in an emerging market you must stay informed and keep an eye on the stability of the country in which you have invested. Things can change in a hurry and many instances in ways we do not expect. In my retirement account, I allocate at least 15% and up to 30% in the international choice. If you do not feel comfortable with investing in a single country, there are ETF's and mutual funds for regions of the world as well so look to those as well. Regardless you need to be buying as it seems the rest of the world is in a panic.

Are you looking for an investment that may not be priced as high as US equities? Are you looking for a way to diversify your assets, possibly increase returns and decrease your overall portfolio volatility? Then you may want to consider looking abroad to the emerging markets. In the last year to year and a half the emerging markets have been hit hard and are poised to get back to their historical returns. One reason these markets have been hit is recent unrest in their political systems and a second reason is the Federal Reserve is cutting back on their bond buying, and that is causing currencies to decrease against the US dollar in many emerging markets. Emerging markets have had a history of being volatile, but they have also had some excellent returns as well.

So what is possibly the main reason emerging markets have slowed in recent months? As local political situations do influence that countries markets if you own an ETF that invests in numerous markets one country may not have a significant impact on your investment. But the tapering of the Federal Reserve's buying of US bonds, in theory, wIll cause the interest rates on the bonds to increase and make them more attractive to both domestic and foreign investors. And that may cause countries in the emerging markets to see inflation, a tightening of their monetary policy and slow their economic outlooks. Again by investing in a very diversified ETF that is not concentrated too heavily in one country or a geographic area these adverse factors to reduce the value of the ETF as much as if it is heavily invested in a particular country or geographic area.

While investing in emerging markets is an excellent plan investing in a single emerging market is precarious.

As the Federal Reserve continues to reduce the buying of the bonds, it may continue to have an adverse effect on emerging markets. However, some countries have already taken certain steps to reduce the volatility of their markets as they relate to the actions of the Federal Reserve. In many markets, the countries have raised interest rates and intervened in the currency markets. There are five countries, in particular, that may be very reliant on what the Federal Reserve does and how their own government's react to both foreign and domestic issues. The five top emerging markets in question are Brazil, India, Indonesia, Turkey and South Africa. China has taken steps to restructure its economy, and their individual stocks appear to have future bad news built into today's prices.

Now here is where you as an investor will have to do your homework and due diligence. As China is the largest of the emerging markets, it comprises about 20% of the MCSI Emerging Markets Index. As I told you earlier in the blog, you need to make sure one country does not make or break your investment. With ETF's being as inexpensive as they are it is possible to diversify by owning several ETF's that invest in geographic regions. It is also possible to invest in emerging market bonds through the use of ETF's as well as a way to diversify risk.

Emerging markets may be down right now, but their future is bright. As more and more families that live in these emerging markets enter the middle class, these economies will start to move forward. As a general rule emerging markets offer higher growth opportunities than developed markets.

Are you looking to diversify your holdings? Do you think that the stock market is overpriced or too expensive? In a separate blog, I looked at small cap stock exchange traded funds and mutual funds. Well, there is another asset class that has been hard hit in the recent months that could be attractive if you have the stomach to ride the roller coaster that is the emerging markets. Earlier in 2014 the emerging markets were on a tear and some exchange-traded funds rose as high as 18 percent in the first half of the year, then over the second half lost over 10 percent of those very same gains.

So if the US markets were on an upward move almost all of 2014 what caused the emerging markets to decline? The answer to that is two-fold in my opinion is two-fold, and the first part of the issue is the cost of doing business in emerging markets. In many areas of the world and especially emerging market countries interest rates are much higher than in the United Stated and many developed nations in Europe and Asia. And with the end of the Federal Reserve's bond-buying associated with quantitative easing it stands to reason that at some point in 2015 domestic interest rates will rise. As the US interest rates go up the emerging markets will see an additional increase in their interest rates as well. As the rate continues to rise, the cost of doing business in these countries will continue to rise as well.

The second aspect to why emerging markets have decreased in value in recent months has been tied to the price of the principal commodities. Emerging markets that have the price of the equities related to commodities such as gold, silver, and crude oil have all seen dramatic decreases in the base price of the commodities recently. In the case of gold and silver, the price of these commodities has been on the decline for the last few years and could have bottomed out recently. Oil over the last two months has gone from above $100 a barrel to around $80 a barrel in recent trading. If emerging markets are tied to one of these three commodities, it is plain to see why the underlying stock value of the companies who deal with them have decreased as well. With many emerging markets having their economies tied to the export of these commodities and others like them, it is plain to see that they should and have decreased in value.

But investing in emerging markets allows for investors to diversify their portfolios beyond the traditional asset classes most of us are accustomed. But with this added diversification comes a lot of risks and volatility as well. With emerging markets being so volatile, the rewards of investing in them can be great as well. Since 2000 emerging markets have done better than large US-based equities by about five percentage points annually.

Now investing in emerging markets is very similar to investing in small caps. The most economical ways are through mutual funds and exchange-traded funds. But the two are very different in investing approaches and fees that are passed on to the investors in such funds. Actively managed funds tend to do fairly well when compared with a passive fund because fund managers can avoid certain areas or markets and concentrate on the ones performing better. An exchange traded fund is limited to investing in the index it follows regardless of the performance of the components that make it up. Now an actively managed mutual fund will cost about 1.6% in annual fees while an exchange traded fund will be closer to 0.6%. Like in small cap funds, it is sometimes better to pay the management fee and have a chance at higher returns.

Are all index funds the same? That depends on the index and how they measure it. While most indexed mutual funds and ETFs are weighted based on the company's market capitalization. In this manner, Exxon and Apple would be the largest holdings in an S&P 500 market capitalization weighted fund. In a fund that tracks the same index, it could invest according to a percentage of the stocks that make up the index. In the case of an S&P 500 index, all stocks would be owned by a percentage of 0.2% for each company. That means the largest company is owned in the same proportion as the smallest one.

If by doing this, you would take advantage of the smaller company's moves as they grow as compared to a market capitalization approach in an overall view. This is done mainly by equally weighted funds tend to rebalance their positions on an annual if not quarterly basis. This may increase the taxes to a degree as the fund will now have capital gains that are passed through to the shareholders. But it also will enable the fund to sell equities that have outperformed the others and buy the ones that have not performed as well. This is rebalancing the index and just as in a personal portfolio it will over the long haul increase the returns the fund experiences.

By rebalancing this way a fund that invests in the S&P 500 has gone from a fund that is invested mainly in the five largest companies now is an indexed fund that looks more like a mid-cap fund. If you go by market capitalization, the average market capitalization is around $35 billion and in an equal-weighted fund the average market capitalization is closer to a mid-sized company value of $17 billion. As history has shown us, small and middle capitalized companies have outperformed the larger companies in an indexed fund such as the S&P 500. But these added rewards does come at the cost of slightly higher volatility in the fund as compared to a traditional market capitalized fund. But over the last 25 years this has been a minimal risk that has returned to an extra 1.7% annualized. Now that may not seem like much but compound that over 30 years and you can be looking at some significant money losses.

As you would expect, the equal weighted funds are slightly more expensive than that of passive funds but still cheaper than an actively managed fund. While an actively managed fund can cost you anywhere from 1% to 2% an ETF that tracks an index in an equal weighted manner can cost as little as 0.4%. True a passive index fund can cost as little as 0.1% the extra 1% annualized return over the long term outweighs the costs of the two different funds. If you do not believe me go into Excel and perform a future value function and compare the returns of an investment over at least 20 to 30 years and see what the difference is between a return of 6% and that of one that is 7%. Don't feel like looking I will run the numbers for you. Say you invest $5,500 in a ROTH IRA for the next 35 years if you are in your mid 20's and right out of college starting your first job. In the first case, you invested in a passive indexed fund that returns 6% a year and remember from an earlier blog we are making our IRA contributions in the first part of the year. In this fund, you would have an account worth $691,938 after 35 years. Now you took that extra little bit of risk, paid the extra fees and received the additional 1% that same account would now have $872,245 in it. See the power of compounding is that simple and little extra 1% a year, it means an extra $180,000 in your retirement account.

Shop around and look for an investment that meets your investing needs and then find the one that charges the least in fees. But do not compare a fund simply on fees as you need to understand the equities that make up the fund as well.

For several topics now I have talked about saving for retirement and its importance. In this brief piece, we will look at Generation Y or Millennial when it comes to jobs and savings. Now most people would define a Generation Y individual as someone who is between the ages of 18 and 35. According to an article, I read on TheStreet.com Generation Y individuals are more likely to switch or change jobs that are comparable for one that offers a better retirement benefits package. According to the article, about three-quarters of all Generation Y individuals say that the retirement benefits that they are offered play a significant factor in their decisions on what jobs they will accept.

Generation Y workers do indeed value their 401(k) accounts almost 90% in fact. When compared to other generations, the Generation Y worker is offered a 401(k) about 70% in their jobs while Generation X and the Baby Boomers are closer to 80%. While there are fewer jobs that offer Generation Y workers, a workplace savings plan almost 70% of them are saving either through work or a similar plan somewhere outside of the workplace. And they are listening to older investors and financial professionals who say start early as they are beginning to save at the age of 22. Compare that to Generation X workers who started on average at age 27 and the Baby Boomer, who joined the savings party at a median age of 35.

Not only did the Generation Y worker listen to the start early portion that also heard the message of saving more. On average a Generation Y worker contributes about 8% of their salary as compared to Generation X at 7% and the Baby Boomers at 10%. When one considers the employer's match the Generation Y workers participation rate climbs from about 65% to 80%, and they are saving closer to 10% of their salary.

And unlike many other people who are actively saving for retirement in a variety of accounts the Generation Y individual opts for the professionally managed money. I am not saying that these young productive members of the workforce are engaging with financial planners but they use wealth management site that I will examine in an eBooklet in the near future, risk allocated funds or what many people term as target date funds.

While it is always easy to preach save early and often it is good to see an article that reinforces the fact that a whole generation is taking advantage of this and doing it with some professional guidance of some sort.

Do you need a human financial advisor or will one of the up and coming robo-advisors work for you? This is a question that many people are asking themselves in today's financial world. The only one who can answer this new question is you the investor and one who is planning for their retirement. While robo-advisors are gaining in popularity, they now have about $16 billion in assets under management but that pales in comparison to the trillions that are with traditional advisors. But the robo-advisor tout cheaper fees and the fact that they are more objective because they are based on algorithms and, therefore, take the emotion out of the equation. But they may not be able to offer many of the added values that a registered investment advisor can add.

The fact that robo-advisors use algorithms as compared to emotion is one of their main advantages, or so they claim. A second advantage they claim over human advisors is that they are cheaper when it comes to fees with some as little as .25% as compared to the 1% a human advisor typically charges. Also robo-advisors rely heavily on the use of exchange traded funds to invest and diversify your investments. And depending on the funds used these fees may be minuscule as compared to actively managed funds, provide more diversification, and actually reduce costs as the small fee in most instances includes the price to rebalance the portfolio when the time comes.

In recent months, there has been a sharing of ideas between robo-advisors and actual planners. Many planners are now using the exchange traded funds to invest their client's funds in providing cheap investment options and provide added diversification to the portfolios. Also, planners can use the same algorithms the robo-planners use to provide this service as well as providing the additional services that robo-planners just cannot add. These can be tax advice, estate planning, and charitable gifting. In order to adequately plan for and execute those areas a real planner is needed and not a basic robo-planner.

Robo-advisors have been looking at adding a human component to their services in order to better compete with real planners. An example of this can be seen in Vanguard. They have begun to offer a service called Personal Advisor Services with fees of .3% for those who accounts are over $100,000. This service is in the testing phase and may be a new way for traditional advisors and robo-advisors to join and provide a lower cost to investors with fewer funds than what a traditional advisor might take on. And Vanguard is not alone in looking for this untapped market as Charles Schwab is also investigating the possibility of entering this market as well.

If you wish to manage your portfolio there is nothing to prevent you from going to a site such as www.wealthfront.com and answering their questions to get your portfolio mix and in the case of this site they will even tell you what exchange traded funds they would use to invest for you. Then all you need to do is open a brokerage account with a discount brokerage firm to buy your funds. Here it is up to you to keep track of your positions and rebalance when needed and you will also be responsible for any commissions associated with the account. In the case of this robo-advisor, a small fee of .25% would cover your brokerage fees related to buying and selling of assets.

What is right for you? Well for someone who does not have much in the way of assets or a complicated financial situation a robo-advisor may be the perfect fit for you. If estate planning, taxes, or gifting are part of your financial plans, a real advisor is better suited to your needs.

Do you invest in mutual funds? There is a website that started as a rating agency for mutual funds and now has ratings on much more and is a treasured resource for financial information. Using www.morningstar.com, there are three basic steps that will aid in your use of mutual funds in your investment strategy. If you do not want to use Morningstar Yahoo Finance is also a very useful and best of all free site. Go to one of these sites or a similar site if you desire and type in the ticker symbol for your mutual fund to check out some information that is useful. After you have pulled up the fund by the ticker symbol look for the year to date and one-year returns to see how your fund or potential fund is performing. Please, remember that in mutual funds as in any equity-based asset past performance is in no way an indication of any future returns. Also, as we have been in a strong bull market for the last five years, these funds are tending to have stellar returns over that period.

The next thing that you will want to do as a mutual fund owner is to compare the funds performance with that of other funds with similar asset bases. An example of this would be a fund that invests in larger blue chip companies would be compared to similar funds or even an indexed S&P 500 fund. In this review, you will want to examine what assets make up the fund in order to get a good gauge on what you may or may not wish to compare the fund. If you did own a large cap mutual fund, it would make little sense to compare that to a fund that invests in small caps or even say emerging markets. This is a good place also to see how the fund did in 2008. Compare it to the last five years to see how that particular fund will react in what could have been one of the worst years for stocks.

Now if your mutual fund did poorly in 2008 and over the last five years, you might want to consider seriously selling and getting into a more profitable fund. Depending on what assets make up the fund, there could be a variety of reasons for a poor performance. In the previous paragraph, I mentioned small caps and emerging markets. Both of these sectors were hit hard in 2008, and the case of these two the last five-year bull market to a large degree has been avoided in these sectors. Another area that could cause a fund to have a period of poor performance when they should be experiencing gains is a change in the management of the fund. If you are investing in an actively managed fund, a change in key management positions could have disastrous effects on the fund's performance.

While I would rather see, people buy and invest in exchange traded funds if you are looking for actively managed funds a mutual fund is your best bet. But when buying them do not just look at performance and remember to see what the fund charges in fees. Actively managed funds will have higher fees than an indexed fund or a passively managed fund it will have to have a higher return to make up for the fees it charges.

Personal Finance: A Grouping of Financial Topics
By Kirk G. Meyer

Are you looking for an investment that has attributes of an equity and fixed income? Have you considered a REIT? Right now, Real Estate Investment Trusts offer some of the best opportunities in the last few years. While they are currently down as compared to stocks they historically are, so that is not a primary concern. But buying opportunities exist in markets like this and now may be the time to look into a well-run REIT. Since 2009 many REITs have had returns in the neighborhood of 200%. And if you go back to the early 1970's REITs have averaged a 13% return over the last 40 years. So a few bad months or even a bad year will not negate the positives that well managed REITs offer.

Why are REITs still considered a good investment if they are not keeping up with the broader stock market? As I hinted at earlier REITs have a historical cyclical cycle with equities. When equities are up REITs are down, and the reverse is also true. But right now REITs are attractive and undervalued because the underlying basics of the REIT are sound. REITs are not cutting their dividends, buildings are not setting empty, rents are stable at the moment and there have been very few credit downgrades in REITs. Technically REITs are sitting pretty as they tend to use short-term rates as a basis, issues long term stable bonds and mortgages. The real estate market may not be what is was in 2006 but it has bounced back considerably since the meltdown of 2007-2009.

In recent times, REITs did become pricey or maybe even overpriced as returns were slashed. In some instances,

REITs returns were equal to that of the S&P 500 or a ten year Treasury. And tax wise income from a REIT is not treated the same as a dividend from an equity investment. So you need to consider that as well when you are investing in REITs. And historically most REITs adjust their dividends in the first quarter of the calendar year so if you find a good REIT late this year keep an eye on it and consider buying it prior to the announcement of a dividend increase as people have a history of chasing returns and artificially driving up prices at least on a short-term basis.

As REITs are a pool of actual real estate, they, in theory, will appreciate in value because, as a rule, real estate appreciates in value over time. This will be the underlying factor in the price of a REIT going up or down depending on what the values of the property in the REIT do. The dividend is a payment of the profits of these properties after expenses. REITs have to pay out at least 90% of their profits as dividends, or they will lose their status as REITs. So well managed REITs that control their expenses and invest in stable properties should see an increase in their underlying value, and this should also allow for modest raises in their rents to pass along as dividends. Look for well-managed REITs that are trading at a discount or ones that have Net Asset Values under 100% or near that level. Otherwise you will be paying too much for the REIT, and you may take a loss but remember REITs are not trades they are long term investments.

Do you want to invest in the stock market but fear you have missed all the right opportunities? There are two choices that I currently see that make sense to a degree. I will take a look at one of these two options in this post and will consider the other for a future post. The asset class that we will examine at a later date are the emerging markets. This market has been relatively flat for the last few years and may be poised to remain that way as interest rates begin to rise as economic conditions improve. Of course raising rate will have an effect of the second as well, but we will come to that a little later, the second asset class is small capitalization stocks in the US. With the S&P 500 and DOW reaching new highs in recent months, small caps are an investing opportunity. It is no wonder people are hesitant to buy right now as that would fall into the buying high that is not the best way to make money in the markets.

As I just alluded to you, do not want to be in the buying high category of investing, so let's look at why small caps are attractive right now. Small caps, thus far, in 2014 have been relatively flat and have not participated in the massive stock runs that large cap and blue chip companies have experienced. And the best part of this asset class is that historically since 1926 small cap companies have beaten the larger capitalized companies. While, just like large cap stocks, small caps have experienced bull and bear periods and have averaged two percent points more than large cap stocks over the long run. While I do not recommend a buy and hold strategy, the exception could be a good small cap mutual fund or exchange traded fund.

So why do small caps on average have a higher return than large caps? The simple reason is there is more risk in buying and owning a small cap so therefore they should have a higher return. How much riskier as small caps than their larger counterpart? Over the last ten years the index that tracks small cap stocks, the Russell 2000, has been over 30% more volatile than the S&P 500. But as I told you earlier that these stocks are the exception to not buying and holding. Being volatile is not a primary concern over the short term as these are indeed long term investments. Do not let the ups and downs bother you and remember that you are a long term investor when it comes to small cap stocks.

While there is plenty of information and analysis to follow if you are going to own a large cap, the reverse is the case for small caps. Most small caps have very few analysts that follow them, and thus that creates a lack of exposure on these diamonds in the rough. In a perfect world, a stocks price is based on all known data that is to create a fair and equitable price for that stock. Well, small-cap stocks do not have that exposure and thereby lack the amount of public knowledge that large cap followers enjoy. But any piece of news that comes out about a small cap could cause significant shifts in prices that could go either up or down depending on the news. With a small cap, if a large investor or any institution buys or sells in a large quantity it is going to have a significant impact on the price of the stock. But then again, remember with small caps we are ignoring the volatility and in these picks for the long haul.

Along with the volatility that small caps experience, interest rates have a bigger impact on these companies than they do on large caps. Smaller companies have a harder time in accessing money to fund expansion and growth when rates are higher because it will cost them more to fund this expansion.

But do not over think the current likes and dislikes of the markets or to time them. Know that under certain circumstances, different sectors react differently which can create buying opportunities even when we have markets like we do know that are setting all time highs. Now to define a small cap stock. A small cap stock is one whose market capitalization is under $5 billion. And the lower the capitalization, the more profits you can expect to make provided the company is fundamentally sound. The reason for this is there is more room for movement towards the upside price wise and more room for the company to grow. Of course, this greater potential for rewards does not come without greater risks so keep that in mind when you purchase a small cap.

But I do not recommend buying individual small cap stocks unless you have the time to do your research and follow the company as an analyst would as any small negative comment could destroy any potential gains. So I advise buying small caps in either a mutual fund or an exchange traded fund. The key here is to find a fund that invests in small caps in the market capitalization that you are seeking. Keep an eye on expense ratios to keep more of the gains in your investment and out of the hands of the fund managers. But unlike large cap funds, be prepared to pay for the expertise of a fund manager and in these instances I do think that provided the fund does better than the averages, a good fund manager is worth the fees they charge. Otherwise, look at buying an exchange traded fund with similar characteristics of a mutual fund you like at a lower cost.

Personal Finance: A Grouping of Financial Topics
By Kirk G. Meyer

Are you saving for retirement? Do you invest all your money in retirement accounts such as a 401(k) or IRA? There is also a place in your savings for a taxable brokerage account provided you put the correct assets in the taxable accounts. Everyone should contribute to a company-sponsored 401(k) if the company provides a matching program. If yours has a matching program, which is free money and you should never shy away from an instant return. Regardless of anything else always contribute up to the company match even if your plan does not have the best investment options. After you contribute up to the match, I recommend contributing up to the limit in a ROTH IRA if you qualify for one. I may be taking an adverse outlook on things, but I do not see the tax rates going down in the future. Depending on the asset it makes sense to keep taxable bonds, bond funds, equities that pay high dividends and REIT's as in many instances their dividends are taxed as ordinary income.

Other advantages of a taxable brokerage account are there is no penalty if you were to need the money before you retired or age 59 ½. In the event, you withdrew the money from a retirement account prior to the age of 59 ½ you would not only pay taxes on the money but you will get hit with a 10% early withdrawal penalty. Another consideration is 401(k) plans, and traditional IRA will have mandatory withdrawals at age 70 ½ regardless of if you need the money or not. And if you did not take the necessary minimum withdrawal you are looking at a 50% penalty on what you should have withdrawn.

So what do you want to keep in a taxable account? Assets that have a tax benefit unlike those mentioned above. Municipal bonds are not taxed at the federal level and if you buy a bond or a bond fund that is comprised of bonds issued in your state of residence they are state income tax-free as well. However, the AMT tax may still apply even on nontaxable municipal bonds so when in doubt seek the advice of a financial planner or tax expert.

Individual stocks that you intend to own for over a year are an excellent asset to a taxable account. Provided you own the stock for at least twelve full months the gains are treated as long-term capital gains and taxed at 15% if your income is high and cold be zero for lower income households. In most cases, capital gains will be a lower tax rate than your ordinary income. This approach can also be used for tax efficient ETF's and mutual funds as well as the capital gains rule applies to them as well with the big exception that you will pay taxes regardless of if you reinvest the funds or take the distribution in cash. It is only a benefit to own ETF's and mutual funds if they limit dividends and capital gains to a minimum.

While everyone needs to save for retirement, a taxable account does have a place in anyone's plan. Depending on the asset will determine where it should be placed. However, do not let taxes alone dictate your investments as all retirement and savings are considered a real thing. But if possible limit the amount that you will have to pay taxes.

If you are an investor, there are some mistakes that are common to the majority of us. Investing as in life, there are no guarantees of anything other than uncertainty. If you were like most of us and were invested in 2008 and 2009 you experienced one of the worst periods ever for investing, regardless of what you invested in during that period. And now we are experiencing all-time highs in the very same markets that five years ago were hard hit and cut in almost half from early 2008. Here are some common mistakes looked at and how to possibly avoid making them in the first place.

Do not freak out when the market does fall. And yes it will drop as it always has no matter when or where you invested. There are bull and bear markets throughout history provided you open your eyes and look. And how you react when the markets fall will have a direct impact on your returns. Many investors did not freak out in the 2008 and 2009 market free for all until the market was at or near the bottom then they got out of the markets. This is the absolute worst time to get out of the markets as your losses are going to be at their highest. If you had sold in the spring of 2008 because the markets were falling to a degree, at that time you would have saved yourself some serious pain. But many people did not see the DOW losing almost half its value in less than a year. Remember hindsight is always 20/20 so do not beat yourself up. And in the five years since the bottom in early 2009 the DOW has gained back all its losses and then some to close recently at all-time highs some 10,000 points from where we were at the beginning of 2009. Now I am not saying to try and time the markets because that is a losing proposition as well. Be patient and pay attention to what the market is doing. Have an investing plan and stick to it no matter what. By being patient and having a well thought out plan, you can save yourself a lot of possible pain in your investments.

While it is enough not to get caught freaking out when the markets fall, the same goes when the markets are going in the opposite direction. Intelligent investors who practice patience will not allow themselves to get caught up in market upticks as well. Remember I mentioned the investing plan earlier? That plan will keep you disciplined in both down as well as up markets telling you when to buy and sell. While the goal is to buy low and sell high far too often, it happens the opposite way. Remember I said many people sold and got out of the markets in late 2008 or early 2009 those same individuals got back into the markets after they had already seen severe movements up. Hence, they sold cheap and were buying high. Develop an investing plan that will serve you well both in bull and bear markets then have the discipline to stick to your plan.

Are you an investor or a trader? That is a question you must ask yourself when buying or selling and especially when you are developing your investing plan. I do not advocate for anyone to be a trader as the odds are against you that you will succeed on a long-term basis. If you want to invest in a reckless manner chances are you would not be reading this blog on personal finance. If you wish to have the fast success stories of instant riches let me include you in on the secret, those investments are few and far between. Yes, they happen but more often people lose money when they actively trade instead of developing a long-term investment strategy. Now I also do not advocate a buy and hold mentality by any means. Good companies can go wrong for a number of reasons thereby making their stocks go from good to bad. Once you buy stock in a good company, you need to make sure you are doing your homework and making sure that the company and its stock stay on the positive side of things. If you buy and forget then, you are also inviting disaster into your returns.

Now I know many financial professionals do not like or even acknowledge Jim Cramer's Mad Money, but he addresses the next issue weekly on his show. And that are you diversified or not? It is never good to have all of your investments in one or two stocks or sectors. Ideally you should be invested in at least five sectors or businesses that are not inter-related or connected. By doing this, you spread your risks out over a much broader array of investing choices. Now this really did not save many people in 2008 and 2009 but if you were diversified in blue chip companies then chances are you lost less than others and have made it all back and then some in the last five years. By spreading the risk over many sectors in the stock market or better yet over many different asset classes as well, you can achieve stock market-like returns with far less risk.

Now that you are properly diversified in your investments it is time also to look at the art of rebalancing. If you have read many of my blogs, you are aware I am a believer that is rebalancing it essential to overall portfolio health. If you have done what you should have by developing an investing plan, this will be a portion of that very plan. If you invest in two asset classes, say stocks and bonds. Stocks are having a good year and are up big while bonds have not had as good a year and were flat. Most people would be happy sticking with what they had originally purchased but now the problem is you identified percentages that should be invested in each asset class. With the stock having gone up so much, and bonds remaining flat, your portfolio is out of balance. So now you need to rebalance by selling the asset that has appreciated and buy more of the asset that has declined or remained flat. By doing this, you will lock in gains and have a portfolio that is matched to your investing plan. As you get closer to retirement or are experiencing some other life event, you may need to examine your investing plan and adjust your percentages for different asset classes.

While there is no one list of all questions to ask or mistakes that have been made this blog does provide you a good starting point and can serve as a reference.

Education

Do you have children who are getting ready for college? Have you considered there are more things that need to be addressed besides writing a check for tuition? If you have been planning for your child attending college, hopefully, you were prepared and contributed to a 529 plan or made arrangements with some other means to pay for the cost of college. If you are a young couple or parent, it is never too early to start saving for the cost of college. Consider this, on average inflation over the past ten years has been about 3% while the cost of college has outpaced that and education costs have an inflation rate of closer to 5%. The key to paying for college is to use tax-advantaged accounts, often save and start early and let compound interest work in your favor. But this blog is not about how to pay for college but rather how a child attending college affects your insurance policies.

Let's first look at health insurance. Most systems allow for adult children to remain on the parent's policy until age 26. Now the problem is many kids do not stay around where the policy has an in-network option for healthcare. If your child goes to college very far away, the only choice for their healthcare may be out-of-network providers or care for emergencies. Despite having coverage, your child may not be adequately cover in the event they get sick. To supplement a parent's coverage, it may be wise to look at the college itself for a student policy. While many of these policies limit coverage to a campus clinic or a nearby hospital that is affiliated with the college, they are relatively inexpensive and can provide a great peace of mind to both your child and yourself. A final option is to go to the healthcare exchange and purchase a policy outright through the exchange. While these policies may not be eligible for the subsidy because your child is most likely still a dependent the costs are really affordable and may provide a better range of coverage than a parent's policy or a policy purchased by the college. Weigh the options and shop around for the best policy for the money. No one knows what is in someone's future health wise, but it is better to be prepared.

Now when your child goes off to college, they take many of their possessions with them on this maiden voyage into adulthood. If you child lives in the school's housing your homeowner's policy will cover around 10% of the value of the items, they bring. The reason this is limited is because they are not in your home anymore and are at the college. The liability limits will be the same as they are at your residence. Of course, you may purchase additional riders to cover high ticket items that your child may have brought to college with them such as laptops. These extra riders are inexpensive and can cost anywhere between $50 and $100 a year depending on the amount of coverage that is required. If your child rents and apartment or house they will need renters insurance to cover their possessions and it is wise also to make sure that they have at least $500,000 in liability insurance. A basic policy that includes about $15,000 in possessions and $500,000 in liability coverage can be between $125 and $150 a year.

As far as car insurance it will depend on if your child takes a car to college with them or not. If you keep a child on your policy and move over 100 miles from home and do not take care with them, your premiums can decrease as much as 40%. And the best part is when they are home or drive a car at college they are still insured on your policy. And of your child does take a car to college you may even see an increase in your premiums depending on where you live and where the college is located. Encourage your child to get good grades and maintain a B average and your premiums may decrease between 5% and 15%. It may even be cheaper to have your child on their policy and take them off of yours completely. As with health insurance understand your policy and shop around for the best policy under the best conditions.

Are you the parent of someone who will be going to college? Are you a current college student? Are you a grandparent of future college students? How can you prepare for college in a tax advantageous way you ask? Well, look at state-run 529 college savings plans for some of the most flexible and efficient ways to pay for college. It is estimated that there are some $191 billion invested in 529 savings plans, and if you have funds in one you need a strategy to draw the funds down when it comes time to pay for college. But 529 plans may not be the answer to everyone and every situation.

You need an investment strategy for your 529 plan the same you would for your personal investments. Many have the plan rebalance from equities into bonds as your child gets older and approaches their college years. But in the event you do not adhere to that approach you need to get much more conservative with the plan around your child's freshman year as any downturn in the markets will most likely not have the time to recoup your value in such a short period. In your child's high school years, your 629 portfolio needs to be composed of a few equities, about half in fixed income and a medium percentage of short-term assets.

When it is time to withdrawal funds from the plan, it is important to take out an amount that covers the allowable costs. As these are growing tax-deferred, you will have penalty and tax consequences if you take out more than you need. But in the event you do a withdrawal more than you need you do have some options that will allow you to avoid taxes and penalties.

They are open a new 529 plan with the excess funds, prepay the following year's tuition or just pay the taxes on the excess you took out. Another thing that needs to be considered is who will the 529 check be made payable to when the withdrawal is done. In most instances, a check made out to the child is acceptable and will be considered to have gone to college expenses. A check made out to the parents will be looked at a little more carefully. And in the event the check is made out to the institution it may affect your child's financial aid.

If you are comfortable with your financial situation, there may be more efficient ways for you to pay for your child or grandchild's education. While a 529 plan will grow tax-free parents and grandparents can contribute to the plans with no problems but if your child does not go to college you have few options. One is to name a different child as the beneficiary of the plan. Another is to withdrawal the money and pay the taxes on the gains and use it for whatever you want. But grandparents may give up to five years of gifts at one time to 529 plans but will then not be able to make a contribution in that child's name for the next five years.

Some tax advantageous ways to transfer money to your children or grandchildren is to give them up to $14,000 a year in real investments in their name in an irrevocable trust that may have the stipulation that it is to be used for college or until they reach a certain age. That way you have gifted the money to them and avoid the gift tax because it is under the annual exclusion. But the best way to avoid taxes, trusts and gifts is to keep the money simply yourself and invest it in a manner that is acceptable to you. Then when the time comes pay your child or grandchild's tuition straight to the institution and there are no limits on what can be paid in that manner. For grandparents who want to reduce their taxable estate, this is an ideal way to reduce your estate and help out your grandchildren at the same time.

With proper planning, there are several ways to save for college. If you can think ahead and plan appropriately, you may be able to pay for college without the need for student loans. College, like retirement, takes planning ahead and sticking to an investment plan regardless if you use 529 plans or invest in a brokerage account and pay the tuition yourself. Develop a plan and invest for the future.

What are you doing to save for your children's college expenses? Just as with your retirement the sooner you begin saving, the better off you will be when it comes time to write that check for college tuition. And in today's environment where the cost of education is vastly outpacing inflation it is even more important to start early and use the best possible savings method. Based on historic costs and the rate that the cost of higher education has advanced the cost of a four-year education at a public school could be as high as about $225,000 for a child born today and the cost of a private education will most likely be even higher.

But there is an easy way for you to save for a child's education, and that is through a state-sponsored 529 plan. While there are other types of savings plans, I feel the 529 plans are the best for several reasons. A few of these reasons are in many states there are tax advantages for contributing to the state's 529 plan, there are no income limitations on contributions to the 529 plans, beneficiaries can be changed if the one named does not need or go to college, and contributions are not limited to parents as friends and grandparents can make contributions. In the case of grandparents they can give up to five times the annual gift limits at one time for grandchildren with no tax consequences but would then be barred from gifting to that child again for the full five years unless they are willing to pay the gift tax or use some of their lifetime gift exemption.

Also, it is worth noting that it is doubtful that you would be required to save the full amount for college as with many students there are alternative ways to help fund the expense. Scholarships, work study, grants, and loans are some of the ways to bridge the gaps between what you do have saved and what the actual costs are. Some financial planners think that parents should only try to save between a third and half of the expenses instead of the full amount. And under no circumstance should you be saving for a child's college at the expense of your retirement. Pay yourself first and fund your retirement accounts before you save for a child's education. The reason I say this is because you are the only one you can count on for your retirement where your child can work or take out loans to help pay for college as they will have longer to pay off the debt. With some proper planning and work by all parties involved college can be paid for with little dire consequences on the family.

But not all state 529 plans are created equally. Some states have plans with lower fees than others. Some states offer a wider range of investing options than others. Some states will only offer tax breaks if you invest in that state's plan while other states will give the tax breaks regardless of where the 529 plan is located. Currently Washington state and Wyoming are the only two states that do not have 529 plans so if you live in one of those two states you will be forced to invest in another state's plan. Also, you are only allowed to change a plans asset allocation once every twelve months so look at the plans to see which one will allow you to have the best freedom as it comes to reallocating your portfolio. Most plans will be more aggressive when your child is younger and become more conservative as they approach college. Also, there are fees to consider when selecting a plan where state-run plans are cheaper than plans operated on behalf of the state. And the plan administrator can affect the fees as well as Vanguard funds are generally the cheapest as, in general, investing.

Do an Internet search to help you find the state plan that best works for you and your needs. Remember that not all states offer the same tax benefits so check with your state prior to going out of state for plans. There are numerous things to consider when selecting a state's plan, and I have touched on a few of them and given you some food for thought. If you have any questions, feel free to contact me, and I will do my best to help you figure out the best solution for your situation.

Are you or your children getting ready to go start your college career? If so you probably have a pretty good idea that this endeavor will not be a cheap one and in many instances could be a very expensive one indeed. But as with any expense the costs of college can be mitigated and made somewhat more bearable. The key to being able to afford college is to prepare adequately for it in the first place and if you are a parent that means start saving early and often as your child approaches their college years. For adults, it may mean saving before or while you are in college. And do not forget that both you and your children can apply for scholarships and grants to help defray the cost of college as well. With the class starting in the next few weeks, let's take a look at some ways to reduce your college expenses and make this part of your life more reasonable.

One of the largest expenses outside of the tuition is one's room and board while attending a college that is not close to your home or residence. Last year the average cost of room and board at a four-year college was about $10,000 a year. But there are alternatives to staying on campus that may or may not be more reasonable. One is to not reside in the newest dorm or one that is in the best location as these tend to be more expensive. Also, if you can avoid getting a private room as that will also increase the cost. If possible see about becoming a resident advisor for the college and your room expenses may be paid to you by the college. But if you want to live off-campus consider the roommate route to reducing expenses such as utilities and rent. Also, when living off-campus, you need to consider the length of the lease you will be required to sign and any extra expenses that you will incur such as transportation commuting costs.

Another component that goes hand in hand with room is the board or meal plan that is available to you. These can vary as widely as the room prices depending on the level of service you wish to enjoy. One way to reduce this expense is to opt for a reduced meal plan instead of higher priced options. As these plans are done by the meal and if you can reduce the number of meals you will eat you will create additional savings. The difference can be substantial so look into ways to reduce your meal plan and in return you will be gaining valuable life skills in the way of budgeting and cost comparisons.

Textbooks are another large expense and can be even larger depending on the classes you will be taking. Finance books, as I know from experience, are very expensive as compared to an English course book on average. Specialized courses tend to have the more expensive books but as they are required it is not an option or something you can simply do without. On average books and supplies can run over $1,000 a year at a four-year college. First try to buy a used textbook over the new editions for instant savings at the college bookstore. For additional savings, I always look at Amazon.com and Half.com to see if the book is offered there at a cheaper price. In many instances, you can find it cheaper elsewhere but this will take a little extra effort on your part. Also, book rentals are becoming more and more popular as well further reducing the cost of books. If you do buy, your books take good care of them, and you should be able to resell them to the college's bookstore or on-line.

With some effort and planning, there are numerous ways to reduce expenses associated with college. Get creative and do not be afraid to think outside the box when it comes to ways to pay for something. Get in the habit of budgeting now and create a life-long commitment to doing this. Budgeting is the key to anyone's financial success and well-being. The main thing to remember is to live within your means and plan for things correctly and in advance.

Are you a parent or a grandparent that will help a family member pay for education beyond high school? While there are many choices for people in this situation, one of the best education planning tools for families is state-sponsored 529 plans. These plans offer tax-deferred growth on your investment and are tax-free if used for qualified educational expenses. Also, many states will offer tax breaks or incentives for people who invest in their state's 529 plan. The following are some common misconceptions about 529 plans, in general.

The first and one of the most common mistakes is that you are limited to your state's 529 plan. While many states make it very attractive to invest in their plans by offering tax breaks on your income taxes or lower fees on the investments, they may not be the best options, in the long run. Many states have very different plan options that have better returns, lower fees, or more attractive options to invest in that are more in line with your investment strategy. And yes, you need an investment strategy even for your 529 plan as they do play a role in your overall financial state. Shop around from state to state to find a plan that best fits your needs, but you also need to consider your states plan with tax incentives factored in.

Another area that causes confusion is the limits that one can contribute to a 529 plan. Many people think that they are the same as IRA contributions. While gift taxes may come into play in this area, it is not a primary issue. For individuals, they can contribute up to $14,000 with imposing a gift tax. Married couples can do what is called a split gift and double the contribution up to $28,000 in a calendar year. And when it comes to 529 plans and contributions you are allowed to contribute up to five years at once to a 529 plan without triggering the gift tax. That means an individual can contribute $70,000, and a couple can contribute $140,000 for a single year but then make no more gifts to that family member for a full five years. Each state does set contribution levels so check with the state you plan to invest with to see their annual contribution limits.

Many people also think that they are not allowed to make contributions to a 529 plan due to their incomes. While this is true for a Coverdell Education Savings Account, 529 plans have no such income limitations. When it comes to a 529 plan, there are no income limitations at all, and anyone can open or contribute to a family member's plan.

529 plans also do not have to be held in your child's name. Although it is best to name a beneficiary and a parent or trustee listed as the owner. When it comes to these educational plans, the donor and not the beneficiary is the one in control. That means that a child who has a 529 plan established for them does not get control of the funds once they turn the age of majority and would possibly want to spend the money on something other than education expenses.

Another major misconception about 529 plans is that the money will be lost if the child does not go to college, or they get scholarships to defer the planned cost. This is not the case as beneficiaries can be changed to another sibling, family member, or even the donor. And in the event that there is no one who can benefit from the 529 plan the donor can take the funds and earnings back provided they pay the taxes on the earnings and a 10% penalty. But that is a worst case scenario. Also, there is no age limitation on who can be the beneficiary of a 529 plans which is unlike a Coverdell account.

And these plans can be used for education expenses other than those that are at a four-year university. Many qualified educational expenses are allowed at trade schools or professional programs. When in doubt on if an expense is allowed check with your plan to get a definitive answer.

As far as financial aid goes these accounts may hurt your child's chances to a degree, but the benefits far outweigh the negative effects of having a 529 plans. If your child does get a large financial aid package remember you can always change the beneficiary on the account to another family member without any penalty.

These are some of the more common questions and misconceptions about 529 plans.

Do you have children or grandchildren that will be going to college? Are you saving for your college expenses? What used to work for older generations may not work as well today. If you are around 40 years, old chances are your parents saved for your college in a savings account or maybe a brokerage account that was taxable to either you or your parents. If you were lucky maybe you had a wealthy set of grandparents who paid for your college expenses. But in today's world we have 529 savings plans that are offered by just about every state. These are imperative savings tools for college are inflation has averaged about 3% a year over the last 30 years and the last decade college expenses have experienced inflation of anywhere between 5% and 10% a year. An old fashion savings account no longer will make due, and 529 plans are the answer.

Before we examine the basics of the 529 plan, let's get rid of some common misconceptions many people have about college and their children. First save like your child will not be receiving a full scholarship as that is very unlikely to happen. It is better to save like there will be no scholarships for your child and experience a windfall rather than to have saved too little when it comes time to pay for the college expense. Also, it is a wise move also to save as if you will not be able to cover the entire cost of the education with financial aid. The reason for this may be twofold, one parents have no business financing a child's education as they are closing in on retirement and second many do not want to burden their children with large amounts of debt in today's strengthening economy. And finally it is imperative that before you save for college expenses that you have a written and well thought out plan for your college investing. Sallie Mae released a study that concluded that those who had a savings plans saved on average 80% more than those who saved without a plan. That is a difference that cannot be ignored in my opinion.

So what is a 529 plans? Simply put it is a state sponsored savings plan that offers investment choices similar to that of a 401(k) plan. A 529 plan allows you to make contributions for a child that will grow tax deferred over the child's life until they reach college age and start to spend the funds on qualified college-related expenses. And if the expenses are indeed qualified all the proceeds paid will be federally tax-exempt, and state tax exempted as well. In many states, they offer tax deductions if contributions are made in that state's 529 plan. In order to ensure maximum benefits consult a tax advisor or financial planner. If you or someone, you know wished to make a gift contribution to a child they may contribute up to $14,000 without counting towards someone's gift tax. Grandparents can even contribute up to five years' worth of gifts at one time provided they do not make any additional contributions for a full five years. And with split gifting that amount can be doubled to $28,000 a year.

The main differences between 529 plans can be in investment choices offered from state to state and how the investment is structured. As not all state's plans are the same, it is wise to compare them for historical returns, structure, and fees associated with the investment choices offered. Fees can be a large portion of an investment's return so does not assume all things are equal as chances are they are not. Again consult a professional to ensure you can expect the best returns and tax incentives available. Also, with your investing plan it is wise to decide your risk tolerance level as well. Based on your risk tolerance, your investments will be based on age or more on investments. A portfolio based on age will adjust as the child gets closer to college age and by that more conservative in nature. But do not assume all of the age-based portfolios are comparable as some will rebalance and change investments more than others. Research is essential here as in with fees so make sure you understand the entire investment before you put your money into something.

Saving for college is important indeed but not something to be done without thinking and some research. Just as with your retirement accounts you need to understand what it is you are investing in, the fees associated with the investment, and the risks involved. And you should always have a written plan no matter what type of investing you are doing to ensure you can maximize your return while monitoring your risks. For more information feel free to contact me.

Do you have a child that is about to start a college? Are you wondering how you will help pay or pay for college? The best way to pay for college is to start saving early in a tax-deferred account such as an approved 529 plan. That combined with an approach of selecting a school that is academically a fit for your student and is also a fit financially is the key to success. Look at all options early and figure what amount and kind of aid the institution provides. All schools require the FASFA to determine aid eligibility. Do not wait until your child's senior year to fill this out and find out what amount of aid will be needed. Go to the FAFSA website and use the on-line calculator to estimate your child's need.

Now the FAFSA will tell how much assistance the family is expected to contribute to income being the primary factor. Things such as savings, retirement accounts, and your home's equity do not factor into the equation. Now after the FAFSA is filed out it will determine if your child is eligible for federal financial aid. This could be a guaranteed job through the work-study program, grants, or loans. Institutions use it to determine what grants or scholarships they will offer a student.

The key to selecting a school is the first look at in-state universities, flagship universities in other states, and both large and small private universities. Each is unique and will offer a variety of aid. By looking at all these different universities, your child will surely find one that is a fit for them and their academics. Not all schools have the same programs or degrees especially some of the smaller public and private universities. Also, be watchful for schools that may be placing new importance on a given academic area and by that will be offering extra incentives for students to attend.

Okay, now your future student has found several universities that are an academic fit. The next step is to select universities that will help fund as much of the college expenses as possible. Many will provide full scholarships to students that excelled in high school and tested well on the ACT or SAT. Even if your child was not the best in high school in many instances above average will provide just as useful and beneficial. Many schools are relatively liberal in their merit scholarships and grants. Also, some schools excel in providing aid that will supplant the student and family's contributions and provide a need-based scholarship or grant to cover the unmet need of the student. Look for institutions that provide as close to 100% of the need of its students by researching the schools website. Try to apply to universities where you will be in the top 25% of incoming freshman. That will give your future college student the best opportunity to fund their college experience entirely.

Do your research. Save early for college. And do not limit your child to one school or another. Look at all options available even including Ivy League schools as they have some of the largest endowments that can fund more and more of students need. Apply for scholarships on a national level and never forget scholarships that are local. While a $500 scholarship might not seem like much, it could help cover the cost of books or if combined with other scholarships pay for college in its entirety. The one thing to remember do not wait until your child's senior year to examine schools starts as early as possible.

Are you trying to pay for your kid's college? Not sure where the funds to pay for college will come from? Are their grandparents will help pay for college? Depending on how old your children are can determine the best avenue for obtaining help from grandparents. There are several option to choose from with each having different effects on the student, you the parents and the grandparents.

If there is a shortfall in your child's education expenses after you fill out the Financial Student Aid (FAFSA), there is no need to consider having the grandparents help in saving. Why will they not help save? It is easy your child is about to start a college as the FAFSA is filled out their senior year in high school. In this case, it is best for the grandparents to make a cash gift to the parents for the child's education. In 2014 the amount that can be gifted to you the parents is $14,000 for a single gift or $28,000 for a split gift where both grandparents can each give $14,000 to having to pay a gift tax. If the money is gifted to the parents, it will have little effect on the FAFSA as compared to giving the gift to the children.

There is a reason the grandparents should not pay the school directly in the event they are not able to pay the full amount. And that is any payments made on behalf of the student will reduce the child's financial aid based on the FAFSA. But if the grandparents can afford to pay the entire tuition bill then the answer is much different. In this case, the grandparents do need to pay the institution directly as it will not be considered a gift and could help reduce their taxable estate. And since the payment is not considered a gift there is no limitation as to how much they can pay provided it is paid directly to the institution.

The third option for grandparents that are stepping in late to the college process is to make a bona fide loan to the parents. This must be a written loan, charges interest, and has a payment schedule. If the loan is made to the parents, it does not have to be reported on the FAFSA. After the child's college is over the grandparents can forgive up to the maximum allowed for gift taxes are applied, $14,000 for a single grandparent and $28,000 for a split gift per year until the loan is forgiven. But that arrangement cannot be made in any manner prior to the loan or during the life of the loan or it could be considered a gift and gift taxes would apply.

If the grandparents are involved when the child is younger and instead of paying for immediate college expenses we are in the savings mode there are some options. If the savings plan is in an approved 529 plan, then the grandparents can make gifts to the child's or parent's 529 plan. The main difference is how the asset is accounted for on the FAFSA. If your child is young and the plan is just starting out the grandparents can make up to five years of gifts at once and then not make any to that child or you until the five years is up. That means a grandparent can make a single gift of $70,000 or $140,000 for a split gift to the child or you the parent.

While not all grandparents are in a position to help pay for college, these are some examples of how they can of they are able. As always the best way to pay for college is starting a savings plan early on in the child's life. But under no circumstance should a parent risk their retirement in favor of paying for their child's education. Your kids have an entire working career to repay loans whereas you only have yourself to rely on for your retirement.

401(k) and IRA Accounts

Are you around a decade from retirement? Do you think you have saved enough for your retirement? These are some serious questions that many baby boomers, as well as younger people, ask themselves every day. While there is, no one answer for everyone there is some steps that individuals who are nearing retirement can take to save additional money. It is never too early to take a look at your savings to see if you are on track to reach your retirement goals. In fact, the sooner you examine your situation, the better off you and your family will be.

Many financial planners and people think that they will need approximately twelve times their annual salary to fund their retirement needs. While this is a good rule of thumb, it is by no means a one size fits all for everyone. In fact, the twelve times your salary works fairly well for a couple that earns about $100,000 a year and will need to replace between 80% and 85% of their income. Obviously the less you need to replace the less you may need to save and conversely the more of your pre-retirement income you need to keep the more you will need to save. For higher wage earners, it is recommended that you save upwards of sixteen times your annual salary depending on your circumstances and possible needs. Unless you can project how much of your pre-retirement salary will need to be replaced in retirement, you are saving blind with no real idea of how much you will need.

One way to determine how much you will need in retirement is to have a well-defined budget now to see what expenses you will in fact still have after you retire. Some costs will remain such as utilities, some insurance, a possible mortgage though I hope not for your sake, and some significant expenses of your annual income that should not be a primary part of your retirement are social security taxes and well as your income taxes. Once you have your budget that shows all of your revenue and expenses for at least six months, you will be in a better position to determine what your post-retirement replacement of income will be. In many instances, I think you will find that what you will be in retirement may be lower than what you expected.

So here are some tips to help you save some additional money as you get closer to retirement. In the event, your house is paid for, and you have no mortgage there may be little reason to sell and move unless that is what you want to do. If you are like many retirees you may have a house that is larger than what you actually need but if you do not wish to move and you can maintain the house it may be a benefit to keeping your current house as your family and eventually grandchildren may need the space when they come visit you. If you can sell your house at a good price level and can buy a smaller house where you intend to retire that is a sound decision and one each couple must make on their own. If you do not have a mortgage, there may be little incentive to sell and downsize. If you do have a mortgage, still it may make more sense to sell indeed and downsize into something that you can use the equity from your current house to pay cash for and eliminate the mortgage entirely.

For most now that you are entering retirement you will experience an empty nest so to speak as by now your children should be grown and out of college. If you aided your kids in their college expenses now that they are out of college, you would have an excess of money that will not be an expense in retirement. Instead of spending this money try to save it instead. When most of us no longer have children in college, we start to spend these funds on something else, and it makes perfect sense to continue to save these funds for your retirement. As you have been spending this money on a worthwhile expense, continue to do without using it and save the money in a retirement account or brokerage account. They key here is to save these funds and not spend them on something else.

Another way to save some extra money for retirement is to spend less on a favored low-cost pleasure. When we are younger, we want and desire the most expensive items and luxuries. People like to take the expensive trips abroad when they are working and while they are young enough to enjoy the experience of physically exertive trips. When we are older, we opt for trips that are closer to home, for the most part. Skip the international excursions and opt for dinner out, a visit to a museum or a trip to a national park. While I am not saying do not travel or take nice vacations, it is just as we age our list of places to visit is likely to be more practical.

And finally the way you approach your investments can save you some money as well. Many people will pay higher fees for actively managed mutual funds that can cost 0.8% or much more in management fees. While these funds may outperform the market from time to time, I do not know of any fund manager that consistently outperforms the market on a long term basis. Here in my opinion it is better to get a low-cost indexed fund for about 0.2% or less depending on the index you chose and pocket the difference and let it earn additional money for you. While it may not seem like, much this small difference can equate to about $4,500 or more in additional fees on a $750,000 account. Now I am not sure about you but I would prefer to keep that money for my use and not pay some fund manager.

While everyone is different, these are some basic tips that can lead to additional savings for you and your family. Again not everyone needs to save the same amounts or multiples of their annual salary. But these are some good rules of thumb to go by. Again do a budget and see what your need will be then estimate a return on your money and also an estimate of how long you will need it to the last. With this information, you will be in a better position to save for your retirement.

With more and more companies switching from a traditional pension to 401(k) plans it is more important than ever for you to be vigilant and know the most you can on your retirement account. Over the last 36 years, 401(k) plans have been the best invention or the worst depending on where we are at in the economy and how people feel about their investment choices. Also, many people do not feel qualified or comfortable managing their retirement accounts and would prefer a professional assist them. Most people had no problems with their 401(k) plan or its administrators during the bull market of the late 1990's and everyone seemed to hate the same plan during the stock market crash of 2008 and 2009. Of course, even the professionally managed accounts regardless of where they were located did not escape the last stock market crash as it was a once in a hundred-year event in many opinions. Now let's look at five ways in which you can maximize your 401(k) plan.

The first thing that you need to know about your 401(k) is what are the fees you are paying the plan's administrators to manage the funds? Regardless of the plan administrator there will be costs for managing money is not a free endeavor and people do get paid to manage the funds. That is just being realistic as there is no such thing as a free lunch but if your plan's fees are much more than a percent (1%) then it may be time to talk to your company about changing administrators. Here is a disclaimer though in that regard and it is the larger the company, the greater the amount of money that is involved. Larger plans can charge lower fees as the administrators will make up the difference between higher fees and volume of additional assets under management. To see how much say a half a percentage point will cost you and your retirement funds over a 35 year period just use Excel and plug in your expected rate of return minus your current fees to get a projected value. Then find a comparable plan that charges a different fee and do the same. In most instances, even a half a percentage point can make a huge difference over the life of your account. As an example, $25,000 invested with a 7% return and an expense fee of .5% will grow to about $225,000 over 35 years. The same investment with a 1.5% fee would only increase to about $163,000 over the same period.

If you read my blog on a regular basis you know I am a big believer in ROTH accounts, and it is no different when it comes to a 401(k). The benefits of a ROTH account are better for lower wage earners as the taxes that are being paid relatively small compared to someone who may be in their primary wage earning years. Also, ROTH 401(k) accounts do not have income limits as ROTH IRA's so if your company offers a ROTH 401(k) anyone is eligible to contribute to them. Tax-free money in the future is always a good thing, and it allows for tax diversification when it comes to your retirement planning as well. And if you leave your job and roll a ROTH 401(k) into a ROTH IRA there are no minimum distributions at age 70 ½ as with a Traditional IRA.

A majority of companies use the auto-enrollment option for new employees and in doing so they will place 3% of your salary into the 401(k). Some firms will increase that amount as your wages increase but most will not do so, and they will leave your contribution at 3%. Also, most automatic investing will place the funds in the most conservative investment choice or a target date fund. In my opinion both of these options are not really that good as a traditional fund will not outpace inflation as a rule and I find most target date funds to be a tad conservative as well and not a right choice if it can be helped. If you can afford it, I suggest you save 10% of your salary in your 401(k) to ensure you will have enough when it comes time to retire.

If you do not contribute 10% of your salary to your 401(k), then please at least contribute up to the amount that your company will match if it does that. Otherwise, you are leaving free money on the table and let's face it an instant positive return is something you never want to give up. After you contribute at least an amount equal to the match try saving the amounts of your raises and live on the same amount as you did the previous year. That way you will not notice the loss of any additional funds as you have set it up on an auto-pilot type scenario. The maximum that a person can contribute to a 401(k) is $17,500 in 2014 and for those over the age of 50 they are allowed an extra $5,500 for an annual limit of $23,000.

And a while ago I wrote a blog on how many individuals do not take advantage of financial advice. If your plan offers any financial planning advice, it may be worth the effort to examine what it is they offer. In some instances, there is a conflict of interest but in many there are some excellent benefits being missed because people just do not take the time to take full advantages of their benefits package.

While investing in a 401(k) is not all that difficult it can be overwhelming at times. Take your time to read and understand what your plan offers and how much it will cost you in fees.

Do you have a 401(k) plan? Better yet if you have one do you understand it? Most workers now have company-sponsored 401(k) plans and when they first started many were less than desirable when it came to investment choices. But in recent years 401(k) plans have gotten more and more options and have seen expense ratios fall. With a little effort, anyone can take control of their 401(k) and in return their retirement. The following are some areas that may not be the best for employees, but there are ways to fix the issue and make your 401(k) work for you.

Many employers are now enrolling new employees in the company's 401(k) plan automatically. In recent years, 401(k) plans have seen the participation of eligible employees grow due to this action by employers. But a drawback to the auto-enrollment is some companies have reduced the amount they will match due to the increased participation. While younger workers are saving the benefit from the company in the form of matching may not be as high as it was prior to this action becoming the standard course of action by employers. Another drawback is twofold in nature. Many companies set the initial savings for the employee's 401(k) at about 3% and then they will default the money into the most conservative of the investments that the 401(k) offers. The problem with this approach is 3% is not even close to what someone should be saving into their 401(k) as many financial planners recommend at least a 10% contribution. Secondly by investing in the most conservative investment the employee while they may not lose principal chances are the gains they make will not keep up with inflation. Now starting out it may be difficult to save 10% of your salary but when you are younger and starting out raises are relatively common. The key here is to set up automatic increases in your contributions if your plan allows for that. The second is when you do get a raise increase your contribution percentage so you will not notice you have saved more due to the fact it is automatically taken from your check before you even see it.

One of the largest complaints by 401(k) participants was that they were expensive for participants and that they had few options. In the last ten years, expense ratios have dropped almost .1% mainly due to litigation that was instigated by employees against their companies. Now larger companies have access to funds that have lower expense ratios but that is a result of economies of scale. But prices are coming down for all employers in general for their plans and the expenses associated with them. Regardless of the expense ratios it is important always to contribute up to the company match, or you are throwing free money away. Irrespective of the expense ratio, free money is an immediate return on your investment and will outweigh any costs associated with the 401(k). But if your plan does have unusually high fees fund up to the company match then fund a ROTH IRA with the difference in low priced ETF's or indexed mutual funds.

Many larger funds now have some form of fund management for your 401(k) contributions. While as of now this is limited to more major employers who have a lot of assets under management in a 401(k) plan, they may become available to medium and smaller plans as they become efficient. This management services will aid in picking asset classes or even rebalance your assets for you to achieve your retirement goals or to stay within your risk tolerance ranges. But as you are in this plan for the long term and not for short term gains the best approach is to find a small expense indexed fund within your 401(k)'s plan and invest in that. Over the long haul, this has proven to be an effective investment strategy. And again if your plan does not offer what you consider to be good choices contribute up to the match then fund your IRA to its maximum then switch back to the 401(k) to save additional money until you have maxed it out as well.

And to answer the old question of when to start saving that is start saving as soon as you can. The power of compounded interest over 30 plus years will amaze you. If you want to see what it will cost you to wait 5 or 10 years open an Excel spreadsheet and use the Future Value function. Fill in your variables and see what it will cost you to wait. Five years can make a huge difference in what your account can end up within 30 or 35 years. Play with the numbers and see for yourself.

If your company has limited, options for investments in the 401(k) plan remember always to invest up to the match, so you are not leaving free money on the table. But if the plan is substantial on your company's stock contribute up to the maximum then fund your IRA. After the IRA is funded, go to a brokerage account and buy equities that are tax efficient in such an account. Remember dividends and capital gains are tax-advantaged, so equities are a good choice for a brokerage account.

Not all 401(k) plans are set up to be advantageous for the employee but with a little work on your part and creativity you can still save effectively. Remember retirement for most of us is many years away and with proper planning it can be comfortable for you. If you are closer to retirement still contribute to your company's plan but it may be wise to seek the guidance of a financial planner to help iron out the smaller details.

Are you preparing for retirement? Are you maximizing the various options for retirement accounts? Provided you meet the income guidelines you can open either a ROTH IRA or a Traditional IRA and in the event you are self-employed or work for a smaller business you can have a SEP IRA as well. But one of the best ways to generate large sums of money for retirement is to take advantage of your employer's 401(k) plan especially of they offer a company match. That is free money that will add to your retirement nest egg regardless of what the markets do. As I have said before, always pay you first and always contribute up to the percentage that there is a company match. Then if you can contribute as much as you can as these funds will grow tax deferred until you withdrawal the funds after age 59 ½. So how do you maximize your 401(k)? Here are some simple steps to help you on the way to a healthy retirement.

A little money put in a 401(k) in your early 20's can lead to big paydays in retirement thanks to the power of compounding interest. According to some statistics if you contribute to your 401(k) for 30 years and combine that with your potential Social Security you can realistically replace about 60% of your income at retirement. As I showed in the blog on savings if, you save $4,000 a year for about 35 to 40 years with a return of about 8%, you can retire a millionaire. Not an unrealistic goal depending on how much you elect to put in your 401(k) from an early age and get a decent return on your investment.

If you are not sure of your investing style or ability to tolerate risk, you may want to find a financial planner that will assist you for a fee. There are plenty of on-line tools that can tell your tolerance for investment risk and with a little research you can find a good ETF or mutual fund to invest in for the long-term.

No matter how good you think you are with finance everyone needs a budget to know how and where their hard-earned money is going. Develop a budget that allows you to not only live a comfortable life but one that will allow you to save for retirement. Take an honest look at where your money goes and see if you can find ways to make savings and then turn those savings into additional contributions to your IRA or 401(k).

Now consider that the 401(k) has been around for about 40 years. This makes those retiring now and those who will retire going forward rely heavily on the 401(k) for their retirement income. Also, it is time to consider that most of us will not be like our grandparents or maybe even our parents and work at one job for our entire career. So what happens when you change jobs, and both have 401(k) plans that you have participated in? Well, you have two basic options when this occurs.

One is to cash out the IRA when you turn 59 ½ and pay the regular income tax on the gains you have achieved over the years. That means leaving the money with your old employer but also means keeping track of the plan's administrators. A second similar option that keeps the money in a 401(k) plan it to roll the money over into your new employer's plan and continue to do this every time you change jobs. That way the money will follow you, and you only have to keep track of your current plans administrator.

Another option is to roll the funds over into an IRA and not your current employer's 401(k) plan. Not all companies will allow you to roll over a 401(k), so a Rollover IRA is an option. But make sure you have the old employer's 401(k) administrator pay your IRA administrator directly, or they may withhold taxes and early withdrawal penalties from your amount. The Rollover IRA will give you more investment options and give you more control than rolling it over into a new 401(k). But with that decision comes investment risks of possibly having too many investment choices to choose from.

Not all 401(k) plans are created equally so watch out for the hidden charges. Your old employer may have a great plan with low costs meaning it would be wise to leave the funds with them instead of moving them to a new 401(k) that is not as efficient or a Rollover IRA. Check and compare the plans before you do anything.

Saving early and often is the key to a golden retirement. Use IRA's, and 401(k)'s to save money in a tax-deferred or tax-free manner depending on it is a Traditional or ROTH account. Use budgets to get the most out of your hard earned money and save the maximum you can early while you are young. Then invest wisely and watch the power of compounding interest work in your favor.

Personal Finance: A Grouping of Financial Topics
By Kirk G. Meyer

Does your employer offer a ROTH 401(k)? Is it really beneficial to contribute to a ROTH 401(k)? The basic answer to that last question is yes provided you are young enough and do not plan on taking any withdrawals for at least ten years. Like a ROTH IRA, the money will go into the account taxed so any gains will be withdrawn tax-free when you retire after age 59 ½. But unlike a ROTH IRA there are no income limitations on a ROTH 401(k) and no need to convert a Traditional IRA to a ROTH IRA. Under the current tax code, employees under age 50 are allowed to contribute up to $17,500 annually. For those over the age of 50, the IRS allows you to contribute an extra $ 5,500 per year. And provided you retire after the age of 59 ½ and have had the ROTH 401(k) account for a minimum of five years the withdrawals will be tax-free.

This makes sense for several different related reason. One, when you are younger your earnings, are less, so you do not notice the tax consequences as much as someone who is in the prime of their earning career. By plugging some numbers into Excel you can see that the growth of a real tax free investment and not merely a tax-deferred investment can lead to some serious differences depending on how long you can let the money compound tax-free. But if you do not think your tax bracket will be as high as it is now while you are working the ROTH may not make the most sense for you.

But in retirement you will need to consider several variables that could influence your tax bracket. Social Security may be taxable depending on your family's situation. Pensions could be a taxable source of income as well. Interest and dividends will be considered a source of income for you as well. And if you make a withdrawal from a Traditional IRA or 401(k) account that is seen as ordinary income and will be taxed as well. If you have any further questions on what may or may not be taxed in your retirement years consult a financial advisor or tax professional.

If you do not wish to make the mandatory 401(k) withdrawals, you have the option of converting the ROTH 401(k) into a ROTH IRA tax-free. Now the remaining question that is an option for some employees is should they convert their Traditional 401(k) into a ROTH 401(k). Like converting an IRA, you will be required to pay the taxes on the converted amount in the year the conversion is made. Unlike converting an IRA, you will not be able to change your mind on a 401(k) conversion.

Check with your employer to see what options are available to you where you are working. Consult a professional to get an idea of what your retirement may look like. However, keep in mind no one knows what the future will hold for investments or taxes but you need to be able to make the most informed decision that you can make based on today's facts. ROTH accounts are an excellent source of possible wealth accumulation for anyone, but especially those who are younger or will be able to let the money accumulate tax-free over a longer period.

Does your company offer a ROTH 401(k)? If so, have you considered contributing to it rather than a Traditional 401(k)? Personally I contribute all of my funds to a Roth account in my government Thrift Savings Plan, which is the government equivalent of a 401(k). However, all of the matching funds I receive have to be placed in a Traditional account as taxes have not been paid on those funds yet. So it goes to reason I will have two streams of income when I do, in fact, decide to retire 1. Being a taxable source and 2. Being a tax-free source. Considering that it is vital to have some of both types of income in retirement depending on what you need to achieve.

A little history on the Roth 401(k) as they were first started in 2006 and basically allow for you to save up to $17,500 in 2014 in after-tax money and $23,000 if you are over age 50. And unlike a ROTH IRA there are no income limitations on a ROTH 401(k) so anyone who works somewhere that they are offered can participate in a ROTH account. ROTH IRA's are phased out at certain income levels for individuals and couples because this is not held to the same standard. All withdrawals from a ROTH 401(k) are tax-free provided the account has been active for five years, and the participant is at least age 59 ½. And more employers are offering ROTH 401(k)'s now estimated to be at 50% as compared to just 11% in 2007.

Need some reasons as to why a ROTH 401(k) is a better option? Here are a few of them that come to mind. Consider this, you put a dollar in a traditional 401(k) and get the tax advantages now of reducing your taxes by a dollar. That dollar then grows for the rest of your working career until you decide to take it out along with its earnings. Now you saved say 25% on your taxes for that dollar but you will now pay taxes on the dollar along with all of its accumulated earnings possibly resulting in placing you in a higher tax bracket than you would have been otherwise in retirement. That is because withdrawals from 401(k) accounts are treated as ordinary income by the IRS. If you need to withdrawal a large sum for some reason, this could put you in a higher tax bracket than you would have otherwise been in. Now consider a ROTH 401(k) account with the same dollar. You pay the taxes now, and if you are just starting your career your tax bracket is most likely relatively small, and that dollar will grow just as the Traditional 401(k) account did earning you more money. Now you met the guidelines of a ROTH account and decided to withdrawal your dollar and its earnings. Now these funds are 100% tax-free and do not affect your income taxes as the money has already been taxed, the earnings are considered taxed as well, and the entire amount is tax free for income tax purposes. Now if you pull out a large amount from a ROTH 401(k), it will not place you in a higher tax bracket. And to be honest I do not see taxes or the tax brackets being reduced all that much over the next 30 years as more people retire and there are fewer workers earning money the government will have to keep taxes relatively stable as to ensure the funding source for government operations continues.

While all 401(k)'s require minimum withdrawals at age 70 ½, there is a way around this for ROTH 401(k) accounts. As a ROTH 401(k) participant, you are allowed to withdrawal the funds and roll them over into a ROTH IRA that in turn does not have any minimum withdrawal requirements. And by doing this you can create a legacy account for your heirs with the use of beneficiary designations on the ROTH IRA allowing the beneficiary to make minimum withdrawals over their lifetime while enabling the account to earn money still. If you have any questions about this process, feel free to contact me or seek a local financial advisor to assist you.

A ROTH 401(k) also allows for you to diversify your taxes by providing tax-free income in your retirement years. While it is true that many will be in a lower tax bracket in retirement having a tax free source of revenue will aid in many respects. One it will have no effect on your Social Security benefits like a Traditional 401(k) might. As I mentioned earlier large withdrawals from a ROTH 401(k) will not be treated as a large influx of income for income tax purposes. And finally if you decide to retire before you reach age 65 and Medicare starts making withdrawals from a ROTH 401(k) will not increase your income for health insurance under the new health care law enabling you to get government subsidies possibly when you purchase your interim health insurance policies.

While ROTH 401(k) accounts are relatively new, they have many positives and few negatives for people saving for their retirement. I would advise anyone to contribute to a ROTH account over a Traditional one as the benefits are better in my opinion.

I hope you are contributing to your 401(k) plan at work. If you are not now is the time to start. If your employer offers a company match, it is imperative to contribute at least the amount that the company will match. Otherwise, you will be leaving free money and an instant positive return on the table. While everyone does not have a financial planner or maybe the assets to require one it is never a bad idea to at least consult a fee-only planner to help develop a financial plan and a retirement plan for your 401(k). In instances where you are not comfortable deciding what investments you should be investing in many plans offer managed funds such as target dated funds. While these plans may make investing easier and more of an automated function, they do come at a higher cost in the way of fees.

While there may seem to be advantages for managed accounts within 401(k) accounts, these management services can offer widely different strategies. In a recent study by the government, it was determined that eight managed account providers represented about 95% of assets under management. With such little in the way of choices for managed accounts, there are not that many options for 401(k) participants. But these eight firms do offer a relatively broad and diverse group of options using different investment options and asset allocation and rebalancing options. But this does not ensure that the management company is living up to its fiduciary responsibility.

While not every managed account offers personalization some do, but the benefit often goes unused. Two of the eight used personal information on the participant to allocate the account's assets. The firms had the participant's age, gender, income, account balance and savings rate. The good news is the majority of the manager's required additional information such as risk tolerance and spousal assets. The majority of plan participants do not provide any of this information to the managers of the plans thus rendering the manager at a disadvantage. What does this mean? It means that you as a plan participant are not receiving the full benefits of what you are paying for in the way of fees. If the information is not provided then, the plan participant will most likely be invested in something that is similar to a target dated fund.

One thing that participants need always to consider is that there is an inherent conflict of interest between the plan manager and you the participant. It is not always in the best interest of the participant to keep their funds in the plan once they have retired or leave the company. But it is in the manager's best interest to keep the participant's funds in the account. In these instances, it is wise to do your research and decide what is best for you and your funds.

As with any activity that is actively managed it will cost you a fee. The fees for managed funds are higher than those for passively managed funds. If you can and have the time, it may be more advantageous for you to select your investments that are something I advise in the event your plan does not offer management of funds. And I tend to encourage people to avoid target dated funds as

I find them to be more conservative than what a person needs. Many people do not have the assets or need for a full-time financial planner so managed 401(k) plans are a good option provided you take full advantage of the services and benefits that are offered.

While managed 401(k) plans do cost more I see advantages in their services over say a pure target date fund. But as mentioned earlier it is critical for you, the participant, to provide all of the required information so you can have a manager that can provide you the best service that is possible. Why pay for an actively managed fund if you do not utilize it to the fullest. But as with any investment it is not good enough for you to have a manager looking over your investments it is crucial that you do understand them enough to question the manager.

Do you have many 401(k) accounts? Are you considering rolling over a 401(k) into an IRA account? Before you take action on older 401(k) accounts, there are some things to consider prior to putting those funds into an IRA account. Sometimes it is not in the best interest of the owner of a 401(k) to roll these accounts into IRA accounts. The notion of rolling a 401(k) into an IRA account may go against what many financial planners advise. Everyone needs to look at their situation and not take a generic view of someone who may or may not know your circumstances.

If you are between the ages of 55 and 59 ½, you may want to consider leaving those funds in your 401(k) account for one main reason. If you are between these two critical ages, a rollover IRA may not be in your best interest. Yes, it does make sense if you are still working to consolidate many 401(k) accounts into one account for ease of management and tracking. Many 401(k) plans will allow you to roll over prior plans into your existing plan so check with your plan's administrator. That is one way to consolidate multiple 401(k) accounts into one central location. Now if your current employer does not allow this, I do recommend doing a rollover of old 401(k) accounts into an IRA. But if you are currently working for the company that administers your 401(k) plan and are over the age of 55 here is the benefit of, not rolling that 401(k) into an IRA. As most everyone knows who has a 401(k) or an IRA, you cannot make withdrawals until the age of 59 ½ without being hit with a 10% penalty. Here is the exception to that rule. If you are over the age of 55 and separate from your company, you are allowed to access the funds from that 401(k) account without penalty. Now it is apparent why rolling older 401(k) plans into your existing plan is a plus as this rule will only apply to the plan in which you retired. Also, if you had rolled a 401(k) into an IRA, you are bound by the 59 ½ age limitations for withdrawals.

The next reason is not nearly as widely known but is one that is very effective if you can indeed use it. In the instance where you can use this technique consult a tax professional or a Certified Financial Planner to ensure you do not do more damage than good. If you have, stock in the company you work for that is in your 401(k) this tip is for you. Now it is important that you own the stock of the company and not a fund that mirrors the company stock. Where this technique works is when the stock has appreciated a great deal. In this case, you take the amount that you contributed to the 401(k) account that is invested in actual company stock and transfer the stock to a brokerage account. This technique is called a Net Unrealized Appreciation transfer. Here you will be responsible for the taxes on the amount you contributed to the 401(k) plan and not the value of the stock you transfer. Then when it is time to sell the stock you will pay taxes on the capital gains of the stock instead of regular income taxes had it remained in the 401(k) or a rollover IRA. As you will pay taxes on the amount, you originally contributed in the 401(k), this distribution could cause you to bump up into a higher tax bracket. For this reason, you need to seek the advice of a financial professional when you use this method.

A third reason that many overlook while trying to consolidate accounts and centralize funds is a 401(k) plan offers excellent investment options. Now investment choice is not the only thing to consider here as you need to think of the fees the plan charges as well. I know in the case of my retirement account, the Thrift Savings Plan, we have adequate investment opportunities and some of the lowest fees I have seen in any funds. And yes this even includes some of Vanguard's primary indexed exchange traded funds that have some of the lowest prices in the industry. Do your homework and consider all the variables before you rollover a 401(k) into an IRA.

Now I am not saying that you should never roll a 401(k) account into an IRA because there may very well be some reason to do exactly that. But before you do you need to examine all aspects and figure out what the consequences will be if you do. Many people do not feel comfortable managing their money and seek financial planners. While there is nothing wrong with that, and it may very well benefit you, not everyone needs the assistance of financial planners.

Have you heard the President's new IRA idea? It is one that is linked to one if the most successful 401(k) type of investments around, the Thrift Savings Plan or TSP. This new IRA type of investment is called the MyRA. This is an attempt of the President to get more people saving for retirement who otherwise would not be doing so. And the proposed MyRA would be mainly designed after one of the investment options in the TSP. And like the factors that make the TSP so popular the MyRA will have low minimums, virtually no fees, and will be invested in an ultra-safe investment option.

Now unlike the TSP the MyRA will be open to all investors who are looking for a primary return and a guarantee of no loss of their principal. And why not base it on the TSP as it is a simple retirement plan that has extremely low fees and returns that are benchmarked to an index of some sort. The current TSP has two bond funds with the most conservative being the G Fund, which invests only in short-term US Treasuries that are issued just for the G Fund. The key to these is that they are short-term in nature but pay interest as if they were intermediate bonds. This is the investment option that the MyRA will offer to participants. The second bond fund is a broad index fund of all types of domestic obligations. The three equity funds are all tied to a benchmark such as the S&P 500 for larger corporations, a small capitalization fund and an international fund that invests in established foreign markets. The TSP also offers five lifecycle funds for target date investors who do not want to worry about asset allocation. This is what makes the TSP work so well; it is simple and there are no confusing choices from which to select investments. Many 401(k) plans offer dozens of options with most having higher fees than an indexed fund.

These factors keep most Federal employees who have retired in the TSP instead of taking their money out and placing it in an IRA. With over $400 billion in assets, these funds can operate at fees that are close to zero. It is this factor that will allow the MyRA to offer no or low fees to investors who want a safe guaranteed investment. And the economies of scale will provide the volume to keep the costs that way just as in the TSP.

Personal Finance: A Grouping of Financial Topics
By Kirk G. Meyer

Are you saving for retirement? Do you know what it is you are doing when it comes to your retirement accounts? It is critical saving for retirement, and you need to be doing that as early and as often as you can. But there are several different types of retirement accounts that you can choose from so let's look briefly at each. They are a Traditional IRA, ROTH IRA, SEP IRA, and SIMPLE IRA. Unlike a 401(k) plan that is through your employer an IRA is an account for you that has different requirements, qualifications, limitations and rules that govern them.

Most people are familiar with the Traditional IRA that is funded with pre-tax dollars, and the earnings will grow tax-deferred. Depending on your income, you may be able to deduct some of the contributions from your income taxes. Withdrawals can begin at age 59 ½ without facing penalties. If you do take money out of this account, you will pay taxes on the earnings as well as a 10% penalty for an early withdrawal. The exceptions are if you are buying your first home, higher education expenses or a qualifying medical condition allowing you to take a withdrawal without penalty, and the proceeds will be reported as income. Also, once you reach are 70 ½ you are no longer able to make contributions to the IRA and will be required to make minimum required distributions based on IRS tables. The maximum that an individual can contribute in a year is $5,500 for those under age 50 and $6,500 for those over age 50.

A second option is the ROTH IRA, which is made with money that has already been taxed. The basics of the account are the same as a Traditional IRA with the exception that there are no minimum withdrawal requirements at age 70 ½. Also, the income guidelines are different, and any contributions will not reduce your tax liability. For couples, the maximum income that is allowed for a full contribution is $181,000 and $114,000 for singles based on 2014 figures.

The main difference is whether you believe your taxes are higher now or will be higher in retirement. Personally I think younger people have advantages of a ROTH IRA as they are in a lower tax bracket as a rule just out of college thus reducing the tax benefits at the time of the contribution. I do not see the tax rate or brackets being reduced in the future and plan for a tax rate similar to the one I am paying now when I retire.

The third IRA is the SEP IRA or Simplified Employee Pension, which lets business owners allocate funds for their and their employees retirement. Any sized business can contribute, but there are some specialized rules that accompany the SEP IRA so consult a CPA when establishing these to ensure all the laws and rules are adhered to when operating the IRA. In 2014, a person can contribute $52,000 or 25% of their compensation whichever is less. There are definite tax advantages here for small business owners, so please do consult with a CPA or tax professional.

The fourth type of IRA is the SIMPLE IRA or Savings Incentive Match Plan for Employees. This is a plan that allows you and your employer to contribute to a Traditional IRA set up by the company. Employees have the option to contribute to these accounts while employers do not which is a little different than the SEP IRA that the employer contributes and it is at their option provided it is equitable to all.

As you can see, there are many IRAs available to individuals and the maximum for those who are self-employed. If you have further questions, please email me or contact a CPA, tax professional or financial planner.

Do you contribute to an IRA on an annual basis? When in the year do you contribute? Are you one to make your contribution early in January or do you wait until closer to the tax and contribution deadline? Depending on your timing over the long haul, the delay could cost you some serious money later on down the road. As an IRA contributor, you may make your contributions anywhere from the first of January until April 15th of the following year.

By waiting to make your contributions later in the year, you are taking valuable time away from the tax-advantaged status and the power of compounding interest and gains. Also, people tend to make poorer investment decisions closer to tax time as there is a sense of urgency in their contributions. But by making the contribution earlier in the year you will gain valuable time for the asset to appreciate in value. This will also help the account outpace inflation by adding the extra time to compound its value.

And we are talking some serious compounding. Let's look at some numbers and time frames. If you were to contribute $5,500 to an IRA every year for 30 years, your working years and prior to retirement, what would the difference be in making the contribution at the start or end of the year assuming a 7% return. For the early saver, they would have $597,769, and the late saver would have $561,402 for a difference of almost $36,000. That could be an extra year in retirement depending on your situation. Not a bad tradeoff for making a contribution that you planned on making anyway, just earlier.

Also, when you make a contribution at the last minute, you may not be making a wise selection of your investment. In many instances, the funds people put in their IRA is placed in low yielding assets such as a money market account. Those who invest early in the year have more time to make wise decisions and can invest with the knowledge that they have performed their due diligence and are investing in the asset that is best suited for them.

One way to fund your IRA at the start of the year is an easy one. If you are getting a tax refund and file your taxes early put the refund to work for yourself by investing it in your IRA. Between savings and the refund I hope you can get close to the maximum $5,500 annual contribution limit for those under the age of 50 and $6,500 for those who are older than 50 and allowed a catch-up contribution. Maximize your contributions regardless of anything else and try to make them as early in the year as you can to maximize your potential gains.

Does the sound of a tax-free income appeal to you? Then you need to consider a ROTH IRA definitely. A ROTH IRA will grow not only tax-deferred but with tax-free growth. And unlike a Traditional IRA you are not required to make any withdrawals at age 70 ½. If you have a Traditional IRA, you can always do a conversion to a ROTH IRA regardless of age or earned income limitations. If you are in a lower tax bracket now, it may be a good time to convert some of your Traditional IRA into a ROTH IRA and do some good estate and tax planning. Remember a distribution from a Traditional IRA is taxed as ordinary income and so would your ROTH conversion. But if you plan on leaving the funds in your ROTH IRA for over 5 years and have some room in your tax situation before you are bumped into the next highest tax bracket this is definitely something you may want to consider. And if you are still working many employers now offer ROTH 401(k) plans but they do have some differences from a ROTH IRA.

In order to open a new ROTH IRA you must have earned income in the year you open the account but you may contribute at any age as the money you place in a ROTH IRA is taxed where a Traditional IRA is tax deferred and you may not make contributions after age 70 ½. If you are under the age of 50 you may contribute $5,500 to an IRA for 2013 and 2014 and if you are over the age of 50 you may contribute $6,500 with phase-outs based on your income. The phase-outs for 2013 are $127,000 for single filers and $188,000 for joint returns and in 2014 they are $129,000 and $191,000 respectively. For ROTH 401(k) plans for individuals under 50 they may contribute up to $17,500 and for those over 50 they may contribute $23,000 for both 2013 and 2014. December 31st must make ROTH 401(k) contributions, and IRA contributions may be made until April 15th of the previous tax year.

If you do not have earned income, you may still open and have a ROTH IRA you will just have to do it through a conversion of a Traditional IRA. And unlike ordinary contributions you are not limited to a conversion IRA with exception to tax consequences. One way to minimize the tax bill is to convert a Traditional IRA over several years ensuring you do not bump yourself into a higher tax bracket. But make sure you have the money already outside of an IRA when you do the conversion or you will be adding extra taxes onto those encountered by the conversion IRA with more in taxes from the Traditional IRA to cover all the expenses. When you consider a conversion IRA it is best to meet with a tax advisor or financial planner to make sure you do not bump yourself into a higher tax bracket, convert so much you hit the surcharge tax of 3.8% or affect your Medicare Part B and D if you are over age 65.

Now you also need to plan for if and when you will do a conversion from a Traditional IRA to a ROTH IRA. If you are in a higher tax bracket now and you project, you will be in a lower one once you do retire it is better to do the conversion after you retire. However, if you are already in a lower tax bracket convert as much as you can before you reach the lower limits of the next tax bracket.

Now here are some unique features of a ROTH IRA that you may or may not need to be aware of. Like the money, you put in a ROTH IRA is taxed you may withdrawal that money after five years from the conversion date if you are under age 59 ½. If you have had the converted IRA for at least five years and are older than 59 ½, there are no restriction on your withdrawals. Now the five years begins on January 1st of the year in which you did the conversion and will extend five years until the January of the 5th year. If you convert an IRA in 2013, the date of the conversion would be considered January 2, 2013 and, therefore, the five years would be on January 1, 2018. The five-year conversion rule applies to each conversion and not the IRA as a whole.

As far as using a ROTH IRA as an estate planning tool they are excellent choices for that purpose. ROTH IRA's may be left to anyone regardless of their age and depending on who it is left to will determine the rules that will apply to it. If you leave a ROTH IRA to a child, grandchild or anyone other than a spouse, they will have to start taking minimum distributions the year following your death. That allows young people to enjoy a lifetime of tax-free growth in a ROTH IRA. If the ROTH IRA is left to a spouse, there is no requirement to take the minimum distribution. While leaving a ROTH IRA may defer the taxes on the IRA itself it will still be included in your taxable estate. In the event, you will leave an IRA to a charity do not under any circumstance convert a Traditional IRA to a ROTH IRA as charities do not pay taxes on the gift under either circumstance. If you convert a Traditional IRA to a ROTH, you are just paying unnecessary taxes.

If you convert a Traditional IRA to a ROTH IRA and for some reason you made an error in doing so you have until October 15th of the following year to characterize the IRA back. If you do not have the money to pay the conversion taxes you may change the IRA back or if the value of the IRA has a dramatic decrease you may want to switch it back as well. You can also convert a Traditional 401(k) into a ROTH 401(k) but that is a permanent change that cannot be undone. Also, ROTH 401(k) accounts are subject to minimum withdrawals starting at age 70 ½ unless you are still working for the company that holds the 401(k).

Well, by now you are aware that I think a ROTH account be it an IRA or a 401(k) is one of the best retirement tools the government has given us. As more and more baby boomers retire meaning, there are more people entering Social Security and Medicare systems it will be more vital that future retirees have their savings in some form or another. With only about a quarter of Fortune 500 companies offering pensions and many ending their pensions this year or in the coming years it is going to be extra important for workers today to save in some manner. And the most popular saving techniques are a company 401(k) plans and IRA's. So why a ROTH IRA? Here are a few reasons why I think a ROTH is the better way to go when it comes to an IRA.

First is the tax advantages of ROTH accounts. When you are younger, and earning less you probably are in a relatively low tax bracket, so there is no reason to go with a Traditional IRA because of the tax deduction. It is not much to begin with and your taxes are low anyway so pay the tax on the $5,500 that you can contribute in 2014 unless you are already over 50 then you get an additional $1,000 in catch-up contributions for a total of $6,500 a year. Now let's say you are 25 and just out of college and do manage to contribute just $5,000 a year to a ROTH IRA for 40 years until you retire at age 65. If you earn a conservative 7.5% on that money, you will have over $1.2 million your account. And since the taxes have already been paid for the contributions that are tax-free money you will be taking out. Not a bad deal if you ask me as you only invested $200,000 over the 40 years, and now you get $1 million tax-free.

Now to contribute to an ROTH account you need to meet some government requirements. First the money you contribute must be earned income. Meaning if you are in your teens and have a summer job and are thinking of investing for your retirement you can provide you contribute no more than you earned into the ROTH account. Meaning if you made $4,500 in a year you could contribute a maximum of $4,500 to a ROTH IRA. Also, there are income limitations for contribution to ROTH IIRA accounts. If you are single and make over $114,000 or married and earn over $181,000 a year, you are not eligible to contribute to a ROTH IRA directly. But there is a way to get the money into a ROTH account with proper planning. What you need to do if you make over the income limitations is contribute to a non-deductible IRA and immediately convert it to a ROTH IRA. All you will have to do, in this case, is pay any taxes on any gains between the time you invested in the Traditional IRA and when you make the conversion to a ROTH IRA. To ensure you are doing this correctly and legally consult a qualified financial planner.

In a ROTH IRA, you can withdrawal the principal you have contributed. And if it is a converted IRA you may provide you have had the ROTH account for a minimum of five years. This means if you have had the account for 5 years on converted accounts, and made contributions of $20,000 you are allowed to take that principal out before age 59 ½ without penalty because taxes have already been paid on those funds. You are not permitted to take out any earning or profits in the account just the contributed principal otherwise you are looking at a 10%

penalty. While I do not recommend taking money from any retirement account before you retire, this does provide options for someone who is in desperate need of additional money.

Some other benefits of a ROTH IRA are you can make a withdrawal for the purchase of your first home. Unlike just taking out the principal, you are allowed to withdrawal up to $10,000 in earnings as well without the 10% penalty being imposed. If you were married and each had a ROTH account, you would be able to take out the principal and a total of $20,000 in earnings without penalty. Just as above you must have had the ROTH account for a minimum of five years.

This also goes for paying for a child's college education, so it gives you additional options when you are faced with saving for retirement and possible college expenses. Another tax-advantaged way to save for college expenses is to open a state-sponsored 529 plan in which you make contributions to the account, and it grows tax deferred until your child or another family member incurs qualified college expenses which the 529 plan will pay for tax free. If you take the funds out of the 529 plan for reasons other than for education, you face taxes on the gains and a 10% penalty.

Again, the ROTH IRA has some excellent qualities besides being a tax-free investment. It allows the owner some freedom in making withdrawals under certain conditions allowing for people to purchase a first home or to fund a child's college educations. But again, I stress saving for one's retirement is vital in today's world more than ever and I do not suggest or recommend using a ROTH IRA or any retirement account for any purpose other than your retirement. But if you have limited options it is always there in the event you do need it.

IRA's can be invested in traditional things that most people associate with IRA's such as equities and bonds. But you can also invest IRA funds in other things as well such as CD's, real estate, and precious metals. If you want to invest in equities, I suggest a discount on-line broker to minimize commissions on trades. For a mutual fund or many exchanges traded funds, I would suggest investing in the actual company that runs the fund. For low-cost funds, I recommend Vanguard as they offer a wide selection of investment options, have low management fees, and allow you to change funds within a fund family at no cost. For a CD or money market account, I would recommend a bank but if you want better rates look to on-line banks such as Ally or Capital One 360. If you wish to invest in real estate, there are many complicated steps, and you must do it through a self-directed IRA normally with a designated trustee to manage your IRA. There are many such firms so you can Google self-directed IRA and a list of companies that do these IRA's. And for precious metals you need to buy through a company that offers IRA's and for a fee they will purchase your metals and store them for you until you sell them.

As you can see, there are many advantages to a ROTH IRA, and there are many investing options. Their key to a wealthy retirement is to save as much as you can and start as early as you can. The compounding difference between someone who saves for 40 years and someone who only saves for 30 years is dramatic. Remember our example from earlier in the post? Someone who is 25 and saved for 40 years had $1.2 million at age 65. Now if you waited ten years and started saving at age 35 and only for the 30 years until you reach age 65, you would only have about $560,000 in the account. That is less than half! Now you can see the advantage of starting early.

Do you earn too much for a traditional IRA or a ROTH IRA? If you do there is an option available for high-income earners but it is not always the best choice. For higher income earners, the tax-deferred advantage may not outweigh the simplistic brokerage account when it comes to taxes. As April 15th approaches, everyone is thinking of making contributions to their IRA's.

For a ROTH IRA, an individual must earn less than $129,000 and a couple $191,000 in order to contribute. The positive of a ROTH is it grows tax-deferred, and all proceeds are tax-free. A double win and a powerful ally to compounding interest. If an individual earns less than $70,000 and a couple less than $116,000 they can contribute to a traditional IRA and get a tax deduction in the year, they make the contribution. But unlike the ROTH, the growth is tax deferred but the gains are taxed as ordinary income when they are withdrawn after age 59 ½.

For high-income earners, there is an option, and that is to contribute to a traditional IRA with no tax advantage and then let the contributions grow tax deferred. But, in theory, this is not the best course of business as any proceeds would be taxed as ordinary income and chances are your tax rate will not go down all that much in retirement. So many investors do invest in these IRA's and then convert them into a ROTH IRA after the fact. And if this is done shortly after the IRA is established the taxes will be minimal as it will only be on the appreciation since the IRA was opened. Then the proceeds will grow tax deferred, and the gains will be tax-free when withdrawn.

If a high-income earner does not wish to open a traditional IRA and convert it to a ROTH, there is a reason it may not even make sense to open the IRA in the first place. Unless there is a ROTH conversion, the gains in a traditional IRA are taxed as ordinary income that will most likely be higher than 15%. Had you as a high-income earner invested in a brokerage account you would be taxed on an annual basis so the growth would not be tax deferred but would get good tax benefits. If the account is established and the security is held for a year, any gains would be long-term and therefore taxed at 15% as would dividends. Chances are this 15% tax rate could very well be lower than your ordinary income tax rate.

Always save for retirement in some manner. But save in a way that is most beneficial to you both tax-wise and savings wise. Sometimes a combination of many different retirement savings plans provides the best return and protection for you as the investor.

Are you planning on converting a Traditional IRA to a ROTH IRA? If so you may want to consider not only the Federal tax consequences but also any state tax consequences. Now if you think you will be in a higher tax bracket when you retire it makes good sense to convert the IRA now provided you can afford to pay the taxes associated with the conversion. Where you live will also have an impact on if a conversion makes sense for you. A ROTH makes sense for numerous reasons but the two biggest affect our choices are what tax bracket we will be in when we retire, and second all of us with ROTH accounts hope that Congress does not change the rules on us at some point in the future.

Now if you do think you will be in a high or higher tax bracket after retirement ROTH accounts do make sense. Pay the taxes now and enjoy a tax-free retirement. But you also need to take into consideration state taxes on income in your retirement. There are a few states, but not many that do not have an income tax and those that do have fairly high rates when you consider a conversion. So when you are planning a conversion now take into account state income taxes as you will owe those in addition to the Federal income tax. So do think of the entire tax consequences when you are considering a Traditional IRA to a ROTH IRA conversion.

Many people who retire move from states with high-income tax to states with lower or no income tax. So if you are paying taxes in a state with high-income tax the benefits might not be as good when you move as you have now paid income taxes in the higher state and will not have any taxes to a ROTH withdrawal in your retirement years in the low or no income tax state. The same goes for your conversion IRA's, and that is it may not make sense to convert an IRA to a ROTH when you live in a state with high-income tax and plan on moving. The key to remember here is what you think your tax situation will be in your retirement years and will the state you live in have a high, low or no income tax.

Now it is always a good idea to start with a ROTH IRA when you are young as you do not know where you will be when you retire or what states will do with regards to income tax. But letting your money grow for 30 to 35 years tax-free in an IRA is always a good idea. That and when you are just starting your career, in theory, your tax bracket is lower as your earnings are not as high yet. Unless you are converting large sums, a ROTH IRA is always a good way to go for retirement.

Now that you are saving for retirement in an IRA be that a Traditional or ROTH IRA you are ahead of most at this point. But did you know that there is a third type of IRA? For some, there is a third choice at least called the SEP IRA. SEP stands for simplified employee pension and is an IRA that allows employers to contribute to the IRA for their workers. And even better yet it works for self-employed individuals as well, and they can contribute to their own SEP IRA. Now you may be asking yourself why would I want a SEP IRA and not a Traditional or ROTH IRA. The answer to that is the amount you can contribute to the IRA. For Traditional and ROTH IRA in 2014 you can contribute $5,500 and $6,500 a year for those 50 and older. For a SEP IRA, you can contribute 25% of your pay up to $52,000 a year. Now that will allow you to save some serious money for your retirement as compared to the two more widely known IRA's.

And as compared to a 401(k) where you are limited to the plans choice of investments a SEP IRA is only bound by where and who you have administered the IRA. This opens up the investment choices to almost all of the mutual funds, ETS, bonds, equities, precious metals and even real estate. All you need to do to have just about any option there is as far as an investment is to have a self-directed IRA where you pay a small fee for someone to administer the IRA for you. In the event, you do not go with a traditional broker check with a financial planner to see what options do make the most sense.

Here are some more details on SEP IRA's:

- Only the employer or a self-employed person can contribute to the IRA, but employees are also able to contribute to their own IRA's as well.
- Contributions are on a pre-tax basis.
- The account grows tax-deferred so you can buy and sell assets in the account without capital gains tax at the time of the transaction.
- Withdrawals are taxed as income.
- They are 100% vested at the time of the investment.
- Must be the same for all eligible employees.
- Early withdrawals occur prior to age 59 ½ and are 10% plus taxes.
- At age 70 you must start taking withdrawals.

While they are not available for everyone, they are a very useful tool for retirement planning. Look at the SEP IRA as an option and if you have any questions seek the advice of a financial planner.

Personal Finance: A Grouping of Financial Topics
By Kirk G. Meyer

This topic will address some issues that I was made aware of a few chapters ago when I had dinner with a family that also happen to be good friends of mine. Without getting into too much detail, I am appalled on many levels with what happened to my friends. First for those of you who are not aware I am one course shy of completing a Master's of Science in Financial Planning, and I am also a licensed life insurance agent in the state of Tennessee. First I will explain what has me so upset about this situation then I will explain the solution for those of you who may be in a similar situation.

First my friends are naturalized US citizen who owns their own business. They have a beautiful family and work as hard as anyone I know for their livelihoods. Now I know for a fact I am outraged at their insurance agent who took complete advantage of their good and trusting nature. This agent sold them a whole life insurance policy that had a monthly premium that was well into four digits for the two of them. They were sold this policy with the intention of using it for their retirement as they have no need for additional life insurance. This agent told them the accumulated cash value would be theirs tax-free when they needed the money. They did not however explain that this is their money and is considered a loan against the death benefit that is due with interest when they do, in fact, die. The agent sold them this policy as a retirement asset and not as life insurance. If the agent did have my friend's interest at heart, they could at least have sold them an annuity that is a retirement asset and not a whole life policy. The second aspect that I am not certain of but suspect with a high degree of certainty is that they do employ a CPA to help with their tax situation. It amazes me that the CPA never mentioned what the rest of the blog will be about, and that is Simplified Employee Pension (SEP) plans. It amazes me that these people who have people such as my friends trust them are not providing useful services and advice. These professionals should have their client's best interests in mind and not their own.

A SEP is simply a retirement plan established by employers and individuals who own their businesses. The plans are IRA based on the nature of more liberal contribution guidelines and act similar to other business's 401(k) plans. In the case of a SEP, the employer can make tax-deductible contributions for the employee. In these instances, the employer can receive a tax deduction for the contributions made to all eligible employees. So in the case of my friends they could have made contributions to a SEP plan for their retirement while lowering the taxes owed by their business. A win-win situation that any CPA should have been aware of if they had their client's best interest at heart.

Now the contributions to a SEP plan are not taxed at the time of the contribution to the employee but any accumulated value including all earnings will be taxed as ordinary income when they make withdrawals after age 59 ½. As I stated earlier, a SEP plan is an IRA-based plan, and these funds have to be placed in a Traditional IRA for the employee. Some firms require the IRA to be designated as an SEP-IRA; however it is on the basis a Traditional IRA and is treated as such.

The following people may establish a SEP IRA, and they include owners of sole-proprietorships, partnerships, corporations and non-profit organizations with one or more employees including the owner who, in theory, could be the only employee. Employees may not establish SEP IRA's unless they are, in fact, the owner of the business. In the event, your employer wishes to contribute to a SEP IRA it is the responsibility of the employee first to establish the Traditional IRA that the funds will be deposited into. SEP IRA's are relatively easy to administer compared to other qualified plans with lower fees as a general rule. Also unlike a qualified plan SEP IRA's are discretionary, and the employer decides if a contribution will be made in any particular year provided it is done fairly and equally to all eligible employees.

In order for an employer to establish a SEP IRA there are three criteria that need to be met. First it must be a formal written agreement to provide the benefit to all eligible employees. The second step is for the employer to provide each eligible employee information about the SEP and the guidelines of the plan. The third is for the employer to ensure that a SEP is established for each eligible employee. Failure to do any one of these three things could negate the SEP's tax advantages for the employer. In order for an employee to be eligible they must meet the following conditions: be at least 21 years old, earn at least $550 for the year, and has worked for the employer for 3 of the previous 5 years. Those three requirements are recommended, and any employer may elect to set their set of requirements that ensures it does not disqualify themselves. About the only limitation on earnings is that an individual cannot be part of the SEP if they earn over $255,000 a year. For the current year, SEP IRA's are limited to 25% of the employee's salary or pay up to a maximum of $51,000 which is indexed. For any questions, it is best to consult a tax planner, financial planner, or a competent CPA.

In order to calculate how much an employee will receive the employer has a few options at their discretion. First is the pro-rata method that gives all eligible employees the same percentage of their salary as everyone else. The second is a flat-dollar formula that is simply everyone receives the same dollar amount regardless of their salary or pay. And the third is Social Security Integration where higher wage earners may receive higher SEP contributions. In this method, the employer assigns a percentage of the accumulated total of the employee's compensation. Using a unique formula the employer allocates a percentage to each eligible employee. This method must follow regulatory requirements, or the SEP may be disqualified.

As the SEP IRA is a Traditional IRA, those rules apply to the SEP account. One main difference is that an employee may make a withdrawal to pay for medical insurance for themselves, their spouse, and their dependents under the following conditions: the individual has lost their job, they have received unemployment compensations for at least 12 consecutive weeks, they receive the distribution in the year or following year they received unemployment compensations, and they receive the distribution within 60 days of being re-employed. Withdrawals may also be made penalty-free in the event of disability provided they can provide proof that they are not able to be gainfully employed. There are special withdrawal stipulations for beneficiaries so check with a specialist in the event you inherit a SEP IRA. If the owner has qualified higher education expenses, the SEP IRA may be used for those qualified costs as are the first-time homebuyers. When taking out an early withdrawal, it is always advisable to check with a qualified professional.

As you can now see, it was a great dis-service that the life insurance agent and CPA did to my friends. With a little knowledge, the life insurance agent could have sold them an annuity for their retirement years that would have made much more sense than a whole life policy. Many people viewed annuities as an inadequate financial tool but used correctly they can be very advantageous to someone in their retirement years. And if the agent had their best interests in mind they would have referred them to a financial planner. As for their CPA, he should have recommended that they establish a SEP-IRA for themselves years ago to accomplish two things. One they would be saving a substantial amount for their retirement and two they would have lowered the income taxes they would have owed from their business. A true win-win for my friends. I cannot stress this enough, but you should always know and trust the financial experts with whom you do business with. And always use one that takes the time fully to explain any products they sell or services they offer. Do not assume that they are ethical and are looking out for your best interests and not their own.

Do you own an IRA? Depending on how you became the owner of that IRA will dictate how you must make withdrawals from the IRA. As is the case with all traditional IRA's Uncle Sam wants his share of the taxes associated with the IRA that someone owns. And all traditional IRA's at some time will have required minimum distributions (RMD). But how and when the RMD starts and is treated depends on how ownership was established for the IRA.

If someone is the original owner of the IRA, their RMD will begin April 1st of the year after they turn age 70 ½. In these instances, the RMD must be done prior to December 31st to avoid very costly penalties from the IRS. In the event, someone does not take their RMD the IRS will impose a 50% penalty on what should have been the RMD. As an example, if someone's RMD is $5,000 the penalty would result in the loss of $2,500. As an original owner, the RMD is determined by using IRS Table III or the Uniform Lifetime Table. This is the table used for most owners and their spouses. The exception is when a spouse is more than ten years younger than the owner who is 70 ½. In these cases Table II or the Joint Life and Last Survivor Table. These couples will see a lower RMD than a couple whose ages are within ten years of one another.

A spouse who inherits an IRA has a few options available to them. They may keep the IRA as a beneficiary and will be required to take the RMD when their deceased spouse turned 70 ½. In these instances, the spouse will use Table I which all beneficiaries must use. Or the spouse may roll the IRA over into their own IRA where RMD's will not be required until the spouse that inherits the IRA turns 70 ½. Whether to keep an IRA as an owner by rolling it into an existing IRA or as a beneficiary checks the corresponding tables and see which results in the lower RMD.

Non-spouse beneficiaries must use Table I and may not roll the IRA over into their own IRA. But these beneficiaries make RMD's a little differently than a spouse or original owner. If a beneficiary is 55 when, they inherit, an IRA their RMD factor is 29.6. The following year their RMD factor would be 28.6 as it is reduced by one each of the following years. That is compared to a RMD factor of 28.7 according to Table I. Over time the RMD factor will decrease faster for a non-spouse heir as compared to an original owner.

The key is to know when you have to begin RMD's, know what table to use and calculate the correct RMD amount or face hefty penalties.

Are you a grandparent? Do you want to leave an IRA to a grandchild? If so there are some methods that you need to follow to ensure that the full benefit of the IRA is passed on to your grandchild. First is to list the grandchild as a beneficiary on the IRA allowing them to take out the minimum yearly withdrawal based on their age and the IRS tables. If you leave the IRA to them as a beneficiary, then they are allowed to take the minimum withdrawals out over their lifetime allowing the IRA to continue to grow tax deferred or even tax-free. If you leave the IRA to a grandchild by means other than the beneficiary designation, they will only have five years to withdrawal the entire amount from the IRA.

If your grandchild is a minor, you will need to take certain steps in order to leave the IRA to them. One is to list them as the beneficiary and select an adult as a custodian to oversee the IRA until they reach the age of majority. The custodian can be their parent or any other trustworthy adult you see fit to manage the account until your grandchild is no longer a minor. The other option is to create a trust for the benefit of your grandchild and select a trustee to oversee the trust on behalf of the minor grandchild. This can be an effective way to ensure there is some more control over the funds for a longer period as you can dictate the terms under which the funds can be accessed, and this will be enforced by the trustee. A trust can extend the control of the trustee past the age in which a minor becomes an adult and can ensure the IRA will stay intact longer as compared to a simple beneficiary designation that names a custodian. But in both instances it is imperative that the IRA be left to your grandchild by the means of a beneficiary designation and not by any other means.

As far as taxes any IRA left to a grandchild will be subject to the generational skipping tax as most grandchildren are over 37.5 years in age difference from their grandparent. If the IRA that is left is a Traditional IRA, it will be subject to taxes on the withdrawals based on the purchase price of the assets. If the IRA is a ROTH IRA, it will enjoy tax-free withdrawals for the assets.

Leaving an IRA to a grandchild is an excellent way to pass on your estate to younger members of your family in a way that allows the funds to continue to grow with minimal withdrawal requirements. But before you do any estate planning such as this consult an expert to make sure you are gaining the maximum benefit and passing along the maximum benefit to your grandchild.

Have you inherited an IRA? If so you may want to read this posting in particular as the rules are vastly different from an inherited IRA from your own. First if you are a spouse and named as a beneficiary, you are allowed to roll the inherited IRA from your deceased spouse into your own and continue as if nothing has changed. By doing that, it allows deferral withdrawals until age 70 ½. If you are younger than that for a traditional IRA, you are not required to make withdrawals. If you inherit an ROTH IRA, there are no such requirements for a spouse. The key here is for the surviving spouse to name a proper beneficiary with the company that holds the IRA so further heirs can benefit from tax-deferred growth. So what happens to you if you inherit an IRA and are not the surviving spouse? We will look at that next.

If you are anyone other than a spouse and inherit an IRA here are some of the differences, you will face. First if the surviving spouse does not name a beneficiary and leaves the IRA to their estate, it will defeat the advantages of tax-deferred growth. The simple reason is yes their children will get the funds as they wished through the estate after the probate process. But they will have to make their final withdrawal from the IRA at the end of the fifth year, and they will not have the advantage of a child who inherited the IRA as a named beneficiary. If you name someone other than a spouse as the beneficiary, they are allowed to take the minimum withdrawals out of the IRA based on their projected lifetime. What this means is someone who is about 50 gets to spread the IRA withdrawals over the next 34 or so years where someone who inherited the IRA through their parent's estate will only have five years. By naming the person as a beneficiary, they provide their heir about 30 years of tax-deferred growth that they in turn can leave to their heirs as a lump sum payment. All of this is all dependent on the heir by transferring the money to the IRA to an inherited IRA. If heirs do not do this, they are subject to possibly having to take the full amount of the IRA as a lump sum payment with all the possible tax consequences.

It is important that the beneficiary roll the IRA into an inherited IRA directly. If an heir receives a check made out in their name, they are barred from rolling the funds into an inherited IRA. They will have possible tax ramifications depending on the type of IRA that was left to them. So it is important that anyone who inherits an IRA contact the managing company and convert it into an inherited IRA and never ask or request a check to do this yourself as that is not allowed. By doing this, it is in contrast to rollover IRA's where you have 60 days to invest the funds from one IRA into a new IRA.

Once your heir has converted the IRA to an inherited IRA, they will have their lifetime to take the payments and spread out any possible tax consequences. But it is important that they make their minimum withdrawal from the IRA by December 31st of the year following the death of the original owner. If they do not make the minimum withdrawal by December 31st they will pay a 50% penalty on the amount, they should have withdrawn. The rules as slightly different if there are more than one heirs and they are of various ages and these steps are not followed so check with a tax professional if this occurs to you and your family.

In the event, you have an heir that has credit or financial problems you may consider a trust as your beneficiary instead of your children directly. The Supreme Court recently ruled that inherited IRA's are not protected from creditors as individual IRA's are. The main drawback of this process is trusts can be expensive to establish and can be extremely complex in nature. Currently, 43 states do not offer explicit protection for inherited IRA's.

For more information on minimum distributions see IRS Publication 590, Individual Retirement Arrangements, or go to www.bankrate.com and look for their IRA distribution calculator.

I am a firm believer that in today's political environment taxes will go nowhere, but up even for those of us in our retirement years. If you can, I suggest using ROTH IRA's, and 401(k)'s to your benefit so you may enjoy the fruits of your labor tax-free when you do retire. Now ROTH IRA's do have income limitations, so they are not for everyone especially high-income earners. But there are no restrictions on a ROTH 401(k) provided your employer offer that option to you. Basically both work like this, you pay taxes on the money now in your current tax year and the money will grow until you retire or reach age 59 ½ and then all of the proceeds that you contributed are tax free. Now if you have a ROTH 401(k) and your employer gives you a match that portion of your 401(k) will be considered Traditional and taxes will have to be paid on those proceed but until you make withdrawals the money will grow tax deferred. Here are some advantages of a ROTH IRA.

First you must realize you can contribute up to $5,500 to a ROTH IRA, and if you are over the age of 50 you are allowed a catch-up of an extra $1,000 for both 2013 and 2014. If you are using a ROTH 401(k), you may contribute up to $17,500 a year and an extra $5,500 if you are over the age of 50. ROTH saving instruments are good though no matter what your age is, and retirement is an important aspect of your life and one that it is never too early to plan for and take action on.

The biggest reason to use a ROTH investment is it is tax-free when you make withdrawals after age 59 ½. If you need to make a withdrawal before that age and it is from a ROTH IRA that has been in place for at least 5 years you may withdrawal the principal without any penalty but that is not the case for a ROTH 401(k) as there is always a penalty for an early withdrawal of 10% plus taxes. That is not a proper use of a retirement account so make sure you pay yourself first; but, also make sure you will not need the money prior to your retirement. Retirement and emergency funds are different, and you do need both but in a pinch you can tap into a ROTH IRA if necessary.

And unlike a Traditional IRA where you have to start making withdrawals at age 70 ½ there are no age limitations on a ROTH IRA because you have already paid the taxes on the money, in theory. But with a ROTH 401(k) you do have to start making withdrawals at age 70 ½ unless you are still employed by the company your 401(k) is with. And since you do not have to take mandatory withdrawals you can leave a ROTH IRA to children or grandchildren using the beneficiary mechanism which will allow your heir to take minimum withdrawals based on their life expectancy resulting in many more years of tax-free growth. If you leave any IRA to someone through any means other than the beneficiary method, your heir will only have five years to let the money grow before they are required to withdrawal the entire amount.

What if you are a high-income earner? Simple use a Traditional IRA or a nondeductible IRA and then convert it to a ROTH and pay the taxes in the year of the conversion. But this can be difficult with various tax laws, so it is best to consult a tax specialist when you go this route.

Annuities

A few weeks ago I posted a rather long blog on annuities and here is a brief summary of what you need to know about annuities. First let's be honest and all agree pensions are a retirement tool of the past and are not a retirement option for the millions of people currently working. Workers today will rely on their retirement plans like 401(k) or an IRA in addition to Social Security if it is still there when you are ready to retire. An annuity can act as a supplement to Social Security and your other retirement accounts, or it could replace what a pension used to provide retirees.

An annuity is an insurance product that will produce income on a monthly, quarterly or annual basis depending on what you purchase. Annuities are funded by you with taxed dollars and will grow tax-deferred until you begin taking your payments. Unlike other retirement accounts there is no limit as to what you may contribute to an annuity and you are only taxed on the gains of the funds you paid in and not the full amount as technically you have already paid taxes on the funds you contributed.

No there are hundreds of different types of annuities and each annuity may offer different add on's that could guarantee a particular return or may pay you for the rest of your life a specific amount regardless if you have paid in enough money in the event you live a long time and are receiving payments for decades. But the more you add to or change an annuity the more you can expect to pay for it in fees. Anything over 4% is too much to pay for what you will get as a rule, and you should try to keep fees as low as possible to maximize your tax-deferred growth for as long as you can. Also you need to always be aware of surrender fees as they are usually very high and can last for many years so make sure you examine the fine print of any annuity before you buy it and understand all of the fees that are associated with the annuity.

And as you will be associated with the annuity for many years to decades make sure you are dealing with a reputable company that is financially stable. Your retirement is not something you should just trust to any company, and you need to deal with reliable firms that offer competitive annuities with reasonable fees.

Do you need a piece of mind in retirement? Are you looking for a somewhat safe investment for your golden years? Then individual annuities may be for you. While just as in any investment there are certain risks and annuities can be instruments with very high fees. But they can offer you some piece of mind for a steady return, or at least in theory depending the annuity you pick. And although they are long term investments they can act as an insurance policy for you in your retirement years that does provide you protection from not outliving your income if you chose an annuity with a lifetime payment.

Annuities can offer you some protection in a downturn of the markets if they are set up to provide you a guaranteed rate of return. And like many retirement accounts they do grow in a tax-deferred account that will only be taxed on the gains and not the principal when you do receive your payments after age 59 ½. But you need to be aware of surrender fees that can eat a substantial portion of your investment in you need to withdrawal the money before you have met the company's number of years that you have to keep the annuity with the company. This can range anywhere from six to eight years and can charge you as much as 7% of your investment if you withdrawal the fund early. On the plus side, the percentage that you have to pay typically decreases as you get closer to the end of the surrender period.

Many insurance companies offer incentives for you to move your existing annuity to their annuity and in many instances a variable annuity. These annuities do offer you an opportunity to have outstanding gains in your annuities value but also come with higher fees than a fixed annuity so beware of the fees. After all the more you pay in fees, the more your investments will have to earn for you to make more money. An example is if you have an annuity that charges fees totaling around 1% and pays 5% you are netting a 4% gain in your investment. With a variable annuity you can invest in pools of money that are similar mutual funds that will charge a management fee in addition to the standard fees associated with the annuity and can be as high as 4% when added together. That means the investments you chose in your variable annuity will have to make more than 3%, depending on the riders you chose, and that means in order for you to make money in the annuity you will have to have a return of more than 3%.

Annuities can be a valuable tool for your retirement, but they are a complex product that you need to understand before you buy one. There lots of fees, surrender charges and a multitude of options and riders you can add to your annuity to make it a product that does work for you and your needs. Some of the choices you have with annuities is immediate or deferred, fixed or variable, and how long you want to receive your payments. Once you figure out those three things, you can start to shop for an annuity that meets your needs and has fees and charges you can accept. And always remember that your annuity is considered a safe investment but it is also only as safe as the financial soundness of the issuing insurance company so make sure you do your homework and make sure the insurance company is sound and has a good financial history. After all of that research on what you want and need, and you find a sound company you are in a better position to purchase your annuity. And never buy any financial product that you do not understand and if you do not know something ask a professional for their help until you do understand what it is you are buying.

Personal Finance: A Grouping of Financial Topics
By Kirk G. Meyer

Are you between the ages of 55 and 64? Are you preparing to retire in the coming years? Have you saved and invested well enough to provide an income stream during your retirement years? As nothing in life except death and taxes are guaranteed there are some steps, you can take to help ensure you will have an income stream in your retirement years in addition to Social Security.

No one has the answers to how much you will need in retirement, but you know what you have spent over the previous years and what you are likely to spend in your retirement as well. What you need to do while you are working and after you retire track or budget your expenses you will have an excellent idea as to what you will need from your investments and Social Security to survive month to month when you are no longer working. I am nowhere near my retirement age, but I use a budget spreadsheet I developed to track my income and expenses on a daily basis that shows monthly comparisons in statistical and graphic form. If you are interested in my spreadsheet, please visit www.kirkgmeyer.com and click on the store. The spreadsheet is a digital download, and it is very easy to use and works with Excel.

Now that you know what your budget is you will be able to determine better how much income your investments will need to generate for you to pay your bills. Hopefully, you have been investing in your company's 401(k) plan or an IRA in your working years and have a sizeable sum. Now you could invest in Blue Chip stocks and rely on the dividend payments but you have the risk of the dividend being reduced or cut and the risk that the underlying value of the stock will go down. Neither is a risk you would want to take in your retirement years. Another option is to invest in the bond market and rely on interest payments from the individual bonds, a bond mutual fund or ETF. The problem with this is bonds are not paying attractive interest rates currently. A third option that I think maybe the better option is to buy an annuity with your 401(k) or IRA if you do not want the risk associated with stocks or the interest rate risk associated with bonds. Many annuities will guarantee a fixed payment for a set number of years or the remainder of your life. The amount of the payment you will receive will depend on the amount you invest and the length of the payments.

I recently read an article in Kiplinger's Retirement Report that compared two websites that projected an annuities payment for someone who retires at age 65. On one private company's website, a $500,000 initial investment in an immediate annuity an individual would expect to receive $26,810 annually in payments. This site uses current interest rates, annuity pricing, life-expectancy projections and other factors and feed it into the program to establish an annual payment.

Now the Labor Department also has an on-line calculator to project annuities annual payment on a $500,000 initial investment for an immediate annuity. This website assumes an interest rate of 7%, a contribution of 3% and does not take inflation into account. With these assumptions, the annual annuity payment would be over $35,000. Now almost a $9,000 difference is a substantial amount showing that not all annuity calculators are created equally, and you need to know what goes into the assumptions and how accurate they appear to be to you.

No one knows what the future will hold in the investment world, but annuities can provide a steady source of income for retirees. One major factor, which neither of these sites took into consideration is the gender of the person who is buying the annuity. Look for sites that not only use projected interest rates but current ones as well, consider your health, gender, and inflation factors when they project your annuity payment.

Are you a Baby Boomer who is about to retire or maybe you have recently retired? Regardless, you are most likely looking at your golden years and wondering do I have enough money to last me in my retirement? I am hoping you have investments in IRA's, 401(k)'s or a brokerage account to help get you through these years in comfort. Chances are you may or may not have a pension that you will collect as you seem to be about the last generation that will have this luxury. And of course you will be collecting Social Security if you are at least age 62 and opted for early payments. Now, what do you do if your expenses are greater than your new monthly income? One answer may be an annuity.

Depending on the amount of money you need to make up and for how long you will need the payments will determine what kind of annuity you will need to buy and how much you will need to invest initially. Buying immediate annuities right now with interest rates at historic lows may not be your best option but regardless it is an option if you are already retired or will retire very soon. An example is of you invested $100,000 in an immediate annuity you would receive about $6,900 annually for the rest of your life. However, if you had purchased the same annuity at age 60 and deferred any payments until age 65, you would receive about $8,700 annually for the rest of your life. In that example, you will get a $1,800 a year benefit for just five years of deferring payments and letting the money earn interest with the life insurance company. Now think of what the payments would be if you could invest the same $100,000 as early as age 50? That would be equal to a good piece of replacement income for you for the rest of your life. But there is no law stating you have to fund an annuity with a lump sum and if you plan according and start early in your working years you can accumulate a substantial nest egg that will pay you on an annual basis in your retirement years.

Also there is no rule that you have to start taking your payments at age 65 and you could defer the payments until age 70 or 75 when you think you will have depleted a good portion of your investments and will have a greater need for the additional income. The only exception is if you have an annuity in an IRA account you are required to start taking payments at age 70 ½ or face a penalty. Now if you defer payments until later in your life, you will see a dramatic increase in your annual payments because your life expectancy will be shorter than if you started at age 65. But here you run the risk of not living long enough to recoup the money you invested.

Now if you are married or want to leave the payments to your heir or heirs you have this option as well but the monthly payments will be reduced some. In the event that the annuity is left to an heir other than your spouse, the payments are limited to a particular number of years. Several years ago life insurance companies introduced "longevity insurance" that began payments at age 80 or 85 with high annual payments because the insurance companies figured you were not going to live that much longer. And people took the risk and invested in these accounts with an all or nothing approach with the chance they could die before payments began. Now most companies will allow you to defer payments anywhere from two to 40 years again with the idea the longer you defer, the higher your annual payment will be. Now some policies will allow you to change when you elect to receive payments once, and most all policies build cash value.

Now you may be asking what are the tax consequences of an annuity? I am not a tax specialist, and these are general ideas so always check with a tax specialist for your particular tax needs. But as a general rule unless your annuity is in a ROTH IRA there are some tax consequences to your payments. As most annuities are paid for with, after-tax dollars, a portion of the annuity payment will be tax-free as the taxes have already been paid for on that portion of the payment. Any portion of the payment that is not from your principal investment will be taxed as ordinary income for the recipient. Now if you outlive your principal in the annuity, the entire amount will be considered ordinary income for tax purposes. If you decided to cancel the annuity and take your cash value any principal of the cash value is not taxed while any interest accumulated and paid to you will be taxed as ordinary income provided you are older than 59 ½.

Miscellaneous Planning

Do you think estate planning is for the rich? Do you think you are too young to be thinking about estate planning? Well, there are seven simple steps anyone who cares about their family needs to take to simplify your estate after you die. And yes everyone will die it is just unknown when. Will you be prepared when you do is one of the important questions that need to be addressed. So let's look at the seven simple steps that everyone regardless of net worth or age needs to do to establish some simple estate planning. For a few of these steps, it may be a wise decision to consult a legal professional in your state to ensure that it is done appropriately and legally.

1. First everyone needs a will to ensure that their assets will go where they wish them to go. In a will, you will name an executor who will oversee your estate, distribute your assets according to your instruction in the will and pay your debts and estate taxes of there are any. If you die without a will and are married with children in most states, your spouse will receive half your estate, and your kids will split the remaining half. If you are single, the state will divide your assets to your living blood relatives. When someone dies without a will, their assets are distributed based on your state's laws of intestacy and will most likely go through the probate process.

   If you do not wish to have a will and you do want to avoid probate, a revocable living trust can be used to pass your assets to your heirs. But do not rely solely on a trust as you still need a will for many important matters, and it is the building block on which your estate plan is made. Trusts are an excellent planning tool if you have minor children and wish them to inherit your assets and a trust will name a trustee to manage the assets and disburse them to your children according to the terms of the trust. But a trust cannot name who should be the guardian of your kids a will does that. If you do not name a guardian in your will a judge will decide who will watch over your minor children, and you need to ensure that their future is determined by you and not a judge. And in the event you do not use a trust to leave your assets to your minor children a judge will appoint someone to oversee the assets until the children become of age and can inherit the assets themselves.

2. This is a very simple way to help establish your estate plan, and that is to name beneficiaries on all accounts that allow that designation. If you name a beneficiary, you do not need to list this asset in your will, and it will not have to go through probate and will pass directly to the person who you name as the beneficiary. Certain assets may be given directly to named individuals if you use such tools as right of survivorship or payable-on-death in place of your will. Using these tools will simplify your

estate and minimize the assets that will have to pass through probate in the event you do not use a trust. Here is the part you need to pay attention to and adhere to when you do use these tools, and that is to keep the person you named current and up to date. If you are married chances are your spouse is the designated beneficiary. But what happens in the event you get divorced? Your now ex-wife is still the beneficiary unless you take the time to change it. So stay current on this.

3. Most of us will not need to worry about federal estate taxes but for a small percentage it is a reality. If you are married, you may leave all of your assets to your spouse, and there is an unlimited exemption for spouses on estates. And in the event you do have a rather large estate the first $5.25 million may be estate and gift tax free and you may double that for married couples to $10.5 million provided you do some simple estate planning beyond what I am discussing here. But beware as there are fifteen states and the District of Columbia that have estate taxes that may be different from federal estate taxes so consult a professional where you live in order to be compliant and do some basic estate planning to minimize estate taxes.

4. Here is another simple estate planning tool that anyone can and should do, and that is simply to leave a letter detailing your wishes that may not belong to a will. If you have a certain way you wish to be buried or how you want your funeral this is the way to accomplish that goal. Also items with sentimental meaning can be left to individuals in a letter provided you give it to someone you trust. But be aware these letters may not be considered a legal document where you live but chances are your family will want to follow your instructions, so it is best to leave them in a detailed letter.

5. Everyone should have a durable power of attorney to protect them and their interest while they are still alive. Should you need assistance or become incapacitated you need a durable power of attorney to give legal rights to someone you trust to watch over your financial and medical needs while you are unable. If you use a simple power of attorney and become incapacitated, a judge will appoint someone as a conservator or guardian for your affairs. A durable power of attorney will avoid this, and the person you wish will undertake that role. The person you name has to be someone you trust to carry out your wishes so give this a lot of thought. And remember a family member may not be the best person to do this as history is

riddled with stories of family members doing what is in their best interest and not that of the individual who drafted the power of attorney. One way to avoid this situation is to name co-trustees, so one person does not have complete control.

6. In the event you need medical attention and are not able to make decisions for yourself you need a living will and a medical durable power of attorney to ensure your wishes are adhered to. A living will established what medical treatment you want to get in the event you are not able to make the decisions and a medical durable power of attorney designates the individual who will ensure your wishes are followed by the medical staff attending to you. Also, make sure you address Health Insurance Portability and Accountability Act (HIPAA) requirements or your medical information may not be related to your appointed designee.

7. And the final and hopefully simple step is to organize your files and digital files for easy access in the event you die or become incapacitated. All relevant paperwork that your trustee or executor will need has to be made available to them and accessible.

Depending on the complexity of your estate you may want to seek professional assistance for some of these steps such as wills, trusts, durable powers of attorney and living wills. Do not go the cheap route on these items as this is a critical part of your plan, and you want to make sure your wishes are followed. A very basic estate plan does not need to be expensive and can be done for between $1,200 and $2,000 depending on where you live, what you need to be done and who you have do the work. Shop around as not all lawyers are the same and as the saying goes you will get what you paid for or at least I hope you do. Look at your situation and do some proper planning for your estate. And no, it is never too early to plan and in fact I encourage everyone to do just that.

Do you think of your estate planning? With today's heavy reliance on digital information and the Internet, it is important that when someone is creating an estate plan that they include their digital information as well. By making this valuable information known and available to someone involved with your estate it will ease the burden on the estate's administrator or family members. Most people already know that an estate plan will handle physical possessions such as a house or investment accounts. But today it really does need to include all of one's digital information as about 90% of adults in the US use the Internet in one form or another.

Digital information can hold both a monetary value as well as a sentimental one for people. In today's world, people use technology for many different reasons. Many people use on-line accounts to manage bank accounts or brokerage accounts that may be accessed easiest by use of the Internet. Other methods that need to be considered for are paying bills and managing one's affairs. If these accounts are not listed somewhere and accounted for in an estate plan, it may make managing your affairs demanding. Passwords, encryption, and privacy laws can make it virtually impossible for someone who is going to manage one's estate unless steps are taken in advance.

To avoid this it is a good idea to include these items in a will or trust and designate someone as a fiduciary to execute the wishes of the will or trust. This can be done by simply taking an inventory of all of the digital information that will be of use. This means listing all sites that you use along with usernames and passwords. This will aid and speed up the processing of your estate. While it is not a wise idea to make this list part of a will it is a good practice to list where the information may be obtained upon your death. This is mainly done because the contents of a will do become a matter of public record.

Do not forget to list any social media that is used. Some sites allow pages to become memorials and in other instances close family members may just ask for the pages to be removed. Think ahead and plan your digital estate with the same care as you do your physical one.

Are you in the mood to give to charity? No matter what your economic situation is, you should give something to charity. No matter how bad you think, you may have it there is always someone somewhere who does indeed have it worse than you. Regardless of if you give $10 or $100,000 it is the right thing to do. If you cannot afford to give cash, many charities accept donations of property provided it still has some use left in its life. And neither of those is an option you can donate your time to the charity as most accept volunteers to do work.

If you are making a sizable donation of cash or a cash equivalent to a charity, ask the charity if there is a better time to donate as compared to just making a donation. Most charities get most of their donations during the holiday season so it may be better for them to get your gift in the spring or summer. Also, check with the charity to see if they prefer to get a lump sum or have it spread out over months or years. But no matter what there are advantages to you for giving. Not only is the donation a tax deduction but the feeling for helping others who are less fortunate is worth something as well.

If the cash donation is enormous or you are donating an appreciated asset such as a stock position that you have owned for at least a year and it is worth considerably more now than it was when you purchased it there are several option for making your donation. One option is a charitable gift annuity where you give cash or an asset to the charity, and they will in turn buy an annuity for you or your beneficiaries. There are some tax situations here that should be discussed with a tax professional if you go this route for your donation.

If you are in the position that you have an asset that has appreciated a lot giving it to charity may make the most sense. As the cost basis in the asset is low and by selling it you would see a large capital gain that would be taxed an option is to donate the asset to a charity. By giving an appreciated asset to the charity instead of selling it and donating the proceeds you are not taxed on the gains, and you will benefit from the full appreciated value of the assets as a tax deduction.

If you want to make the donation and are not sure what charity to donate to there is an option for you as well. You can give cash or assets to a donor advisor fund that are operated by many mutual fund companies. The beautiful thing about this avenue of donating is you get the tax advantages now but do not have to name a charity in many instances what could be years. There is a plan administrator that will oversee the account and does have the final say in what happens to the funds but in the majority of instances the donor's wishes are complied with and met.

Charities exist for a purpose, and that is to help those who are in need of help. No matter if it is a monetary donation or a donation of time making any donation is the right thing to do. Some people are in a better position to help more than others but no matter what your economic means are there is something you can do to make someone's life easier or make their day a little bit better.

Do you have permanent life insurance and typically give to charity? Are you in a position where you may not need the proceeds of a life insurance policy? If so you may consider donating your permanent life insurance to your favorite charity. There are two approaches that you may take in giving a life insurance policy to a charity. Both are effective, and both have advantages and disadvantages.

In once scenario, you may name the charity as the beneficiary of the policy and they will thereby get paid upon your death. In this case, you would continue to pay the premiums and the charity would receive the death benefit. An advantage of this method is that you keep ownership of the policy and thereby may continue to name or rename beneficiaries as you see fit. A disadvantage is that you will not be able to realize a tax deduction for a gift to a charity until your estate files its taxes after your death. Another advantage of maintaining ownership of the policy is you may name multiple beneficiaries on the policy splitting the gift between more than one charity.

If you decide to go with the second option, you will assign ownership of the policy to the charity and continue to pay the premiums. This option is permanent, and you are not able to change your mind on the donation or who the beneficiary may be. Your cost of the policy or the cash value at the time of the gift could be considered your tax basis for deduction purposes. There are not that many charities that will accept ownership of a life insurance policy due to legal and administrative issues. The reason for this is that they would be responsible for the management of the policy. However, larger charities and even some universities are beginning to accept these gifts.

If you do donate a life insurance policy to a charity by transferring ownership one way to pay the premiums is to donate appreciated equities that have been held over a year to the charity. The charity will accept the donation giving you further tax incentives, and the charity will sell the security and they will not be responsible for any capital gains taxes and neither will you. In fact, you will receive a tax deduction equal to the full value of the gift at the time.

If you have a retirement account that is around the same value of a life insurance policy, you will have some things to consider. In these instances, it may make more sense to donate the taxable retirement account to the charity and leave the life insurance policy to your family. While the proceeds of the insurance is taxable to your estate, the proceeds will be provided to your family tax-free to them. Also had you left them the taxable retirement account they would be taxed on the withdrawals as ordinary income.

Are you in a marriage with a stay at home spouse? If so there are things that you can do now that will aid you when it is time to retire later. It is hard enough to plan for your retirement years when both spouses have incomes and retire as in theory you both will have higher social security benefits and I am hoping you both have 401(k) accounts from your employment. But in the event one spouse has stayed home for any number of reasons that does not mean you cannot make adjustments and plan accordingly.

The government has placed a relatively high value on stay at home spouses, and that is seen as a spousal social security payment of up to 50% of the wage-earning spouse. This amount will vary depending on how much the working spouse made and at what age the two of you start taking your social security benefits. The longer you delay them, the more your benefits will be.

But as we all know social security will not meet all of your retirement needs, so you need to establish an IRA for the stay at home spouse. There is a rule that allows spousal IRA's regardless of if the spouse has any earned income. But you need to make sure that the working spouse makes enough money that you can afford to have the IRA. Also, if there is a retirement plan for the working spouse's employment there may be limits as to what portion of the IRA contributions will or could be deductible. And if you meet the guideline a ROTH IRA is the best option to let the savings grow tax-deferred, and the withdrawals are also tax-free as the contributions were tax prior to going into the IRA.

If you are a self-employed individual, your spouse may be eligible for retirement plans afforded to self-employed individuals. If your non-working spouse helps you with your home business why not pay them a salary that is appropriate for the work they do and make them an employee of your home business. This will maximize income in a tax-sheltered investment, and you can avoid current taxation on that income.

And if you have assets that are all in one spouse's name under current IRS tax code you are allowed unlimited gifts to your spouse. Those gifts can be in the form of cash, stocks or anything of value. You may also have assets as joint tenancy where ownership will pass to those named in the event of one of your deaths. But in the case of an IRA or 401(k) only one beneficiary can be named so it will usually go to the spouse of the working partner.

Just like married couples who both work there are tools that can make it easier for couples where one spouse stays at home. It is not impossible to have a comfortable retirement, but you need to start planning now. Just as with anyone retiring, it is never too early to start your planning.

Do you have a mortgage that you want to pay off? Do you want to make extra payments, so you are not on a 30-year mortgage? If you answer yes to these questions, there are some steps you can take to shorten your mortgage. First make sure your mortgage does not have a prepayment penalty as to not cause any unnecessary fees. The first step you can take to shorten your mortgage is to make an extra payment early in the year. By doing this at the beginning of your mortgage, a single payment can shave around four years off your mortgage and save you thousands of dollars in interest payments. Also by paying the extra payment early in the year will allow you to use year-end bonuses to make the additional payment. If you make a full extra payment on your mortgage, then try paying extra every month or rounding to the next hundred dollar mark. An example says your mortgage payment is $630 you would make a payment of $700 with the extra $70 reducing your principal. A third payment approach is to see if your mortgage lender will allow you to make payments every two weeks similar to your pay. This will allow you to make one extra payment during the year as there are 26 two-week periods in a regular year, and the thirteenth payment will be applied towards your principal as well.

A second approach to shortening your mortgage is to see if you can afford to refinance from a 30 year to a 15-year mortgage. Your payments will be higher than they were, but you will save a lot of money over the 15 years you will not be making mortgage payments. The mistake just about everyone makes when they refinance is they have 20 years remaining on their current mortgage. Now a refinance is done when rate go down so you will save money based on the interest rate alone. But remember you have been paying for ten years and only have 20 years left. The key to this is to refinance into a 15-year mortgage and not another 30 year as that will just put you back to where you were prior to the refinance. A smart refinance, and shorter mortgage terms can save you tens of thousands of dollars over the life of your mortgages.

When getting a mortgage buy what you can afford and not what they approve you for as there is always a difference in the two. Pay extra as often and whenever you can to lower your principal balance faster. And try always to get the shortest mortgage you can afford as well. Use these simple tools and save yourself thousands in interest payments.

Personal Finance: A Grouping of Financial Topics
By Kirk G. Meyer

Are you like so many people and have excess debt you have to worry about? Do you have a plan on how to best pay off this debt? As the economy slowly improves, it seems that most Americans are digging the financial debt hole a little deeper than it was last year. And when this happens people start to panic and may not make the best decisions with regards to their debts. It is never a good sign when someone goes to a payday loan, title loan, or shifts balances from one credit card to another. These are temporary fixes at best and in many instances financial pitfalls that can become almost impossible to get out from under. While it is true some states are beginning to regulate title and payday loan companies they are by nature a predatory company that really does not care if you ever pay them back provided you continue to pay something and take out additional loans. And I do not even want to think about what the fees and interest rates on these types of loans are because they will just upset me and make you sick, but I have seen them over 125%. So how do you pay off your debts? Let's look at some approaches.

On this website I sell a Debt Reduction Tool that is an Excel spreadsheet that with some input from you will tell you when a debt will be paid off, how much you will pay in total, and the interest you will pay on that debt. It is a simple tool to use but one that is very powerful and useful. Now there are two approaches to using a tool such as this. One is based on the interest rate the debit charges, and the other is by the balance of the debt. There are financial planners that will advocate each method, so I played with the tool I sell and ran some numbers. I came up with about a dozen debts that consisted of credit cards, letters of credit, personal loans, and a mortgage. In this test, I used relatively large debts with average interest rates and monthly payments. In the first approach, I used the method Dave Ramsey suggests and that is to pay off small debts first, get a sense of accomplishment, and snowball the excess payments into the next debt. In the second test I used what Suze Orman suggests and that is to pay off the highest interest rates first and then go down the list that way also snowballing the payments, so they get bigger for the following debts. In my example, the debts were paid off roughly at the same time with a negligible difference in the amount of interest paid considering there was about $35,000 in personal debt and a $110,000 mortgage. The approach that had you pay the higher interest rate first saved you only about $1,000 in interest payments over the entire period of payments. The main key to any success here is to avoid creating any new debt while you are paying off your existing debts. Use the cash and avoid credit at all costs in order to get out of debt and begin saving for large ticket items and your retirement.

Another key to reducing debt is to utilize a healthy and realistic budget. Again I sell one based on an Excel spreadsheet on this site as well as an affiliate that has an even better group of spreadsheet that can be used in budgeting, planning, mortgage, and many other functions. No one like to budget but unless you know where your money is going you will never understand how you will afford to pay off debts. Treat budgeting and getting out of debt like a plan you would use to lose weight or reward a child for doing their chores. And that is when you reach a milestone treat yourself to a small reward. For bigger milestones maybe your reward can be something bigger. But in your budget please do not take a drastic approach to budgeting and not budget any funds for recreation or entertainment. If you remove those activities, you will be doomed to fail with your budget as they are important and necessary for one's happiness.

By now you have prioritized your debts and budgeted to see where your hard earned money goes. Now if you are in the red, there are some issues here. You may need to re-evaluate your budget items and reduce some or remove them altogether if you have that option. But in many instances you may still be in the red meaning your expenses outweigh your income. In these instances, it is important to reach out to your creditors and explain your situation to them and even share your two spreadsheet with them showing them you are serious about getting on top of your finances. If you have a good history with the company, they will most likely work with you in forming a payment plan or reducing your interest rates that they are charging you. They key here is to keep honest and open communication with the creditor and pay at least something every month and on time. If you work out a payment plan live up to it and do not miss any payments or the creditor may switch the payment and interest back to what it was prior to your agreement. In today's economy creditors know many people are hurting, and most people do want to pay their debts and avoid bankruptcy. Again be honest with everyone and get everyone on the same page as to what you can afford to pay in the current environment. Your creditors may surprise you.

Watch out for debt management and debt settlement companies as they may not be the best option for you depending on your situation. Debt management companies are normally a non-profit entity that should belong to the National Foundation for Credit Counseling. While entering into a debt management program may be reported to the credit bureaus and could have an adverse effect on your credit score they can be useful if you have no other options. And by making on-time payments your credit score should rebound over time as well. In my opinion avoid credit settlement companies altogether. They charge high fees for their services and in many instances you could have gotten the same type of settlement or payment plan with your creditor by doing what I suggested in the previous paragraph.

While this is not an all-inclusive list of things to do to pay off your debt they do provide a good starting point. If you have a high-interest rate on your mortgage and do plan on staying in the house for at least five years a refinance may be an option for you to reduce that expense. With student loans setting up automatic payments and paying for a 12 month period, may get you a reduction in the interest rate the loan charges. The key here is and always will know where your money goes, know what your debts are and what they look like in total charges, and be honest with your creditors. In many instances, all you need to do is ask. The worst they will tell you is no and that will only leave you where you are now anyway. If you have been a good and loyal customer creditors will work with you on any issues you may have. For any of the spreadsheets I have mentions, please go to the Financial Tools tab.

Are you using technology to make managing your finances easier? If you are, are you worried about security? Chances are if you use any form of technology you are also aware that there is some risk that goes with the territory. But the technology can be used and if you take certain precautions limit your exposure to some of the risks that go with making our lives easier. Regardless of if you use any form of technology to make your financial work easier risks can be mitigated by using some common sense and follow certain rules.

One area that technology has made easier is on-line banking. Regardless if you are on a computer or using a smartphone the things that you can do is almost limitless. With on-line banking you can check balances, transfer money between accounts, see if a check has cleared, verify if there have been any unauthorized charges to your account, or if you have a smartphone deposit a check with your phone's app by taking a picture of the check. Even though, there has been a recent trend of retail merchants having credit/debit card information stolen if the truth be told financial institutions have some pretty good security as they are liable for most fraudulent charges. Most banks and credit card companies have little or no liability to the consumer but getting them to cover the fraudulent charges can sometimes be a tedious task. The cost to consumers for these products is free in most instances and considering the convenience they provide a small fee is not unreasonable. $9.95 a month for bill pay can save you if you mail many bills, and automatic bill payment can save you in fees in the event you forget to pay the bill manually. Overall banking is pretty high tech and relatively safe for users.

Insurance is another area that has benefited the consumer from embracing technology. Many insurance companies are paperless and by going on-line it allows you to keep up to date on your claims and any payments that are not covered by your plan. This access also enables users to monitor deductibles and benefits. And now smartphone apps even allow consumers to file a claim with the use of the app technology and the camera on their phone. Many insurers even have a home inventory service that policyholders can access through the Internet. And like banking the insurance companies are highly regulated and prone to fraud even when technology is not an issue. Most insurance companies provide free apps and services for a better insurance experience.

Personal finance is no different as it has seen technology make budgeting and saving all that much easier. With sites such as www.mint.com that allow users to enter all kinds of financial information to the site and monitor their financial positions. No matter if you are saving for a car or retirement these sites and apps for smartphones make this task all the easier. How can you expect to save if you do not have a proper budget? Well, www.mint.com is an excellent tool that allows the user to track and monitor all things financial. You can link it to credit cards, banks, brokerage accounts, your mortgage, and even retirement accounts through your employer.

The area of taxes has been leaning towards technology ever since Turbo Tax became a standard tax preparer software for home use. I have been filing my taxes online for at least the last ten years and I vaguely remember that if you wanted an IRS form you went to the US Post Office now you just go to www.irs.gov and search for the form you need. It is free to e-file your federal taxes, and the price of the software will vary depending on how sophisticated your tax needs are and range from free to about $150. Many states offer free e-filing as well so now anyone who has access to the Internet can file their taxes for free or a minimal cost. If you prepare your taxes and have a lot of things to maintain and keep for your records I have, use, and recommend Neat Receipts to manage things like receipts. You can get a new portable scanner for about $180 and if you do not mind a used one try eBay.

Technology is great if used correctly and the risks can be minimized with a little common sense and thinking. The power of computers and smart phones is incredible so why not take advantage of all that they have to offer.

Personal Finance: A Grouping of Financial Topics
By Kirk G. Meyer

Are you saving for retirement? What retirement accounts are you taking advantage of? There are several different retirement accounts available to most people. The key is to use them to your advantage and start early saving as the power of compounding interest is something to behold. Anytime you can save for a period of over 30 years your savings will grow at an unbelievable rate. If you do not believe me go into Excel and us its Future Value (FV) function and play with returns, payments, and the number of years you will have the funds in savings. It is an easy way to see what could be in say 30 or 35 years if you started saving now.

The first place people need to save is their company's 401(k), the Thrift Savings Plan, and most 457 plans. Now there are two types of savings in these accounts provided your company offers them, and that is a traditional contribution where you are not taxed now on the money or a ROTH contribution where you are taxed on the money now but the distributions will be tax-free. You are allowed to contribute up to $17,500 into these plans on an annual basis, and those over the age of 50 may contribute an extra $5,500. Now these figures are adjusted for inflation so in theory they will increase some years and not in others.

Now an IRA is another savings option for those who want to save outside of the workplace in a tax-advantaged account. Now these are like the employer-sponsored plans and have a traditional and a ROTH feature. The ROTH IRA is available for individuals who earn less than $129,000 a year and couple making less than $191,000.

These amounts like the contributions above are adjusted for inflation. For those who earn the maximum amounts, they can make after-tax contributions to a traditional IRA and then have the option of converting it into a ROTH. For a traditional IRA, the contributions may be tax deductible so the savings will grow tax deferred and taxed as ordinary income when they are taken out after age 59 ½. The annual contribution limits for 2014 are $5,500 with a $1,000 catch-up for individuals over the age of 50.

If you are self-employed, have a consultant business, or freelance you may contribute to a SEP IRA. If you make money by any of these means and possibly, others provided they meet the definition for self-employment by the IRS this is an excellent way to save in a tax-deferred account. Currently, you are allowed to save up to 20% of your self-employment income, minus half your self-employment tax, up to $52,000 a year. The contributions are tax deductible and grow tax-deferred and are taxed as ordinary income when you make withdrawals after age 59 ½.

Now if you have maxed out your savings in your company's retirement account, have maxed out your IRA contributions and are not eligible for a SEP IRA you should save in a brokerage account. There are a few reasons why this is an attractive option. One as it is not a retirement account you can take funds out at any time for any purpose and pay the corresponding taxes on the money. Also these types of investments while not tax deferred are tax-advantaged. For most investors, the long-term capital gains tax and dividend will be taxed at 15%. If you are in the 10%-15% tax bracket, your taxes could be zero. While you are paying taxes in the year, the income was realized it is taxed at a much lower rate than ordinary income.

For higher earning individuals who want to save in a tax-deferred vehicle, there are variable annuities. While in the past these vehicles have had a poor image with investors due to their high fees and surrender charges, they have changed in recent years. But it is up to you as the investor if the fees outweigh the tax-advantaged status. There are some companies that offer good choices for low-cost variable annuities so research and look at Vanguard and Fidelity.

There are many ways to save for retirement, and no one way is correct. The best approach is for you to use as many of these options as you can to maximize your investment opportunities and reduce your overall portfolio risk. Company plans are great as they are automatic and in many instances offer a company match but may not provide the best investment options. All the IRA's are right choices as they allow you as the investor to pick and choose what you want to invest in and in most instances you are free to invest in equities, bonds, ETF's, and mutual funds. And annuities even can have a place in your retirement plans but they, as a rule, do not make sense for everyone.

Personal Finance: A Grouping of Financial Topics
By Kirk G. Meyer

Are you one of the millions of Americans with credit card debt? Are you not able to pay off your card every month? Are you barely able to keep up with your bills? If you answered yes to any of these the following tips may be useful for you to help lower your overall credit card debt in 2014.

The first step in getting on top of your credit card debt is to know how much you owe. Get a piece of paper or better yet a spreadsheet and list all your debts in one place. If you want to know how much you owe, how much your interest payments will be and when you can get out of debt try my debt reduction spreadsheet. You can get it at Debt Reduction provided you sign up for my free email news letter.

A good second step if you have a good history with a particular card is to call and ask for a lower interest rate. You would be surprised to find out how many companies will lower your interest rate if you call or write and ask. The credit card business is very competitive, and companies want to keep good customers, so they are willing to lower the interest rates for customers with good history paying.

Now if you purchase my spreadsheet you can list your debts from smallest to largest or by the highest interest rate that is charged. I have done it both ways with my debt, and it is less than a $2,000 difference on my total debts including my mortgage and student loans. My personal preference is to list the debts from smallest to largest paying off the smaller debts sooner and seeing debt disappear giving you extra incentive to pay off the next debt and so on.

If you are following the instructions on the spreadsheet you purchased from me, you are making minimum payments on all your cards except the one that is being paid down currently and even then it may be the minimum. But if you have a budget and are using my spreadsheet you may have extra money you can apply to your current debt you are working on to pay it down faster. Once that debt is paid, you will add what you were paying on that debt to the next debt on the list and pay that debt down faster. While you are not making more than the minimum payment on all your debts you are on the one you are working on first and then it will follow you to the next debt reducing your debts faster than making small additional payments on all your debts.

If you are not paying as you go and getting rid of the balance at the end of every month stop using that card except in the case of an emergency. In other words, stop adding to your debts. If you bank somewhere with bill pay charge something, then pay it off immediately. But beware some credit card companies do limit the number of payments you can make in a month. Know your cards rules on payments but at least pay off what you charge on a monthly basis, so you are not adding to your debts.

No matter what pay your minimum payment on time all the time. If you are banking somewhere with bill payment or use a program like Quicken to keep track of your finances set up reminders so you will not miss a payment. Late payments are costly due to fees and in many instances lead to an increase in your interest rate. Also, many companies will adjust your rate to them based on your history with other companies so being late on one card may lead to adverse consequences on another.

Always be realistic on your time frame to pay off your debts and stay current with what is on your credit report. Errors there can lead to higher interest rates on credit cards or prevent you from getting any new credit. You are allowed one free report a year from each of the three big credit reporting agencies so ask for one from each every four months, so you are monitoring your report year round. Follow these simple steps and watch your debt reduce and in time you will be living debt free.

Do you have a poor credit score? Are you aware how your credit score affects you? A lot of people tend to spend a little too much during Christmas, and it may have a detrimental effect on your credit score if you are not aware of what is and is not on your credit report. A less than stellar credit report can cost you in ways you may or may not be aware of. The single largest area where you can see increases in your costs is higher interest rates for those with lower credit scores. The higher your credit score, the better rates you will get from store cards to credit cards for car loans to your mortgage. It is the key to staying on top of your credit score, so you know where you stand with your lenders. Lower credit scores can even mean you may not be eligible for mainstream credit in any form and may have to settle for sub-prime lenders and you will most likely pay extremely high-interest rates to your lenders to compensate for the risk of lending to you based on your credit score.

For an example of how low credit score can affect you, a score below about 730 can add a percentage point or two to your mortgage. Now while that may not seem dramatic over the life of a 30-year mortgage that can cost you thousands of additional payments in interest charges. And as far credit cards and store credit is concerned you can expect to pay the highest rates that they are allowed to charge to compensate for the additional risk of loaning to high-risk borrowers. And remember low credit scores can even prevent you from borrowing at all. A low credit score can even affect your insurance rates. If your score is low enough insurance companies can be just like financial lenders and charge you higher premiums or refuse to provide you coverage at all.

How can you ensure you get the best interest rates you can or the lowest premiums your insurance company offer? Start by taking advantage of the annual free credit report from each of the three big reporting agencies. And since it is wise to always know what is on your report to ensure you are getting the best rates you can it is also good to use as a tool to monitor your reports for suspicious activity or possible fraud. And while you are doing that check your report for any errors it may contain that could lower your credit score and if they are indeed legitimate errors the credit agencies have 30 days investigate your claim of a mistake and remove it provided it is indeed an error. Ask for a report from one of the three reporting agencies once every four months that way you are monitoring your credit report year round.

Pay your bills on time by every due date to help keep your score healthy. Paying your bills timely can account for anywhere from 30 to 40 percent of your credit score. It is critical that you pay every bill in a timely manner prior to its due date. A second way to keep your score as high as you can be by watching your credit usage and do not spend too much on your revolving credit cards. The lower your outstanding credit usage is to your available credit the better your score will be. In a perfect scenario, you should keep your credit usage at or below 30 percent of your available credit limit. That will help keep your score higher than if you are highly leveraged. And it is not viewed on a whole basis and by having one card maxed out it will lower your overall credit score. Bankruptcy or a short sale on a house can be a negative on your credit report for many years and there is not much you can do to remove these negatives as they will take time to fall off your credit report. But if you have minor blemishes on your credit report ensure they do not become habits, and they will have minimal impact long term.

The key to keeping your credit score as high as you can it to monitor your report for any errors, reduce or manage your use of your credit and always pay your bills in a timely manner. While there are many factors that go into a credit score, these are three areas that you do have control over. Also a part of your credit score is the length of time you have had your credit open, so it is important to maintain accounts that you have had for several years in order to help boost your credit score.

Personal Finance: A Grouping of Financial Topics
By Kirk G. Meyer

Do you have trouble saving money? If so you may need to read the following and make some changes in your savings habits. On average Americans are not good savers with an average savings of less than 5% of a basic paycheck. On average we should strive to save at least 10% of our paycheck not taking into account any employer matching. Yes, that is you should save at least 10% of your salary on an annual basis for either retirement or your emergency fund. Regardless of where the money ends up you need to save this amount from every check.

First you may be doing yourself a disservice if you have too many bank accounts. It has been shown that people who have one bank account tend to spend less and save more. Now that is not rocket science considering if you are not spending as much you are thereby allowed to save more. Common sense in action there but it is a simple way to increase your savings and it also makes your life less cluttered in an already cluttered world. One account is easier to take care of than multiple accounts, and it is easier to manage as well. Also, by having one account, it will mean you have fewer decisions to make thereby allowing you to have more options for saving more. As a rule, the more options you create for yourself the less likely you will be to save when we are ingrained to spend and in most cases spend more on credit instead of saving for large ticket items. Again streamline your life and make things easier on yourself.

Many of us have lost our imaginations as we have gotten older. We need to find them again. People are visual by nature, and when we are visual we are using our imaginations. One leads to the other in most instances. Use specific terms for your savings and use those as goals for you to achieve your savings. As I stated, your saving needs were an emergency fund and for retirement. Picture yourself needing to repair the car or see yourself in retirement. Even better picture yourself in your retirement world and see how you are living. If you are not creative and imagining yourself in a particular place, it is harder to save. There is a reason person who is creative and with active imaginations are happy; they picture themselves as happy and therefore they are happy. See yourself saving, and you will increase your savings. Also, it is difficult to save alone so in line with being creative try saving with someone else. You can have a savings buddy as a friend, co-worker or relative and make a competition see who can achieve their goal first. This approach will make you act more and be accountable for your savings goals as you have now shared them with someone else, and you have a point of reference as you know their goals as well. Think back to when you were a kid, and your parents offered to match your allowance if you saved it for that particular toy. What happened? You saved your money because you had help and encouragement. Do not go it alone and find someone to help you achieve your savings goals.

And finally saving does not have to be a complicated matter. Investing and saving can be or can be different in nature. Buying a stock or mutual fund is not for everyone just as buying a savings bond is not for everyone. But everyone needs a financial plan and a plan for what they will do with their savings. Some people are content with safe investments such as a CD while other prefer stocks. One is not right and the other wrong but each is correct for a particular person. Know your risk tolerance and follow that in your investing strategy.

What will happen to my debt when I die? That is a complex and complicated question that needs to be examined on a case by case basis, but the following are some general rules and some food for thought. Of course, it would be wonderful to leave an estate to our heirs or loved ones but as Baby Boomers retire many are finding they have more debt than assets. Let's face it no one wants to leave a legacy to their loved ones that are a debt. Here are some of the common types of debt that people have and who if anyone will be responsible for the debt.

One of the more common types of debt is the dreaded credit cards. If you have a joint account or live in a community property state, your spouse is more than likely to inherit the debt. Family members or children will not be responsible for credit card debt upon the death of you and your spouse. However, your estate will most likely be held accountable for the outstanding debt and be required to pay the balance out of the estate prior to heirs receiving their proceeds.

A mortgage is very similar to credit card debt, but in case you are married there is an excellent chance you own your home a joint tenant in common and both you and your spouse are on the mortgage. In the event of one of your deaths, the surviving spouse will be responsible for the mortgage debt that is outstanding. If you leave the house to relatives that live with you, they will have to obtain a mortgage in their name or work out an arrangement where they assume the rights and legal responsibilities of the remaining debt.

Student loans that were obtained through the federal government and did not have a co-signor are forgiven upon the death of the borrower. As most federal loans do not require a co-signor, your heirs and estate are not responsible for this outstanding debt. Private loans that were obtained for student expenses are another story and do have to be repaid upon the death of the borrower as most of these require a co-signor to obtain. And in many instances the lender will demand immediate repayment or will accelerate the repayment of these loans upon the death of the borrower.

An auto loan is one that can potentially cause some issues for your heirs or estate. If the auto is owned free and clear, you may leave it to whomever you chose. If there is an outstanding loan balance and you own the auto as a joint owner or live in a community property state, your spouse will be responsible for the debt. If you are single and you leave the auto to someone, they will need to pay off the loan or refinance the loan in their name. If no one wants the auto or to assume the payments, an option is to return the auto to the lender where they will sell it and apply any proceeds towards the outstanding debt. If the selling price does not cover the outstanding debt, the lender may come after your estate for the difference.

Of course, the government will want its share of your estate in taxes. While there are ways to minimize your final income tax return or estate taxes, there is no avoiding them 100%. Here is where this area becomes tricky and that is if you have a debt that is forgiven by a creditor that will now generally become income for your estate and the lender will issue a 1099-C to the estate. In order to ensure your estate is handled correctly, with regards to such issues as taxes have your executor seek the guidance of a tax professional.

Of course, if you have debts and care about what is or is not left to your loved ones it is wise to have an adequate life insurance policy taken out by a proper beneficiary named. If you have read my blog before on any life insurance issue, you know I am not a huge fan of permanent policies and tend to favor a term policy. The reason is fairly simple and straightforward, and that is term policies are very affordable and will provide your loved ones with a higher death benefit. If you are unable to obtain a proper and decent life insurance policy, you can protect your loved ones and heirs with the higher cost insurance on individual debts such as the type offered by credit card companies. But the best thing is to leave no debt to your loved ones and heir at all.

With proper planning you can minimize the toll your death will have on your loved ones by maintaining low debt levels, use and update all beneficiaries, draft a legal and binding will, seek the counsel of an estate planning attorney and leave written instructions to the executor of your estate.

When tax season is upon us and with that comes the stress, anxiety and confusion on our yearly tax issues. As I wrote a while back, Ponzi Schemes have been around for almost a hundred years and take in millions of dollars from novice and seasoned investors annually. But during tax season there are also plenty of people who are running scams on you and your tax concerns as there are people running Ponzi Schemes. Here are some of the more common tax schemes that are aimed and geared at separating you from your money and could cause serious problems with the IRS.

The first may be one of the more common schemes and problems with tax season, and that is a dishonest tax preparer. Beware that not all tax preparers are honest with some skimming money off your return and other simply charge inflated or outrageous prices to prepare and file your return. Also, beware of preparers who offer to or guarantee to get you refunds that are not reasonable or practical. Let's face it do not try to cheat the IRS as they at some point will find out, and they will come after you, not your tax preparer, as a rule. Also, beware of preparers as you do have to give them a lot of your personal information which they can use to steal or sell your identity. It is best to go with reputable firms or preparers that are licensed professionally such as a CPA or licensed financial advisors. And before you agree to hand over all your information make sure you ask them about all the fees associated with preparing your tax return and how and what they do with your information that you have to provide in order for them to prepare your return. You can never underestimate the need for security for your personal information. Also, you need to make sure you are paying a flat fee and not a percentage of your return and always have the return sent to or deposited in your accounts never that of the preparer. Only sign a return that you understand and never sign any blank forms. Again the IRS will go after you and not the person who prepared your tax return.

Another popular scam involves someone claiming to be with the IRS, and they inform you that you owe money. In many instances, they will threaten you with arrest or deportation if you do not pay them. As a rule, they will have your name, address, phone number and even a part of your social security number making them sound very official. In many instances, they will even have a phone number that will register as an IRS call when your caller ID receives the call. In many of these instances the individual that contacts you will ask for payment in the form of a money order, credit card or prepaid debit card. According to the IRS they will never ask for a particular type of payment and do not as a rule call you to inform you of irregularities or issues you may have with the IRS and they typically will contact you via the US Mail system.

Also, beware of people who call you acting as a charity or after a disaster as these individuals are normally in social security numbers and bank account numbers. And never give a donation to someone who says that you can claim the deduction on a previous year's tax return as that is not possible as donations are only tax-deductible in the year that you make the donation.

And scammers do not limit themselves to making contact via phone calls but also use emails to try and gain access to your personal information. Beware of any email that asks for personal information or send you to an official looking website that will collect your information. Many of these emails will state you have missing information from your tax return where they will use the information you provide to either steal your identity or file false tax returns to get fraudulent tax refunds in your name. Also, beware of emails that claim that they will be able to settle a previous tax debt for pennies on the dollar or for a small percentage of what you owe. These individuals are out to steal your identity. As a rule, the IRS does not correspond via email and they never ask you to reply to an email with personal information.

Just because it is tax season, there is no reason to get stressed. Use your common sense if you receive suspicious calls or emails with people claiming to be with the IRS. Remember the IRS will usually contact you through the US Postal service. Never accept someone's word they are with the IRS on a call no matter if they provide a phone number for you to call or a badge number which both can be faked with ease. If you do receive something and you have concerns call the IRS's 1-800 number or go they www.irs.gov and send them an email on their website.

Are you ready for the end of the year where your finances are concerned? Most of us do not think about our finances on an annual basis, but we need to for many different reasons. Many worry about their finances at the beginning of the year, but I would venture to guess the majority do not get around to their finances until the end of the year or the beginning of the following when you do your taxes. And if we were to be honest with ourselves would we have to admit we are really also not prepared for retirement. In general we are just not saving enough plain and simple.

Most people will rely heavily on Social Security and are not doing things now that will make their retirement easier when it does happen. Your retirement account is your funding for possibly decades of retirement and you need to manage it to the best of your ability or find someone who for a manageable fee will assist you in the management of your retirement accounts. A corporate 401(k) and individual retirement accounts are the most common forms of retirement accounts people need to worry about, but management is only a portion of the equation. The remaining part is at what level are you saving?

While almost who works can have an IRA most companies also have 401(k) plans that all employees can participate in. These are two excellent vehicles for retirement that allow for tax savings in some cases and allow your money to grow tax deferred for many years. The fourth quarter is a good point at which to examine your accounts, level of contributions, asset allocation, and beneficiaries.

On an annual basis, you need to check your beneficiaries on any account that has one to make sure they are current and up to date. You do not want spouse #1 to receive what you thought you were leaving your current spouse. Anytime you have a life event you need to make sure you have the correct beneficiaries listed.

In your 401(k) you are allowed to contribute up to $17,500 and an additional $5,500 if you are over the age of 50. Okay, those figures may not be all that realistic to the majority of people but in many companies there is a company match on a portion of what you elect to contribute. Always contribute the full amount that the company matches otherwise you are leaving free money on the table so to speak.

You may or may not think of this and in many circles advisors do not advocate rebalancing your portfolio's assets. Some do not believe it is wise to sell assets that are making money and purchasing assets that are maybe not having as good a return. But by rebalancing your assets you will sell some of your leaders to use that money to buy the ones who are lagging. By doing this, you keep a balance you wished to achieve at the start of your investing. A simple way to look at this is if time-cost averaging is seen as a good way to invest allowing you to buy assets at different price levels this works much the same way. You will sell fewer higher returning assets that will enable you to buy lower returning ones. And since investing is cyclical this will vary from year to year and work much the same way as cost averaging.

If you change jobs, do not leave your old 401(k) with your previous employer but do not cash it in either. If you can, I would recommend rolling it over into your new companies 401(k) if they allow that and have sound investment options. If they do not permit that to happen or are lacking in real investment options roll it over into an IRA where you have control over what it will be invested in and do not leave it to chance or in some cases to be forgotten as you continue to move and change jobs. Never ask for the money in your name as that will trigger possible taxes and other withholdings that are easily avoided if you have them pay the funds directly to a new qualified plan.

It is scary that I have recently seen as few as 3 out of 10 people are saving for retirement. Let's face it Social Security is not going away anytime soon but the chances are that it will look and act in the same manner it does today when someone retires in 20 plus years is remote at best. Do I think I will have Social Security when I retire in about 25 years? Yes, I do, but it will be a different animal than what my parents are getting now. Let's now say you are one of the few Americans who do save for your retirement. Money is tight, and you ask yourself, "Should I borrow against my retirement accounts?" That is what we will look at in this blog posting.

Can you borrow against a retirement account? The answer to that is yes, but the answer is should you? Not only do you diminish your earnings potential on your account you open yourself up to possible tax consequences and penalties. Take a 401(k) loan as an example. Say you borrow $25,000 from the account, and you decide to utilize the maximum of five years to pay it back. Provided you stay with your current job there are no issues as you will be making the payments back into your account. Now say you leave your job for whatever reason, and you still owe $15,000 left on the loan. Here is where you can get into trouble with such a loan. You will have 60 days in which to repay the full $15,000 back to the account, unless you are over are 59 ½, or you will owe ordinary income taxes on that amount and you will owe a 10% early withdrawal penalty. Not a good position to be in if you ask me. Now this position is better than making an outright early withdrawal where the plan's administrator will withhold 25% in taxes in addition to the 10% early withdrawal penalty.

The rules are the same for a Traditional IRA as a 401(k) plan in terms of what you can expect from early withdrawals. ROTH IRA's are a little different as they are funded with after-tax dollars. Provided you meet the time requirements on converted accounts you may take out the principal that was put into the account without any penalties after five years. For new ROTH accounts, you are free to access the principal at any time without tax consequences or penalties.

For both types of IRA's there are particular circumstances that allow for withdrawals but I never advise taking a retirement account if it can be helped. Just because the law allows you to withdrawal the funds does not mean you should by any means. Look elsewhere first and use retirement accounts as a genuine last resort. Remember the money that is tax-deferred will grow much faster than money that is taxed. And if you are younger it has an even more dramatic effect on your accounts.

The short answer is yes you can borrow or withdrawal money from a retirement account, but I advise against it. Look elsewhere for the funds if at all possible and leave your retirement alone and let it compound and work for you. While I think Social Security will be there in some form it most likely will not be sufficient to provide for all your needs and you will need all you can get in your retirement accounts.

Are you a married couple about to enter your golden retirement years? Is Social Security going to be a primary component of your retirement income? If you answer yes to one or both of these, there are certain steps that can be taken that will enable a couple to boost benefits. There is nothing simple about filing for Social Security and in many cases it can be a very complicated matter. The best thing to do is make sure you understand the benefits, visit with a Certified Financial Planner or an attorney that has experience with Social Security issues and then plan a visit to your local Social Security office. The age of retiring and just collecting a monthly check is the history as everyone needs to understand the benefits in order to get the most out of the system.

As a general rule if in a married couple one spouse is expected to live past age 80, the cumulative lifetime benefits will generally be the highest if the spouse with the higher earnings delays their payment until age 70. One reason for this is that for most born in the mid to late 1950's or later your full retirement age is your 67th birthday. For a person whose full retirement age is 67 such as I, for every year that Social Security is delayed my monthly payment will be 8% higher per year until I reach age 70. So if you delayed taking your Social Security benefit from age 67 to 70, the benefits payment would be 24% higher.

Now that is provided that as a couple you can survive without the primary earner's Social Security payments until age 70. And then a primary goal is to maximize the benefits for the surviving spouse after age 80. Now if the primary earner dies the surviving spouse is entitled to 100% of the death benefit once the surviving spouse is at or past their full retirement age. If the benefit is taken prior to their full retirement age, the survivor's death benefit will be reduced. However, all of this is dependent on both spouses living until they both have reached their full retirement age. And obviously one's total lifetime benefit will depend not only on when they start their benefits but how long they will receive them. If your family has a history of early deaths, it may not make sense to delay your benefits until age 70. When to start taking benefits is a decision that you need to make knowing your whole story and is not something that can be learned in a blog. In order to make the best decision for you and your spouse consider all aspects of your life, health, family history, current and future needs and what assets you have saved for retirement.

One way to maximize your Social Security benefits as a couple provided both of you are age 62 at a minimum is for the higher earner to file and then suspend their benefits. You will have to know your due benefits here as a couple as one spouse may be eligible for their benefits at age 62 based on their earning history. But 50% of the higher earner's benefit may indeed be higher and worth getting. But the key there is the higher earner must initiate their benefits in order for spousal benefits to be paid. This is where the higher earner files for their benefits then suspends the payments allowing the spouse to collect spousal benefits despite the fact the higher wage earner is not receiving any payments. If the spouse is not at their full retirement age, the spousal benefit will be less than 50% of the higher spouse's benefit. But if the higher wage earner continues to work they will accrue delayed credits until they reapply for their benefits.

Social Security is not something to be afraid of but it is a topic where you need sound and robust information to base any decisions on. There are many little tips and ideas that are available for retiring couples and in many instances individuals, but you have to be in contact with a qualified person who can give you honest and valuable advice. The Social Security Administration is a good source, but they may or may not have your best interest at heart. And they certainly are not a Certified Financial Planner, who has been trained in financial matters and is knowledgeable on your entire picture as you will have developed a working relationship with them. They should be aware of your history, financial needs, current situation and provided you have been honest with them they will have an idea of your estimated longevity based on the family history you have provided them. If you do not wish to work with a planner do your research on the Social Security website, write a list of questions you will need answered and then plan to visit the local Social Security office to get answers to your questions.

Are you ready to retire? Are you about to retire or start collecting Social Security? Are you aware of how Social Security can affect you in your retirement? Well, Social Security was originally designed to be a supplement in retirement but in today's reality people rely on it more than it was intended to be relied upon. So what is the purpose of Social Security, in general?

First it is not just for retirement purposes as it is also a disability benefit for working individuals. In order to qualify for Social Security disability according to the fund itself you must be unable to work, "because of a physical or mental condition that is expected to last at least one year or result in death." If you meet those conditions and have worked the required quarters according to your age, you may be eligible for Social Security disability. But do not solely rely on this benefit in the event you become disabled as it is a very difficult benefit to get, and you must prove to the Social Security Administration that you meet the definition of a disabled individual. And it will also pay benefits to spouses and children of a recipient as well as those for a deceased worker.

If you take your Social Security retirement benefits early, you will receive a reduced amount for the remained of your life and that of your spouses if you do indeed take the benefit at age 62. If you want to receive the maximum benefit from Social Security and you were born after 1960 you need to work until your full retirement age of 67. And if you delay the benefits until age 70 you will really maximize the benefit as it will add approximately 24% to your monthly payment. But if you want to start receiving the benefits at age 62 you will receive about 70% of your retirement benefit that would have been paid at age 67. And there are tax consequences if you take your benefits at an age prior to your retirement age in the fact that for every $2 earned over $15,120 for 2013 your benefits will be reduced $1 and it could result in lower benefit payments for the rest of your life. If you wait until your full retirement age you are not limited to what you may earn as it will not affect your benefits, but there are restrictions on earning in the year you do reach your full retirement age.

In the event, you want to delay your retirement to age 70 as I stated you could see a relatively dramatic increase in your benefits. By delaying your benefits payment, you could increase your payments between 4.9% and 8.3% per year from age 67 to age 70. Not a bad guaranteed return considering the markets today. But you need to plan ahead if you go this route as life expectancy does come into play here. If you do not think you will live much beyond 70, it may make more sense to take the benefits at 62 or 67 depending on your health, family history, and financial situation, in general. But if you are still working why not delay as long as you can and maximize your benefits.

Now if your spouse did not work your spouse is eligible for approximately half of your benefit when you make your declaration. And in the event of a divorce you get to keep the benefits provided you were married at least ten years prior to the divorce, and you do not remarry. Now let's say one spouse does not plan on earning more than the $15,120 a year they can take early retirement at age 62 while their spouse continues to work. Then when the spouse declares and begins to take their benefits the spouse who retired "early" would see a slight deduction from their new benefit when their spouse reaches their full retirement age. Their new benefit will be the old benefit multiplied by 30%, then subtract that from half of their spouse's benefit, and you will get the new monthly benefit.

Now those are just some of the strange workings of Social Security so always check with a professional or the Social Security Administration for clarification and how current laws affect these benefits. With proper planning, Social Security can be a treasured aid in your retirement plans.

What does it mean to defer your Social Security? Do you benefit by delaying your Social Security payment? Well, there is no right or wrong answer for that as everyone's situation is different but on average you will be better off if you can delay the payments.

There are three ages in Social Security that are important and ones that you need to be aware of if you will be a recipient. The first is 62 which is the earliest you would be able to get a Social Security payment provided you worked the required quarters or about a total of ten years. The second is your full retirement age (FRA) which for those born after 1960 is 67 years of age and for those born prior to 1960 it is between 65 and 67 depending on what year and month you were born. And the third age is 70 which is the age in which no more benefits will be obtained by deferring your payments.

So how do these three ages affect your payments? Well, if you claim Social Security at age 62 your monthly payment will be reduced by your payments, in theory, will last longer. If you wait until your full retirement age you will receive your full payment as calculated by the Social Security Administration based on what you averaged for the highest thirty years of your work history based on your tax returns. And if you delay your payments from age 67 to 70 you will get an extra eight percent a year more for every year you delay the payments. That means if you wait the full three years your payment will be 24% more than it would have been at age 67.

As people are living longer and longer every year many people are indeed working to their full retirement age and in many instances beyond that depending on their job and health. But regardless of when you take your re talking about thousands of dollars more that you will receive compared to taking the payments as soon as you reach age 62.

And when you consider that Social Security will be adjusted for inflation working or delaying your payments until age 70 can mean you will be receiving some fairly substantial monthly checks from Social Security. While inflation adjustments are not guaranteed, they are approved by Congress and are now tied to the inflation index or Consumer Price Index. However, the Obama administration wants to peg the Cost of Living Adjustments or COLA to an index that will provide lower COLA adjustments going forward for all recipients.

Just because you are nearing the age that you can receive Social Security does not mean that you should start receiving your payments. This is an area that can be complex if you are married, and one person was the predominated wage earning, and the other may have been a stay at home parent. In that case the primary wage earner. Social Security payments the breakeven point is right at age 80. Meaning if you live well into your 90's you can file for Social Security as well as the spouse and then suspend their payments allowing the stay at home partner to collect about 50% of the primary wage earner's Social Security payment while theirs continues to accrue and increase in payment value. In these instances, it is wise to seek the guidance of a financial advisor or someone who is very knowledgeable in Social Security payments.

About Kirk G. Meyer

If you enjoyed the book or found it useful Kirk G. Meyer would appreciate any feedback you can leave on Amazon.com. Thank you in advance.

Kirk G. Meyer's educational and work background is fairly diverse. He holds a BS in Business Administration from Haskell Indian Nations University in Lawrence, Kansas and a MBA and MS in Accounting from Strayer University in Washington, DC. He just finished the final courses in a MS in Financial Planning from Bentley University in suburban Boston, Massachusetts. Mr. Meyer works for the federal government in the area of contracts and prior to his current position was a bank examiner for a federal regulatory agency. In addition to his education and work experience, he is also a registered independent life insurance agent in his home state of Tennessee, selling various life insurance and annuities to individuals and families in need of these types of products. His educational background and love of helping others make him an asset to those looking for assistance and guidance in financial and personal financial matters.

How to Contact Kirk G. Meyer

Feel free to email Kirk at kirk@kirkgmeyer.com.

Please follow Kirk's blog at www.kirkgmeyer.com and he welcomes any comments or suggestions on how to make his blog or eBooks better for you.

You can also follow Kirk on Twitter at @kirkgmeyer

You can follow Kirk on Facebook at www.facebook.com/kirkgmeyer

You can follow Kirk on LinkedIn at www.linkedin.com/in/kirkgmeyer

For a complete listing of Kirk's books please visit his Amazon Author Page at Kirk G Meyer.

Other Books by Kirk G. Meyer

Thrift Savings Plan: A Practical Guide to the TSP

The Basics of Life Insurance

A Brief Overview of Annuities

Financial Plans: Just the Basics

Budgeting 101

Final Expense Insurance

www.ingramcontent.com/pod-product-compliance
Lightning Source LLC
Chambersburg PA
CBHW051850170526
45168CB00001B/46

* 9 7 8 1 5 0 8 9 8 1 9 6 1 *